New Frontiers of Customer Strategy

New Frontiers of Customer Strategy

Managing Sustainable, Environmental and Ethical Transitions

Edited by

Thierry Delécolle
Florence Jacob
Isabelle Prim-Allaz

iSTE

WILEY

First published 2024 in Great Britain and the United States by ISTE Ltd and John Wiley & Sons, Inc.

ISTE Ltd
27-37 St George's Road
London SW19 4EU
UK

www.iste.co.uk

John Wiley & Sons, Inc.
111 River Street
Hoboken, NJ 07030
USA

www.wiley.com

Library of Congress Control Number: 2024932214

British Library Cataloguing-in-Publication Data
A CIP record for this book is available from the British Library
ISBN 978-1-78630-850-4

Contents

Introduction xiii
Thierry DELÉCOLLE, Florence JACOB and Isabelle PRIM-ALLAZ

Chapter 1. How Can Customer Relations and Sufficiency Be Reconciled? A Reflection on the Consumption of Second-hand Goods 1
Valérie GUILLARD

1.1. Customer relations and sufficient living: what conflicts? 3
1.1.1. Relationship marketing: spirit and tools 3
1.1.2. Sufficient lifestyle: characteristics, dimensions and links with the second-hand market 4
1.2. Customer relations and the second-hand market 6
1.2.1. The second-hand market: a brief overview in 2022 6
1.2.2. Perception of customer relations in the second-hand market 8
1.3. Conclusion 11
1.4. References 12

Chapter 2. Customer Relationships and Sustainable Development in the Retail Sector 15
Sarah LASRI, Lionel NICOD and Valérie RENAUDIN

2.1. Incompatibility between retail and sustainable development? A few paradoxes to overcome 16
2.1.1. The hyperchoice model versus the expectation of greater sufficiency 17
2.1.2. Selling ever-greener, ever-cheaper products 18

2.1.3. Enhancing the customer experience while reducing energy waste 19
2.2. Customers and employees: accelerating sustainable development in the retail sector? 20
2.2.1. The customer's voice: a gateway to new models? 21
2.2.2. The voice of employees: a driving force in the transition of retailers 23
2.3. Conclusion 24
2.4. References 25

Chapter 3. Corporate Social Responsibility and Loyalty 27
Didier LOUIS, Cindy LOMBART and Nathalie FLECK

3.1. Definitions of perceived CSR and loyalty 28
3.1.1. Perceived CSR 28
3.1.2. Loyalty 29
3.2. The influence of perceived CSR on consumers' retailer loyalty 29
3.2.1. The impact of perceived CSR as a global construct on retailer loyalty 30
3.2.2. A different impact depending on CSR dimensions and consumer profiles 31
3.3. Examples of concrete actions (in line with respect for the environment and philanthropic activities) 33
3.3.1. The influence of a retailer's bulk product offer on consumer loyalty to that retailer 33
3.3.2. Sponsorship, cause-related marketing and CSR-linked sponsorship: three CSR actions to build consumer loyalty 35
3.4. Conclusion 36
3.5. References 37

Chapter 4. Reinventing Loyalty Programs in the CSR Age: Moving toward Prosocial Loyalty Programs 41
Loubaba BELAOUD, Aïda MIMOUNI-CHAABANE and Béatrice PARGUEL

4.1. Limits of the traditional loyalty program in the CSR era 42
4.1.1. A philosophy focused on purchasing behavior 42
4.1.2. A design that conceals environmental and social impact 43
4.2. The academic literature: loyalty program responsibility 44
4.3. Benchmark study: loyalty programs 46
4.4. Interviews with loyalty experts 49
4.4.1. Corroboration of the literature and benchmark findings 49
4.4.2. New findings from interviews 50

4.5. Toward a prosocial loyalty program 52
4.6. References 54

Chapter 5. Toward Greater Sufficiency in Customer Relationships 57
Jean-Baptiste WELTÉ, Virginie PEZ and Isabelle DABADIE

5.1. The systemic collapse of consumerism 58
5.1.1. The impact of marketing and customer relationship practices on the ecosystem: the anthropogenic footprint 58
5.1.2. The impact of new technologies and digital transformation on social ties: accelerating a process of disintegration 60
5.1.3. Consumption and rebound effect. 62
5.2. For more sufficiency in customer relationships. 63
5.2.1. Sufficiency in customer relationships: doing “less” but “better” . . 63
5.2.2. Enhancing the status of customers that practice “sufficiency” . . . 64
5.2.3. Promoting sufficiency through customer relationships. 65
5.2.4. Facilitating commitment to sufficiency through customer relationships. 66
5.3. Conclusion 68
5.4. References 68

Chapter 6. Metaverse Opportunities for Customer Relations 71
Catherine LEJEALLE and Thierry DELÉCOLLE

6.1. An immersive, interactive and persistent universe. 73
6.2. A gamified, esthetic universe 74
6.3. A personalized world of scarcity 75
6.4. A social and community universe. 76
6.5. An innovative universe 76
6.6. Conclusion 77
6.7. References 79

Chapter 7. Towards Transparent and Parsimonious Customer Data Collection 81
Tom VILLENET, Thierry DELÉCOLLE and Grégoire BOTHOREL

7.1. Data as a means of personalizing customer relations and creating a competitive advantage 83
7.1.1. Risks in terms of breaches of privacy for the consumer 84
7.1.2. Risks in terms of strategic dependencies for companies 86

7.2. The new connected consumers and their multiple perceptions of different data collection methods . . . 87
7.3. Why authorize the collection and use of personal data? . . . 88
7.4. How can we encourage parsimonious data collection? . . . 90
7.4.1. Minimizing data collection . . . 91
7.4.2. Relying on transparency when collecting data . . . 93
7.4.3. Giving consumers control . . . 95
7.5. Conclusion: finally, what is the value of data? . . . 96
7.6. References . . . 97

Chapter 8. From Persuasion to Customer Manipulation: The Role of Dark Patterns . . . 99

Florence JACOB, Jeoffrey DROUARD, Séverine ERHEL, Marianne LUMEAU and Raphaël SUIRE

8.1. Dark pattern definitions and typologies . . . 100
8.2. Marketing as usual? . . . 104
8.3. Problematic Internet use due to dark patterns? . . . 107
8.4. Impossible to observe and yet combatable . . . 108
8.5. Appendix . . . 111
8.6. References . . . 111

Chapter 9. Digital Consumption and Inclusion . . . 115

Léa CAUCHARD

9.1. Introduction: when the digitalization of customer journeys raises challenges . . . 115
9.2. Consequences of the digitization of customer journeys . . . 116
9.2.1. A transformation of the user's role during the journey . . . 116
9.2.2. Interaction at the heart of the value creation process . . . 117
9.2.3. User participation . . . 117
9.2.4. A complex user experience . . . 118
9.3. New managerial challenges arising from the digitization of journeys . . . 119
9.3.1. Improving users' relationships with digital technology . . . 119
9.3.2. Still insufficient digital inclusion initiatives . . . 119
9.3.3. Moving beyond a focus on digital uses . . . 121
9.4. Defining the digital inclusion process . . . 122
9.4.1. The role of perceptions in the inclusion process . . . 122
9.4.2. Adopting a two-level approach to the digital inclusion process . . . 122

9.4.3. From inclusion to digital inclusion as perceived by the user 125
9.5. Conclusion: toward digital consumption for all 126
9.6. References 128

Chapter 10. Improving Effective Accessibility of Products and Services for Vulnerable Customers 131
Pierre VOLLE and Sylvie LLOSA

10.1. Effective accessibility of products and services, a challenge for organizations. 132
10.1.1. Definition of effective accessibility 132
10.1.2. Effective accessibility: a challenge for organizations? 133
10.2. The challenges of effective accessibility for vulnerable customers . . 134
10.2.1. How do you define a vulnerable customer?. 134
10.2.2. Reduced effective accessibility for vulnerable customers?. 135
10.3. Ways to improve the effective accessibility of products and services for vulnerable customers 136
10.3.1. How should we respond to the challenge of effective accessibility for vulnerable customers?. 137
10.3.2. How can we rethink journeys to improve accessibility for vulnerable customers?. 137
10.4. Conclusion 141
10.5. References. 142

Chapter 11. The Patient Experience 145
Stéphanie VERFAY

11.1. From the health service to the patient experience. 146
11.1.1. Patient satisfaction as a starting point 146
11.1.2. The patient from an experiential perspective 147
11.1.3. Designing a meaningful experience 148
11.2. Enhancing the value of the patient experience 149
11.2.1. The perceived value of the patient experience 149
11.2.2. A typology of the value of the patient experience 150
11.2.3. Experience value as a lever for appropriation of the patient experience 152
11.3. Conclusion 153
11.4. References. 155

Chapter 12. Adopting Ethical Sales Behavior 157

Eric JULIENNE

12.1. Unethical temptation among salespeople. 157
12.1.1. Salespeople's ethical dilemmas 158
12.1.2. The six principles of influence according to Cialdini 159
12.1.3. Influence or manipulation: what are the differences? 161
12.2. Creating ethical behavior 162
12.2.1. Customer orientation at the heart of sales ethics 162
12.2.2. How can the ethical behavior of salespeople be developed? 164
12.2.3. Ethics and business performance: how compatible are they? . . . 165
12.3. Conclusion 167
12.4. References. 168

Chapter 13. Customer Relationships as a Factor of Resistance: The Case of Smart Feedback Tools. 171

Françoise SIMON and Virginie SCHWEITZER

13.1. The rise of smart feedback tools. 172
13.1.1. Definition of smart feedback tools 172
13.1.2. Deployment dynamics by sector 173
13.1.3. The collection of multiple types of private data 175
13.1.4. Toward a classification based on the nature of feedback 175
13.2. A brand relationship investment. 176
13.2.1. Relational investments supporting customer relationships 176
13.2.2. Smart feedback tools as a promise of empowerment 177
13.3. Consumer resistance to smart feedback tools 178
13.3.1. Multiple sources of disempowerment 178
13.3.2. Forms of resistance 180
13.4. Conclusion 180
13.5. References. 181

Chapter 14. Customer Relations in the Social and Solidarity Economy 183

Hajar EL KARMOUNI and Alix POELS

14.1. Managing customer relations in social and solidarity economy organizations. 183
14.1.1. Democratic governance of SSE organizations and customer relations 184
14.2. CRM in consumer cooperatives: the case of La Louve 185
14.2.1. The cooperative: definition and articles of association 185

14.2.2. La Louve cooperative supermarket. 187
14.2.3. Taking on the intra-role: from consumer to cooperator through work 188
14.2.4. Between customers and cooperative status 189
14.3. Organizing customer relations in a collective interest cooperative company: the case of Enercoop Languedoc-Roussillon 190
14.3.1. The collective interest cooperative company: definition and articles of association 190
14.3.2. The SCIC Enercoop Languedoc-Roussillon 190
14.3.3. A commitment that translates into extra-roles conditioned by the organization's economic times. 191
14.4. Conclusion 193
14.5. References. 194

Chapter 15. Purpose Corporations and Customer Strategy: Toward a Strategy of Customer Education and Empowerment? . . 197
Isabelle PRIM-ALLAZ and Martine SÉVILLE

15.1. Purpose corporations: a response to customers' expectations of "responsible" capitalism 197
15.1.1. Customer demand for "enhanced" corporate social responsibility 197
15.1.2. Companies with a mission to meet customer expectations? 198
15.2. The "customer loyalty paradox" in purpose corporations 202
15.2.1. The transition to a purpose corporation: a challenge for customer relations 203
15.2.2. The transition to a purpose corporation: a tool for winning and building loyalty 205
15.3. Toward a new relationship marketing strategy 206
15.3.1. Purpose corporations: (re)thinking customer relations 206
15.3.2. A renewed promotion and justification strategy around the raisons d'être of purpose corporations 207
15.3.3. Customer awareness and education: a renewed corporate branding strategy 209
15.3.4. A customer education strategy for mutual learning and commitment to the mission 209
15.3.5. Helping customers transform 210
15.3.6. Encouraging customer involvement in defining and carrying out the company's mission 211
15.4. References. 213

Chapter 16. Complex Customer Experience Management with Multi-stakeholders 215
Amélie MARTIN
16.1. From customer experience to its management 216
16.1.1. The origins of the customer experience 217
16.1.2. A first approach to customer experience management 217
16.1.3. The customer journey approach and value co-creation 218
16.2. Integrating stakeholders in customer experience management 219
16.2.1. Moving beyond customer-centric experience management 219
16.2.2. Toward customer experience management focused on stakeholders 219
16.3. Using value propositions to align stakeholders 221
16.3.1. The need to align stakeholders 221
16.3.2. Value propositions as a tool for stakeholder alignment 221
16.4. Conclusion 225
16.5. References 226

List of Authors 229

Index 233

Introduction

Originating in the fields of industrial and service marketing, customer marketing really took off in the 1990s: the emergence of customer databases offered a new way of understanding the consumer, and customer relationship management software made it easy to calculate return on investment [GAB 14]. Transactional marketing gave way to relationship marketing.

Of course, the reality proved a little more difficult. Databases could not capture the customer's every facet, but a large body of research has enriched our knowledge of customer relationship management, its core variables (satisfaction, trust, engagement and relationship quality) and its tools and models (loyalty programs, customer lifetime value, etc.).

The use of computers has been democratized, the consumer Internet has been widely re-populated and a digital business has emerged on the web. The customer has become "augmented" by digital technology, and so have customer relations [N'GO 19]!

Data have never been so easy to collect. Digital marketing, social networks, etc., the range of tools available to marketers, have continued to expand, sometimes side-lining companies from the human relationship: metric-based approaches have sometimes taken precedence over people-based approaches, with the result that customers and companies have become further apart rather than closer [JAL 18].

Customer relationship management has become more developed and professionalized and is now part of the strategic management of customer management: we speak of customer strategies to designate the strategic choices and trade-offs required to make pertinent decisions [VOL 12].

Introduction written by Thierry DELÉCOLLE, Florence JACOB and Isabelle PRIM-ALLAZ.

Theme 1: Frontiers and the Environment	Chapter 1: How Can Customer Relations and Sufficiency Be Reconciled? A Reflection on the Consumption of Second-hand Goods
	Chapter 2: Customer Relations and Sustainable Development in the Retail Sector
	Chapter 3: Corporate Social Responsibility and Loyalty
	Chapter 4: Reinventing Loyalty Programs in the CSR Age: Moving Toward Pro-social Loyalty Programs
Theme 1–Theme 2	Chapter 5: Toward Greater Sufficiency in Customer Relationships
Theme 2: Digital Frontiers	Chapter 6: Metaverse Opportunities for Customer Relations
	Chapter 7: Toward Transparent and Parsimonious Customer Data Collection
Theme 2–Theme 3	Chapter 8: From Persuasion to Customer Manipulation: The Role of Dark Patterns
Theme 3: Inclusive and Ethical Frontiers	Chapter 9: Digital Consumption and Inclusion
	Chapter 10: Improving Effective Accessibility of Products and Services for Vulnerable Customers
	Chapter 11: The Patient Experience
Theme 3–Theme 4	Chapter 12: Adopting Ethical Sales Behavior
Theme 4: Governance of New Frontiers	Chapter 13: Customer Relationships as a Factor of Resistance: The Case of Smart Feedback Tools
	Chapter 14: Customer Relations in the Social and Solidarity Economy
	Chapter 15: Purpose Corporations and Customer Strategy: Toward an Educational Customer Empowerment Strategy?
Conclusion	Chapter 16: Complex Customer Experience Management with Multiple Stakeholders

Table I.1. *Organization of the book and contributions to customer strategy frontiers*

Alongside these developments, humans have also begun to become aware of the consequences of their consumer activity regarding the exploitation of natural resources [VOL 22]. Responsible expectations are emerging among consumers, and companies are beginning to question their practices in order to integrate sustainable development and social responsibility. However, the customer relations field remains relatively permeable to these developments, which are driven by customers, supported by organizations and, more often than not, dictated by changes in the legislative environment. Take the fashion industry, for example. For a long time, this sector thrived during discount sales periods, selling off unsold products and boosting sales through these exceptional promotions. However, a growing number of brands are refusing to do so, both to affirm their engagement with society and to remind us that their products are “fairly” priced all year round. The same is true of Black Friday, a promotional operation imported from the United States, which corresponds to the last Friday in November – the day after Thanksgiving and the first day of festive shopping. To capture this early spending, retailers offer “huge” discounts. However, as you will read in Chapters 2, 5 and 15 of this book, some retailers do not play this game and justify their choice for the same societal and fair-price reasons as those mentioned above. These initiatives reflect a change of paradigm. In the same way as brand engagement, the authors of the various chapters present the questions posed by the arrival of these societal issues and the need for brands to transform their customer relations: not to sell less, but to better satisfy the needs of customers and the stakeholders around them. Among these stakeholders, environmental and social issues are at the forefront of current thinking.

This collective work presents the new frontiers of customer strategy. We identified four themes, which are not mutually exclusive, as in Chapters 5, 8 and 12, which, respectively, link theme 1 (“Frontiers and the Environment”) and theme 2 (“Digital Frontiers”); theme 2 and theme 3 (“Inclusive and Ethical Frontiers”); and theme 3 and theme 4 (“Governance of New Frontiers”). Chapter 16 concludes the book by examining the complex management of the multi-stakeholder customer experience.

Theme 1 – Frontiers and the Environment

Accelerated climate change in recent years has prompted us to question our consumption patterns and the business models of many organizations. The evolution of our consumption can cover a wide range of realities: no longer consuming certain products and services, consuming less, or even consuming better. In all cases, it is all about thinking in terms of sufficiency. As Valérie Guillard justifiably writes in the first chapter of this book, “sufficiency calls into question the way companies are managed, their business models, their marketing strategies and, in particular, their customer relations”.

So, what happens to customer relations in this transition? Is it a hindrance? Or, on the contrary, can it play a decisive role?

Companies’ corporate social responsibility (CSR) and customer relations initiatives are often in their infancy and highly heterogeneous. Customers themselves have widely varying expectations and behaviors. This variation can be found between individuals, in line with their degree of pro-environmental sensitivity, but also within the same individual, who can behave like a chameleon according to the product category (paying close attention to waste management, but regularly taking the plane) or according to their position (responsible consumer versus employee whose remuneration system is hardly compatible with pro-environmental practices).

The issue of responsible environmental customer relations is eminently complex. It sometimes seems that every good deed hides the devil! The following paragraphs provide a concrete illustration of the paradoxical injunctions that regularly emerge when companies and consumers seek to be more responsible.

The question of sufficiency arises strongly for people with high purchasing power, who consume a lot. It is also an issue for people with low purchasing power, who consume less de facto, but potentially low-cost products manufactured on the other side of the world in conditions that are sometimes questionable, and often poorly repairable.

However, deciding to withdraw products from sale because they are not eco-responsible can lead vulnerable populations to be removed from consumption. In Chapter 2, Sarah Lasri, Lionel Nicod and Valérie Renaudin examine the example of a DIY store that has made the conscious decision to stop selling energy-wasting heaters. While this choice is environmentally justified, it also excludes customers for whom the low purchase price of these products remains the only way to access heating.

The development of second-hand or rental products may be an interesting solution. When the brands themselves organize circulation of second-hand objects, they often transform the sale into a voucher for new products, thus forgetting the logic of circularity.

The first part of the book raises the question of the compatibility of customer-oriented marketing with the environmental transition we need to undertake. The very role of marketing in our consumption patterns, but also in developments we may consider virtuous, needs to be revisited.

Chapter 1, by Valérie Guillard, deals with the fact that sufficiency and relational marketing can come into conflict. While sufficiency aims for better but less consumption, relationship marketing seeks to create and maintain a permanent link with customers, and to develop in-depth knowledge in order to develop sales. However, sufficiency focuses on essential needs: when relationship marketing can aim to satiate customers through a high level of consumption, or even to lock them into a commercial relationship. However, as Valérie Guillard puts it so well, "quantity-based thinking is not the same as sufficiency, which is based on less and better". This chapter examines the business model of companies operating in the second-hand market and consumer acceptance of second-hand products. Indeed, second-hand products carry a promise of sufficiency and are naturally part of a circular approach, but the marketing approaches used to promote them sometimes run counter to the desired effects.

Chapter 2, by Sarah Lasri, Lionel Nicod and Valérie Renaudin, discusses the possibility of a new model for retail companies to strike a better balance between profitability, ecology and social responsibility. These authors illustrate the transformations at work within the retail environment, witnessing the tug-of-war of consumers torn between "the desire to consume and the desire to protect the planet". Retailers are the scene of paradoxes, first and foremost the opposition between hyperchoice and sobriety. For these authors, it is a question of getting all stakeholders (employees and other partners) around the table to rethink a new, more sustainable form of retailing, with and for the customer.

Chapter 3, by Didier Louis, Nathalie Fleck and Cindy Lombart, reviews CSR activities: philanthropic activities, respect for the environment, respect for consumers, respect for employees, etc., which make it possible to highlight a set of environmental and social values and objectives, thereby creating intangible assets in terms of image and reputation. They also question the impact of CSR on customer loyalty. If customers express CSR expectations, does a company's engagement with CSR impact customer loyalty? The work presented shows that the philanthropic activities of brands have a positive impact on customer loyalty along different dimensions (transactional, relational or hybrid), depending on the customer's sensitivity to CSR.

Chapter 4, by Loubaba Belaoud, Aïda Mimouni-Chaabane and Béatrice Parguel, invites us to reinvent the loyalty program in the age of CSR. Loyalty programs are key tools in customer relationship management, designed to identify, reward and retain profitable customers. Although they are seen as a win–win relationship between the company and its customers, loyalty programs have mainly been understood by companies as a means of increasing sales, with very little connection to CSR. In other words, loyalty programs are often viewed solely from an economic perspective, ignoring any environmental or social impact, whether positive or negative. This chapter invites us to reflect on how corporate social responsibility could offer loyalty managers the opportunity to transform loyalty programs in depth, in order to renew their appeal while overcoming some of the criticisms leveled at them. By defining the concept of a pro-social loyalty program, this chapter aims to help define the outlines of what a loyalty program could be in the CSR era.

Theme 2 – Digital Frontiers

The continuing digital transition of our economies is contributing to the evolution of customer relations and their management [N'GO 19].

Chapter 5, written by Jean-Baptiste Welté, Virginie Pez and Isabelle Dabadie, is a perfect link between Theme 1 and this theme of digital frontiers. This general chapter aims to advocate more responsible customer relationship management practices, without questioning their validity and relevance in the vast majority of cases. The authors strive to get us thinking about how to do "better" with "less" by systematically and imperatively taking into account the environmental and ecosystemic impact of the actions implemented.

The authors discuss the potential role of customer relations practices in the systemic exhaustion of today's consumer society. They highlight paradoxes such as the rebound effect, also discussed in Valérie Guillard's chapter, "How Can Customer Relations and Sufficiency Be Reconciled? A Reflection on the Consumption of Second-hand Goods". Encouraging people to consume more responsibly may give them the feeling that they are being allowed to mobilize other resources, leading to a zero or even negative effect.

This chapter also shows the pernicious effect of digital transformation, which is leading to an "invisible" pollution that encourages (over)consumption that is supposed to be responsible: overconsumption of data, which multiplies the need for servers, and overconsumption in logistics (in a very significant proportion of cases, home delivery is accompanied by the return of the product to the seller). In addition to the ecological problems it causes, the use of digital tools to support customer relations is not without social consequences. It can lead to dispossession and dereliction, in other words, a heightened sense of powerlessness and abandonment.

The second theme of the book deals with digital frontiers and the digital transformation of customer relations.

Today, this transformation is characterized by new digital media, such as metaverses, but also by the problem of data management and the very structuring of sites and data collection systems through persuasive designs, otherwise known as dark patterns.

Chapter 6, written by Catherine Lejealle and Thierry Delécolle, presents the opportunities offered by metaverses: a growing number of companies are investing in these virtual universes. These universes are persistent and shared, enabling interaction with other people in avatar, 3D or 2D format. The best-known are *Decentraland*, *Roblox*, *The Sandbox*, *Meta* and *Fortnite*. Brands seem to be betting that these new virtual spaces will be more successful than their big brother Secondlife. One of the keys to success will undoubtedly be the ability of these virtual universes to interconnect, which is not yet the case. The authors explore the motivations behind these investments.

Chapter 7, written by Tom Villenet, Thierry Delécolle and Grégoire Bothorel, deals with the transparent and parsimonious collection of datasets. Indeed, the new digital relational spaces, such as the metaverses mentioned above, present the big tech companies and brands with the opportunity to collect a wealth of data on visitor and buyer behavior. For brands, Internet user behavioral data represent a strategic asset for developing sales and steering marketing actions. Collecting these data poses a number of challenges. What is the relationship between citizens and their personal data: reluctance, consent, privacy paradox, etc.? Are all companies equal when it comes to collecting data? What regulatory framework is needed to govern practices?

Chapter 8, written by Florence Jacob, Jeoffrey Drouard, Séverine Erhel, Marianne Lumeau and Raphaël Suire, is dedicated to persuasive design methods and constitutes the second part in the book, articulating the transition from digital to inclusive and ethical frontiers. Regulation is a key issue in these digital environments. The Digital Service Act[1], for example, aims to protect consumers from browsing errors caused by persuasive design (otherwise known as dark patterns). These persuasive designs illustrate the desire of certain digital platforms/interfaces to manipulate customers, and are designed to increase customer connection time and encourage purchasing behavior. In other words, dark patterns are to digital technology what deceptive commercial practices are to offline exchanges. Indeed, if one of the objectives is to capture the user's attention in order to collect as much data as possible, these dark patterns can lead to what psychologists call problematic use of the Internet. At the same time, it is possible to educate and train users of digital tools to recognize manipulation by design. The authors propose an inventory of the different types of persuasive design, with two main categories: structural persuasive design, which exists for all Internet users, and situational persuasive design, which depends on the browsing behavior of the "targeted" Internet user.

Theme 3 – Inclusive and Ethical Frontiers

The return on investment (ROI) vision of marketing is achieved by the calculation of customer lifetime value and comes up against a number of societal as

1 Legislation on digital services to ensure a safe and responsible online environment, available at: https://commission.europa.eu/strategy-and-policy/priorities-2019-2024/europe-fit-digital-age/digital-services-act-ensuring-safe-and-accountable-online-environment_en.

well as financial realities. These strategies are not always the most satisfactory for companies: the growing importance of CSR issues is paving the way for the desire to integrate more customers in order to develop social inclusion and behave more ethically toward customers. While large public companies and mutualist players have been the most inclined to think about these issues, we are seeing the emergence of purpose corporations (Chapter 15 of this book), as well as a strengthening of laws on digital inclusion and society's growing awareness of consumer issues.

The third part of the book defines various concepts, such as digital inclusion and the patient experience, in order to better understand the question of how to establish a different relationship with customers. This part also provides solutions for thinking about customer relations.

Chapter 9, written by Léa Cauchard, enables organizations to think about a more inclusive digital strategy. To this end, the author defines the complex notion of inclusion and outlines its theoretical outlines. She then provides an overview of inclusive digital experiments already underway to reflect on their contributions and limitations. Finally, she develops a new approach to digital inclusion, focusing on both the characteristics of users' journeys and their perceptions.

Chapter 10, written by Pierre Volle and Sylvie Llosa, takes a broader approach to the effective accessibility of products and services, beyond digital journeys. They examine the concept of vulnerable customers and the social responsibilities incumbent on companies. To this end, the authors construct a conceptual image of the notion of the vulnerable customer, which has not yet been explored in research, and then define the actual accessibility of contact points during a vulnerable customer's journey. Based on two recent research studies, the authors then propose two methodologies for improving this accessibility.

In Chapter 11, Stéphanie Verfay explores the emerging concept of patient experience. Indeed, patients are becoming players in their own healthcare journey, while very often being in a fragile position due to illness or uncertainty about the outcome. Long forgotten by marketing, the patient is becoming a sensitive subject to help medical teams work better in cooperation with them. Stéphanie Verfay begins by tracing the development of the patient experience concept in order to define it and anchor it theoretically in the service transformation research movement. To do this, she details the different values that healthcare organizations bring to patients during their journey, and how to value the patient in order to co-construct these values.

Finally, it is also important to consider the question of salespeople's ethics when meeting customers, and this is what Eric Julienne does in Chapter 12. In the first part, the author examines the dilemma faced by salespeople during the act of selling, pointing out the factors that lead to unethical behavior. Second, he presents the techniques of influence, diverted from their sphere of use, in order to manipulate customers to trigger a sale. Finally, he develops an analysis of ethical sales behavior, and the conditions that the company must put in place to encourage its emergence. He shows that these ethics promote salespeople's well-being, customer satisfaction and, ultimately, sales performance.

The role of the salesperson within the organization raises the question of the governance of customer strategy.

Theme 4 – Governance of New Frontiers

The concept of organizational governance is a key subject associated with the long-term survival and success of organizations. This means taking into account environmental and social issues, as well as technological and economic developments, in the decisions made by management. Governance must therefore ensure that the company adapts to change and remains competitive in the long term. The governance of the new frontiers of customer relations, which we see as part of a responsible approach, must guarantee transparency, ethics and responsibility in decision-making (and in the criteria used to make decisions). In the context we have described so far, governance must comply with applicable laws and regulations. What is more, it can take advantage of new mechanisms to innovate, as in the case of the concept of purpose corporations proposed in Chapter 15.

Chapter 13, written by Françoise Simon and Virginie Schweitzer, revisits the question of data transparency through the case of smart feedback tools. Indeed, the emergence of connected tools enables customers using smart feedback tools to track their consumption in real time or their achievement of personal objectives in the context of physical activity. While these uses are of real interest to their users, data capture is also perceived as tracking, and can sometimes lead to forms of resistance (like the outcry against connected energy meters). The authors therefore propose a better understanding of the acceptance of smart feedback tools.

Chapter 14, written by Hajar El Karmouni and Alix Poels, presents customer relationship management in social economy organizations. These organizations are governed by the principle of limited profitability and the participation of stakeholders (including customers) in their governance. As such, the authors raise the question of whether customer relations can be the same in social and solidarity economy (SSE) organizations as in conventional market organizations, and explore their characteristics through case studies of organizations managed as cooperatives.

Chapter 15, written by Isabelle Prim-Allaz and Martine Séville, presents the challenges of customer relations in the field of purpose corporations. These companies have chosen to combine a mission of societal impact with their traditional mission of generating profits. Presenting the characteristics of mission-driven companies, the authors illustrate the paradox of customer loyalty in the context of mission-driven companies, as well as the dual pursuit of marketing and sales objectives, on the one hand, and societal mission objectives, on the other hand.

Finally, Chapter 16, by Amélie Martin, integrates multi-stakeholders into the relationship to manage the customer experience. The author proposes adopting a vision of the customer experience that is no longer customer-centric, but integrates all stakeholders. The multiplication of touchpoints (real and virtual), units of location and players involved in the customer experience poses difficulties in terms of organizational control. Some activities can be totally controlled by the company, while others will depend on all the parties involved: deliverers, installers, etc. The authors return to the origins of the customer experience concept to adapt a broader perspective, not limited to analyzing the behavior of relationship actors in isolation, but also employing a network perspective, enabling us to grasp interrelationships.

This chapter is deliberately included at the end of the book, because in order to support digital, ecological and energy transitions, it is important to go beyond the individual level of analysis to integrate all value chains and their interrelationships.

References

[GAB 14] GABRIEL P., DIVARD R., LE GALL-ELY M. et al., *Marketing des services*, Dunod, Paris, 2014.

[JAL 18] JALLAT F., PEELEN E., STEVENS E. et al., *Gestion de la relation client. Expérience client, Performance relationnelle et Hub relationnel*, 5th edition. Pearson Editions, Paris, 2018.

[N'GO 19] N'GOALA G., PEZ-PÉRARD V., PRIM-ALLAZ I. (eds), *Augmented Customer Strategy: CRM in the Digital Age*, ISTE Ltd, London and John Wiley & Sons, New York, 2019.

[VOL 12] VOLLE P. (ed.), *Stratégie clients*, Pearson Editions, London, 2012.

[VOL 22] VOLLE P., SCHOUTEN J., *Marketing (plus) durable*, De Boeck Supérieur, Louvain, 2022.

1

How Can Customer Relations and Sufficiency Be Reconciled? A Reflection on the Consumption of Second-hand Goods

The ecological transition necessary due to the negative consequences of human activities on the climate and international conflicts raising the question of dependence on natural resources and raw materials are leading us to make sufficiency another possible path for the development of societies [HEY 20].

In its latest report of 2022, the Intergovernmental Panel on Climate Change (IPCC) stated that achieving carbon neutrality by 2050 would imply a sixfold reduction in greenhouse gas emissions in France compared to 1990 levels. Achieving carbon neutrality is a *sine qua non* for limiting global warming to +1.5°C. Otherwise, humanity will have to deal with climate problems (heatwaves, storms and climate refugees) and loss of biodiversity, leading to the disappearance of species and even the services they provide, such as pollination and predation, to maintain natural balances. The reason is as follows: lifestyles that consume too many natural resources, emit too much carbon and are based on production and consumption that are disconnected from "real" needs. The IPCC and scientists call for sufficiency. Adopting a sufficient lifestyle implies temperance, in terms of mobility, food, buildings (particularly insulation and sizing), territories and the production and consumption of goods and services. It is precisely the latter that is the subject of this chapter.

Chapter written by Valérie GUILLARD.

This alternative path for the development of societies, known as sufficiency, calls into question the way companies are managed, their business models, their marketing strategies and, in particular, their customer relations [BOC 20, GOS 22]. Indeed, sufficiency and relationship marketing can come into conflict. Sufficiency involves consuming according to identified, well-considered needs; customer relationships involve creating a permanent link with consumers, which makes it possible to better understand their expectations with a view to selling them what they think they need, or at least end up wanting. While need is at the heart of both approaches, it does not have the same meaning or the same depth. It is up to the consumer (and society) to define their essential (or non-artificial [KEU 19]) needs in terms of the consequences that satisfying them will have on the living world in the case of sufficiency, and up to the company to reveal them (rather than their desires) in the case of the customer relationship. A close, privileged and lasting relationship with each customer is the very essence of relational marketing with a view to increasing sales volumes. Quantity-based thinking is not the same as sufficiency, which is based on less and better, and on diminishing economic models [PAR 22].

Some companies are born with a position of sufficiency in their customer relations. Loom, a sustainable brand, for example, chooses not to promote its clothing or issue loyalty cards or other benefits. The link that this brand builds with its customers is, of course, commercial, but it is also "intellectual" in the sense that the manager periodically sends out, two or three times a year, well-documented reflections on the impact of consumption on the environment. This brand uses phygital to, among other things, better understand how its customers use their clothes, creating a close physical link with them. Other brands, such as La Lessive de Paris (recently renamed Super Flacon), only use referrals as a means of recruiting new customers. They do not offer cards or other loyalty programs. On the other hand, brands that are part of the circular economy[1], such as Le Closet, a clothing rental service, regularly send emails to their customers to tell them about the latest finds and other novelties. Their slogan is "*Portez. Renvoyez. Recommencez*" ("Wear. Return. Do it Again"), which encourages customers to constantly change their outfits, offering them the option of outsourcing their wardrobe within the company. In the same vein, we can also mention the example of the Vestiaire Collective operation in collaboration with Alexander McQueen. Consumers are encouraged to resell one of the brand's second-hand pieces, in exchange for a voucher to purchase one of the brand's products on the new market. Reselling on the used market to buy on the new market is a logic that is far from recent and is widely practiced for all types of products (e.g. Trocathlon), luxury goods and cars. "Do it again", as

1 The circular economy consists of producing goods and services in a sustainable way by limiting the consumption and waste of resources and the production of waste. The aim is to move from a throwaway society to a circular economic model. See: www.ecologie.gouv.fr.

advocated by Le Closet, or selling old for new, as in the case of Vestiaire Collective, without questioning the need, remain the opposite of sufficiency. The question that then arises through these examples is how customer relations and sufficiency are articulated in the particular case of the second-hand market, the spirit of which is to strive for the best while using fewer natural resources compared to new objects, and perhaps even to strive towards a reduction in purchases.

This chapter, whose unit of analysis is the consumer, is structured as follows: in the first part, a few reminders from the literature provide a non-exhaustive overview of the characteristics of customer relations and sufficiency. This is followed by a focus on second-hand goods based on a study conducted with ADEME, CREDOC and Paris Dauphine University in March 2022. Finally, an analysis of a survey of consumers helps us understand how they perceive customer relations in the second-hand market. In conclusion, some thoughts for practitioners are offered.

1.1. Customer relations and sufficient living: what conflicts?

1.1.1. *Relationship marketing: spirit and tools*

Relationship marketing[2] is defined as "all marketing activities aimed at establishing, developing and maintaining lasting relationships with the best customers" [MOR 94, p. 22]. The tools mobilized to develop and maintain lasting relationships are essentially structured around promotional marketing campaigns, loyalty programs and direct marketing, depending on the moment in the relationship with the consumer: before the sale, at the point of sale or after the sale. With the aim of encouraging the replacement of what is already owned or the acquisition of additional goods, or even to build customer loyalty by getting them to return to the brand, companies activate a battery of tools such as vouchers, private sales, promotional gifts or the return of unused items such as schoolbags or clothes. The development of a lasting relationship can also take place at the point of sale through merchandising and the quality of the relationship with a salesperson. This involves establishing a relationship with the customer, informing them, detecting their needs and/or desires, and even offering them services or favors that will keep them coming back, feel listened to, understood and sometimes even flattered. It is also a question of putting the consumer in the right conditions, so that the atmosphere makes them feel welcome, giving them a sense of well-being, which will certainly lead them to come back and tell friends and family. Finally, relational marketing tools can also be

2 This section is not intended to be exhaustive. It aims to present very succinctly some of the elements needed to reflect on the relationship between sufficiency and customer relations. For a more exhaustive understanding of relationship marketing, see [GAB 14] or [JAL 18].

used after a product has been purchased, to perfect its use. The courses offered by certain brands to acquire skills are part of this approach [MON 20].

Relationship marketing is characteristic of a particular context. It marked the 1980–2000 period, a competitive context in which transactions alone were no longer sufficient. But the economic, political and social context is changing. At the very least, since the 2015 Paris Agreements, there has been a growing awareness of the ecological and social crisis. This awareness has recently been reinforced by the IPCC 2022 report, political events (the war in Ukraine) and climatic events (drought), and the emergence and media coverage of a proposal to frame production and consumption activities in terms of sufficient lifestyles.

1.1.2. *Sufficient lifestyle: characteristics, dimensions and links with the second-hand market*

Sufficiency is temperance in eating and drinking [COR 91]. Describing a way of life, sufficiency involves adjusting consumption and production to the needs of individuals in various areas: mobility (e.g. not using the car for journeys of less than 10 km[3] or driving slower), buildings (e.g. adjusting living space to the number of people, but also insulating buildings with bio-sourced or more environmentally friendly materials), food (e.g. eating seasonal, local fruit and vegetables, buying and/or producing them ourselves, eating less meat), territories (enabling soft mobility, composting, using solar panels for public buildings) and responsible consumption (buying products according to needs and that respect living organisms).

Sufficient consumption is embodied in deconsumer practices [DEL 13, GUI 21]. The practices mentioned by consumers include "no longer buying" certain categories of products, such as fast-fashion clothing; making things by ourselves or borrowing; "buying less" by adapting purchases to needs and monitoring the quantity and frequency of purchases; and "buying differently", whether it is better in the local sense, less-processed products or second-hand goods. The latter allow us to "stop buying" new products, thereby reducing the consumption of natural resources in both production and transport. Buying second-hand means "buying differently", in the sense that second-hand purchases give access to the pleasure of unearthing the bargain or the original bargain that no longer exists on the new market. As far as "buying less" is concerned, second-hand purchases can fulfill this objective, particularly for people who are committed to reducing their consumption [AUZ 19]. Indeed, buying second-hand takes time (research time in particular), during which

3 Up to 10 km, the bike is often faster than the car. See: https://www.citycle.com/427-city-moving-time/.

consumers may realize that they do very well without the product: they end up "giving up" and not buying. Second-hand purchases can, however, be at the heart of over-consumption [PAR 17] or even hyper-use when rented: inexpensive, the acquisition of a second-hand good removes the guilt from consumers, who will nevertheless indulge in consumption without straining their budget and, in their view, be environmentally friendly. The second-hand market is doing well: the Leboncoin platform forecasted sales growth of 10% in 2020, while the second-hand luxury goods market is growing at a rate of 12%[4].

Retailers are well aware of the opportunity offered by second-hand goods for their business. Some platforms use the same promotional tools that they use to sell new items. The Ïdkids brand, for example, offers a permanent Ïdtroc platform, an event dedicated to the exchange of second-hand clothing and objects from the Okaïdi, Oxybul, Ïdkifs and Catimini brands[5]. The system is based on the consignment-sale principle: customers are rewarded with vouchers to generate additional sales. General retailers are also offering new services to join the trend toward second-hand clothing in order to diversify their offer and build customer loyalty: rentals, outlets, collection vouchers in exchange for discounts, recycled clothing and repackaging have become innovative new services. The cohabitation of new and second-hand goods in retail outlets (e.g. Camaïeu, Les Galeries Lafayette or platforms such as Pixmania, which sells refurbished computers), or even purchase and rental (Fnac-Darty), has increased. Some retailers, such as Galeries Lafayette, have developed an online platform to bring together private individuals to sell second-hand products. Products are systematically handed over in person and in-store, in exchange for payment by gift card for the seller, which can only be used in the store. Retailers use relationship marketing strategies to attract customers to this offer, which is becoming increasingly popular. The same trends can be found in the economy of functionality, which substitutes buying with renting, for example, on the clothing rental platform Le Closet: "Le Closet is a rental service in the form of a subscription box that allows you to renew your wardrobe on a continuous basis". Continuously renewing your wardrobe seems a far cry from the notion of need. Furthermore, the rental of a garment is necessarily followed by a dry-cleaning service, a polluting activity. Incentivizing clothing rental is tantamount to increasing the negative impact on the living world, if only through dry-cleaning services. Admittedly, ecology is rarely the primary motivation for second-hand purchases: it is the "bargain" that clearly comes first [ROU 08]. Consumers are, however, rewarded for their good deeds, for example by receiving a voucher or contributing to a social gesture (if they bring back a used schoolbag or pair of jeans

4 See: https://ziqy.co/retail/la-seconde-main-un-marche-plein-dopportunites/.

5 See: https://www.idtroc.com/.

[GUI 15]). Receiving a reward stimulates the structures of the reward circuit and induces a feeling of satisfaction or even dependence, in this case on purchasing.

So, by inviting and encouraging this type of purchase, are retailers not going against the grain of a society that is becoming aware of the *need* to change its lifestyle and, more specifically, its relationship with (over)consumption? How do consumers perceive these relational strategies toward second-hand goods sometimes posited as being "at the service" of a more sufficient lifestyle, as they are framed by the notions of recycling, reconditioning or reusing objects?

1.2. Customer relations and the second-hand market

After briefly illustrating the second-hand market in 2022[6], we report on how consumers perceive the customer relationship in this market.

1.2.1. *The second-hand market: a brief overview in 2022*

Note that 62.5% of consumers often visit second-hand buying platforms (on the Internet) and/or second-hand stores without necessarily having a specific purchase project in mind, whereas 66% do so for new items. Buying second-hand has as much appeal as their new counterparts. This type of purchase became stronger or even started for some consumers during lockdown, when they had to go home at 6 p.m. with no opportunity for social activities. So it is often "out of boredom" or "to have a little fun, a little excitement during the day" (woman, 45) that people "look at Leboncoin in the evening on the way home from work, like I look at the newspaper, we look at what's going on in people's homes" (man, 39). These statements echo verbatim other studies according to which Leboncoin was one of the 20 most visited sites during the first lockdown[7]. The second-hand market offers small pleasures (63%). For 86% of those surveyed, it is a way of buying more things for less. Figure 1.1 shows, in percentage terms, the practices used by consumers in the second-hand market compared to the new market.

6 These figures come from a survey carried out with ADEME, CREDOC and Paris Dauphine University on a sample of 1,500 people representative of the French population (55% women; 8% aged 18–24, 17% aged 25–34, 25% aged 35–49, 25% aged 50–64, 25% aged 65 and over; 10% executives and higher intellectual professions, 19% employees, 28% retired, 13% blue-collar workers, 13% inactive, 13% intermediate professions and 4% farmers). The quotations are taken from a qualitative survey of 10 people conducted in the same study.

7 See: https://www.bfmtv.com/tech/20-4-millions-de-visites-en-un-jour-le-bon-coin-a-atteint-son-record-ce-dimanche_AN-202102090271.html.

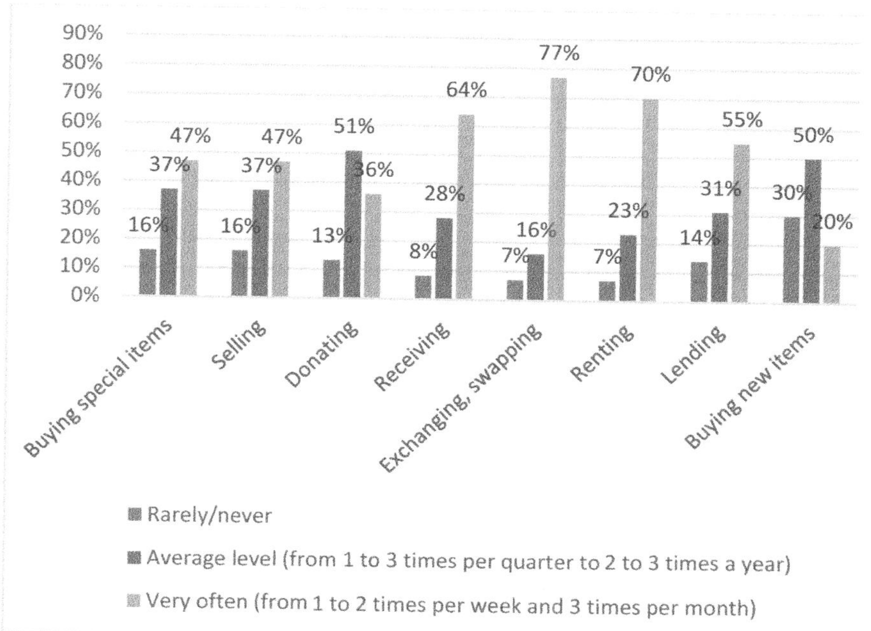

Figure 1.1. *Second-hand and new goods practices and new items (in %). For a color version of this figure, see www.iste.co.uk/delecolle/newfrontiers.zip*

Figure 1.1 illustrates that the most frequent practice is still the purchase of new items: 47% of consumers have never bought used items. The items most frequently purchased exclusively new remain adult clothing (46%), large household appliances (58%), small household appliances (50%) and electronic equipment (53%). These last three categories reflect fears of a lesser guarantee of use over time. Products that are bought as much second-hand as new are games (22%), clothing for teenagers and children (23% each) and furniture (25%).

However, the trend toward the second-hand market seems to be moving toward democratization. Note that 52% of respondents see buying second-hand as "having a similar consumption pattern to the majority of French people" (versus 72% for the new market), 55% as "the norm" (versus 76% for the new market) and 62% as "a habit" (versus 79% for the new market). There are inequalities according to income: 7% of people earning less than EUR 750 a month (4.7% of the sample) buy second-hand items one or two times a month, while 29% never do. For those earning EUR 5,000 or more a month (4.9% of the sample), 1.3% buy one or two times a month, while 40% never do.

However, buying second-hand is a practice that is often communicated as being beneficial to the environment, notably by limiting waste. How do consumers perceive relationship marketing tools (or the lack of) in the second-hand market?

1.2.2. *Perception of customer relations in the second-hand market*

Another survey was carried out with 43 consumers in the form of micro-narratives, to find out how they perceive customer relations in the second-hand market[8]. Customer relations are of course perceived differently depending on whether they concern commercial or non-commercial relations, but also depending on relations between peers (marketplace platforms such as Facebook marketplace, Leboncoin, Vinted, etc.) versus organizations that ensure a physical presence at a point of sale (thrift stores or other second-hand stores such as Envie, Emmaüs, etc.). In the following, we focus more specifically on relationships with a market or non-market organization. Three characteristics emerge from the transcription of the micro-narratives:

– a loss of legitimacy on the part of retailers that make "too much" use of relationship marketing tools upstream and downstream of the sale;

– a gain in freedom for retailers who make little use of them, particularly at the point of sale;

– an opportunity for consumers to gain skills.

1.2.2.1. *Customer relations for second-hand goods: loss of brand legitimacy*

For some consumers, the loss of brand legitimacy may stem from the use of the same marketing tools for the second-hand market as for the new market: promotions, giveaways, packaging, etc., whereas the second-hand market carries with it "another spirit": that of encounters, transmission, "helping each other out" and ecological values in particular [HER 97].

Platforms such as Backmarket are perceived by consumers as functioning "as if you were buying new from a professional seller, so there's normal customer service [...] in this case, the promotions don't shock me, it's a normal platform, they're looking to sell" (man, 29). For others, however, promotions "don't make sense for the second-hand market, it's borderline shocking, it shows that they haven't

8 Some of our reflections are based on an empirical study of 43 micro-narratives (average age: 29): "Unlike life stories, micro-narratives focus on specific consumption situations and practices" [LAD 14, p. 10]. Respondents were asked to write a micro-narrative about one or more customer relations experiences in the second-hand market. The data provided ranged from a few lines to several pages.

understood the relationship expected in this market and that they want to make a business out of it [...] exclusively" (man, 54). Many consumers point to the lack of legitimacy of retailers who offer discounts on prices that are already low. Admittedly, price is one of the main reasons why consumers turn to this market, but they do not expect promotions: "Loyalty programs for second-hand purchases could encourage more consumption of this type of product. I wonder about the legitimacy of this, however, as a second-hand product is already supposed to be discounted" (man, 32).

The perceived lack of legitimacy of certain brands may also stem from the over-consumption that their strategies can lead to among consumers. The latter are not fooled, even if they often "crack", not hesitating to speak of a "scam", perceiving a discrepancy between the marketing strategy deployed (low prices, advertising) and the spirit of second-hand goods, which resonates with ecology: "I buy, it's 8 euros a shirt with the discount, not expensive, no risk when I know perfectly well that I'll never wear it, I clearly don't need it, it's almost a scam I find, it's not the spirit of true second-hand, that which claims to be ecological" (man, 30). Consumers are weary from the sending out of emails, and do not see any sense in this marketing approach: "Vinted sends out emails too often, and it's tiring. They're always trying to push us to consume, which is rather paradoxical for a platform that advocates a more sufficient lifestyle" (woman, aged 23). The same goes for the commercial gifts that sometimes accompany the purchase of a second-hand item. Gifts come in many forms, from keyrings to birthday cards and other promotional items. The presence of a gift bothers some consumers, who once again fail to see the connection between the second-hand item and the gift. The latter, which is new and often of inferior quality, is harmful to living beings because of its composition, origin and, more often than not, its destination: the garbage can [DEL 16].

On the other hand, offers from retailers that encourage decluttering may be better received by consumers. The accumulation of objects can be a real problem for consumers [GUI 13], who do not know how to get rid of them. "I receive promotional emails and incentives from Vinted and Vestiaire Collective. When it comes to encouraging sales, I find it motivates me to sort through my closets, which is a good thing. When it comes to content encouraging buying, I tend to feel sorry for it, in the sense that the second-hand industry should be taking a very strong stance against excessive consumption" (woman, 25). Shopping platforms are transforming themselves by offering services to buy as well as to sell: the Ba&sh brand, for example, offers its customers a "resell" button in their personal space to put previously purchased products back on sale.

1.2.2.2. *Lack of customer relations in second-hand goods outlets: gains in freedom*

When talking about customer relations, consumers often refer to transactions that take place at the point of sale, and more particularly in thrift stores in the case of second-hand goods. Of course, this relationship differs according to the location of the store, as the culture of the place is different: "The relationship won't be the same in a second-hand shop in Barbès as in a small independent boutique in Montmartre" (woman, aged 23). Nevertheless, second-hand outlets are perceived as less formal. Consumers can "look for something in the men's department without (being) told off by a saleswoman: here it's for men only" (woman, 29); or: "I feel free in my purchases, not judged by what I try on" (man, 25).

The merchandising of points of sale in which second-hand items are sold, merchandising often based on searches, seems to influence consumers' relationship with their body: "At least there are big sizes and not just sizes 36 and 38, I find that in thrift stores, all bodies are allowed, you can have the body you have and not be ashamed of it" (woman, 29). The relationship in the lair of the second-hand outlet then generates less social anxiety [DEL 18], with salespeople being less present or even absent: "I feel less excitement than when buying new, the experience is duller [...] for all that the salespeople are less insistent, less oppressive in second-hand stores, the salespeople are more disinterested [...] in the end, I realize that I don't necessarily need more customer relations [...]" (woman, aged 27). Consumers expect less customer service in these outlets: "In thrift stores, there's little customer service, but that's the mood of the place, so it doesn't bother me at all" (man, 24). Consumers do not expect to be flattered by a salesperson when they do not want to be.

Lastly, some consumers want a minimum relationship with the previous owner of the items, but this is not possible on peer-to-peer platforms: "What's a shame is that at a thrift store, you don't know the history of the garment. On Vinted, you can know a little about the seller if you've chatted with her. For example, my Burberry trench coat that I sold at a second-hand shop, I don't know who bought it, but I'm getting a little history" (woman, 20). Some associations (Emmaüs) enable this relationship between two anonymous people who have had the object in their hands by inscribing on a label a little note that the previous owner agrees to write for the future user. The second-hand market can really have this soul, and some consumers are looking for it: the customer relationship must allow it and not spoil it.

1.2.2.3. *Customer relations in the second-hand market: skills development via action*

Consumers may expect platforms to provide them with technical assistance, for example in repairing or even (re)selling an item: "As far as selling is concerned, I appreciate it when the platform or store helps me to transform the products into a good condition" (woman, 31). Some see it as a gain in skills and part of the customer relationship [MON 20]. Making, repairing or giving a new life to an object forgotten in an attic are practices for which some consumers are open, but are practices for which they do not necessarily have the skills. The ADEME-CREDOC-DAUPHINE survey (2022) shows that 52% say they know how to sew, embroider and knit; 63% say they know how to make or transform objects; 85% can repaint a room, but only 36% plumb and 35% do electrics; 24% know how to repair mechanical objects. Only 21% rely on organizations such as Repair Cafés or other associations. These figures, which echo academic studies [CAP 21] and OBSOCO's observatoire du Faire[9], reveal an appetite for this type of customer relationship, based on the acquisition of knowledge and know-how that sometimes characterize second-hand objects. Doing it yourself is often part of a sufficient approach as it allows for prolonged use of objects, less recourse to the market, but also reflection on materials, which pleases consumers by restoring meaning [LOC 19]. "Making" also takes time: it is a practice that does not rely on the ease of acquiring a good that will serve, if not no purpose, at least very little. These skills can be acquired at the point of sale, provided by the company offering the courses and services, often for a fee (e.g. Bricorama), but can also be obtained between peers during the sale of an item, which makes this type of transaction even more attractive. Sellers on platforms such as Leboncoin are often able to give advice on how to use a machine, tool or other object, or show how it works.

1.3. Conclusion

Even in a context of sufficiency, relationship marketing makes sense; sufficiency is based on relationships (with ourselves and with others). On the other hand, the recommendations promoted by academics and practitioners need to evolve in line with sufficiency-promoting marketing [GOS 22]. As some authors explain [BOC 20, GOS 22], new business models based on sufficiency must be envisaged, thought out and created, as must new ways of interacting with customers in order to engage them in the company's mission. Relationship marketing places a premium on the customer's role in value creation. However, the way in which value is created is evolving in today's context, marked as it is by the consequences of consumption on the living world. The creation of value is and will undoubtedly be in the relationship, but in a relationship that is no longer based on the quantity consumed. We believe and hypothesize that value will be created above all through a long-term relationship with customers, supported by well-crafted products and promoted by education. Education for what? To guide consumers toward practices that are less harmful to the living world... if the organization is committed to this approach, and embodies

9 See: https://bpifrance-creation.fr/entrepreneur/actualites/lancement-du-premier-observatoire-du-faire.

these values in its mission statement. Learn what? Learn to consume products that correspond to a real need and not to a lack; learn to know the product (its composition, for example), its origin (where it was produced), its various functions, how to maintain it so as to use it over time and so on. This kind of education (and transparency) should help restore a bond of trust between companies and consumers. The vast majority of the latter never cease to think that they are "being taken for a ride" by paying more for a product, whereas in principle they are in favor of everyone (people, animals) being respected in the production and consumption process (including transport and delivery). Turning to a relationship based on explanation and learning should, moreover, have a positive resonance with consumers who express this desire to learn, to do and to know [CAP 21]. How can we learn? Of course, sales staff need to be (better?) trained in product composition, which would also enrich their jobs and roles. The recommendation of convinced and satisfied customers who become ambassadors for a brand advocating sufficiency will be all the more valuable: the company could then refrain from mass communication on its products.

In the second-hand market, it would seem that a relational strategy modeled on that of new objects reveals to consumers the company's recovery of an ecological discourse for profit, devoid of any sensitivity to the stakes these objects carry: a privileged relationship with ourselves and others, those who have already owned the object; respect for living things because they pollute less; learning a different way of consuming and being, one that requires turning more toward others (making contact, making the effort to go beyond the fear of the unknown, etc.). Numerous relational practices should be reviewed in the light of sufficiency, such as the offering of commercial gifts, which are often of poor quality, or of vouchers to be redeemed in the new market, betraying the absence of any pro-ecological value on the part of the organization that resorts to these practices.

Relationship marketing, as part of sufficiency-promoting marketing, needs to be created to take this new path to sufficiency, particularly through second-hand goods, and like many other marketing tools (communication, pricing, distribution), it can enrich the marketer's profession.

1.4. References

[AUZ 19] AUZARY L., DUBLY S., GUILLORY L. et al., "Devenir sobre en participant au(x) défi(s) "Rien de neuf" de Zero Waste France : analyses des profils, motivations et vécus", in GUILLARD V. (ed.), *Du gaspillage à la sobriété*, De Boeck, Paris, 2019.

[BOC 20] BOCKEN N.M., SHORT S.W., "Transforming business models: Towards a sufficiency-based circular economy", in BRANDÃO M., LAVAREVIC D., FINNVEDEN G. (eds), *Handbook of the Circular Economy*, Edward Elgar Publishing, Cheltenham, 2020.

[CAP 21] CAPEAU F., COVA V., "Faire soi-même et Bien-Être : les éclairages de la Sociologie Positive", *37e Congrès International de l'Association Française du Marketing*, Angers, France, 2021.

[COR 91] CORNARO L., *De la sobriété : conseils pour vivre longtemps*, J.B. Baillière et fils, Paris, 1891.

[DEL 13] DE LANAUZE G.S., SIADOU-MARTIN B., "Pratiques et motivations de déconsommation : une approche par la théorie de la valeur", *Revue française de gestion*, vol. 39, no. 230, pp. 55–73, 2013.

[DEL 16] DELACROIX E., GUILLARD V., "Consumers who avoid relationships: Social anxiety in commercial contexts", *Journal of Consumer Behaviour*, vol. 15, pp. 370–384, 2016.

[DEL 18] DELACROIX E., GUILLARD, V., "Les goodies ont-ils de la valeur pour ceux qui les reçoivent ?", *Congrès de l'Association Française de Marketing*, Strasbourg, France, 2018.

[GAB 14] GABRIEL P., DIVARD R., LE GALL-ELY M. et al., *Marketing des services*, Dunod, Paris, 2014.

[GOS 22] GOSSEN M., KROPFELD M.I., ""Choose nature. Buy less". Exploring sufficiency-oriented marketing and consumption practices in the outdoor industry", *Sustainable Production and Consumption*, vol. 30, pp. 720–736, 2022.

[GUI 13] GUILLARD V., *Garder à tout prix : décryptage d'une tendance très tendance*, Vuibert, Paris, 2013.

[GUI 15] GUILLARD V., JOHNSON G.D., "Un vieux contre un neuf : une étude des réactions des consommateurs à l'égard des offres de reprise", *Décisions Marketing*, no. 78, pp. 29–44, 2015.

[GUI 21] GUILLARD V., *Comment consommer avec sobriété*, De Boeck Supérieur, Brussels, 2021.

[HER 97] HERRMANN G.M., "Gift or commodity: What changes hands in the US garage sale?", *American Ethnologist*, vol. 24, pp. 910–930, 1997.

[HEY 20] HEYER É., LOKIEC P., MÉDA D., *Une autre voie est possible*, Flammarion, Paris, 2020.

[JAL 18] JALLAT F., PEELEN E., STEVENS E., VOLLE P., *Gestion de la relation client. Expérience client, Performance relationnelle et Hub relationnel*, Pearson, London, 2018.

[KEU 19] KEUCHEYAN R., *Les besoins artificiels : comment sortir du consumérisme*, Zones, Paris, 2019.

[LAD 14] LADWEIN R., RÉMY É., "Sacré Noël !", *Revue du MAUSS*, vol. 44, pp. 229–249, 2014.

[LOC 19] LOCHMANN A., *La vie solide : la charpente comme éthique du faire*, Payot, Lausanne, 2019.

[MON 20] MONNOT E., "Les trajectoires d'apprentissage des clients lors de la première utilisation d'un produit", *Recherche et Applications en Marketing (French Edition)*, vol. 35, pp. 50–77, 2020.

[MOR 94] MORGAN R.M., HUNT S.D., "The commitment-trust theory of relationship marketing", *Journal of Marketing*, vol. 58, pp. 20–38, 1994.

[PAR 17] PARGUEL B., LUNARDO R., BENOIT-MOREAU F., "Sustainability of the sharing economy in question: When second-hand peer-to-peer platforms stimulate indulgent consumption", *Technological Forecasting and Social Change*, vol. 125, pp. 48–57, 2017.

[PAR 22] PARRIQUE T., *Ralentir ou périr : l'économie de la décroissance*, Le Seuil, Paris, 2022.

[ROU 08] ROUX D., GUIOT D., "Une mesure des motivations envers l'achat d'occasion, leurs antécédents et leurs conséquences", *Recherche et Applications en Marketing*, vol. 23, pp. 63–95, 2008.

2

Customer Relationships and Sustainable Development in the Retail Sector

In response to Black Friday 2021, French company Aigle launched Positive Friday. Far from offering the usual all-out promotions, it decided to close all its stores and its e-shop in France on that day, and promote second-hand clothing by referring customers to its dedicated Second Souffle website. This example illustrates – through this ephemeral but striking gesture of protest, which goes as far as closing sales outlets on Black Friday – the growing willingness of retailers to participate in a more sustainable retail process, even if it means going against their own short-term interests.

Structurally, retailing is a particularly resource-intensive activity. This is because it involves moving products from the production phase to the consumption phase, in what is essentially a supply chain function. This involves transporting the product from the factory by ship, plane or truck to warehouses, where it is then sent directly to customers or, more often, to points of sale. In essence, this activity generates transport and greenhouse gas emissions. Stores, for their part, also have a heavy carbon footprint: these “factories for sale” are heated and air-conditioned, with lights illuminating products and display cases day and night, and so on. Even if LEDs replace more energy-intensive lighting, if regulations reduce the duration of window lighting, if rainwater recovery systems or solar panels on roofs and parking lots lighten the balance sheet, the store is still an energy-guzzling place. Delivery to the customer also adds to energy costs and greenhouse gas emissions. And when it is not the store that delivers, it is the customers who create much the same effects.

Some new sales concepts reinforce this negative impact on the planet. Business models based on the mass sale of inexpensive products, manufactured on the other side of the globe, are growing exponentially, particularly in a context of flagging purchasing

---

Chapter written by Sarah LASRI, Lionel NICOD and Valérie RENAUDIN.

power. The success of retailers, such as Action, Primark, Shein or even Ali Express, can be explained by the profusion of choice on offer and by extremely accessible prices, regardless of the environmental costs involved. The traditional retailers who have to compete with them are often not to be outdone, throwing themselves wholeheartedly into the latest trends to satisfy their customers. Quick commerce, which consists of delivering groceries from stores or dark stores, local logistics centers located in city centers, in record time (around 15 minutes) is the archetype.

At the same time, however, there is a growing awareness of the impact of retail on the environment. The retail sector is seeking to reinvent itself, make progress, reduce its energy footprint and enter into more virtuous schemes, with numerous initiatives. However, it is not easy to match words with deeds to serve the consumer in a more responsible, yet profitable, way. To this end, retailers are increasingly forging partnerships to move toward a more responsible approach. In recent years, they have moved from legitimacy-based partnerships with NGOs or associations to skills-based partnerships with companies, mainly start-ups [RIA 22]. Naturalia has signed an agreement with Les Petits Bidons, which sells ecological cleaning products made in France. L'Occitane has teamed up with Jean Bouteille to develop in-store bulk liquids. Now is not the time to seek legitimacy, but to take reasoned action, to make taking effective account of sustainable development issues compatible with a business model based on the creation of both financial value and value in the eyes of the customer.

In this chapter, we first identify a number of structural paradoxes that may suggest an incompatibility between retail and sustainable development. These paradoxes often reflect the internal conflicts experienced by customers, torn between the desire to consume and the desire to protect the planet. Yet these customers, who often want everything and its opposite, are increasingly expressing a genuine desire for a paradigm shift in their consumption. They have high expectations of retailers and want them to act more responsibly and transparently. In this way, they contribute to the constraints already imposed on retailers by public authorities. As we shall see, beyond regulatory constraints, it is in the retail sector's interest to play its part responsibly in a complex transition to sustainability, thereby meeting the growing expectations of its customers and employees alike.

2.1. Incompatibility between retail and sustainable development? A few paradoxes to overcome

In this section, we highlight three paradoxical injunctions facing the retail sector today:

– providing hyperchoice but participating in sobriety;

– selling ever greener products at ever lower prices;

– offering an increasingly enriched customer experience while consuming fewer resources.

2.1.1. *The hyperchoice model versus the expectation of greater sufficiency*

Retailers build their product and service offering to best meet the expectations of the customers they have decided to give priority to. As the preferred intermediary between manufacturers and consumers, the retailer selects an assortment. They try to differentiate themselves from their competitors through this assortment, and thus win the preference of their customers.

The temptation to multiply references to cover as many needs as possible is great. Since the 1960s and the establishment of the hypermarket model, consumers have also become accustomed to hyperchoice. This trend has been reinforced by e-commerce, which offers an almost infinite choice, as exemplified by shopping platforms such as Amazon.

Yet this hyperchoice is not inexorable. For traditional retailers, it is possible to concentrate on fewer items, with fewer but better-selected products. In some cases, consumers even appreciate this type of store, as it saves them time and avoids the hassle of comparing special offers and prices, which are sometimes too complex.

When the customer is reassured about price or value for money, in store brands as different as Lidl or Costco, which offer a much smaller number of products per square metre than supermarkets or hypermarkets of the same size, shopping is smoother and the managers can work more on the specifications and logistics of a reduced number of products.

Expanding the product range can also be based on a responsible approach. A large number of retailers, in sectors as varied as clothing, household appliances and telephony, have chosen to add second-hand and reconditioned products to their selection, thereby increasing customer choice by offering alternatives to buying new products, at a lower cost and more respectful of the planet. Retailers are also improving their choice by offering additional services, lending tools or equipment to avoid over-consumption (Monoprix) and promoting repair rather than purchase in their customer service, which is greatly transforming their businesses (Boulanger). In short, these retailers are fully in line with the highly sustainable logic of the economy of functionality [MOA 09].

2.1.2. *Selling ever-greener, ever-cheaper products*

Modern supermarkets rely on a system of wholesale and retail sales to offer consumers low prices. Right from the creation of the first retailers in France and the United States, lowering prices through lower unit margins has been a cornerstone of the retailer's business model. Thus, in 1852, Boucicaut claimed lower prices than its competitors in Le Bon Marché, and Woolworths opened stores in which all products were 5 cents. These pioneers associated the notion of low prices with the image of retail and set consumer expectations for this element of the marketing mix. By way of example, in large food superstores, price remains the number-one choice criterion for customers, after geographical location. With this in mind, retailers such as Walmart, IKEA and Lidl have built their strategies around this criterion. Others, such as Leclerc, through quiestlemoinscher.com, have developed digital price comparators to distance themselves from their competitors. Price has thus become the first-choice criterion for 52% of customers [BRA 22]. Environmental protection and climate change are only the fourth criteria after purchasing power, health and safety. Price optimization is a vital issue for retailers.

In order to achieve low prices, retailers are seeking to optimize costs. This cost-conscious strategy may seem contradictory to the green light given to supermarkets. On the product side, the price of organic products is on average higher than that of other products. This is because the production methods used for environmentally friendly products impose higher production costs on producers than for conventional products. These higher costs are passed on to the consumer in the final price. Sustainable products, which are no longer disposable but designed to last, require an initial investment. For example, a classic soft signal toothbrush costs EUR 2.59, while its refillable version costs EUR 9.39. The two refills then cost EUR 4.89. In the long run, therefore, it is more economical to have invested in this more environmentally friendly toothbrush. Nevertheless, the initial price may put the brakes on short-sighted consumers on the shelves, and all the more so in an inflationary context.

Similarly, the development of short distribution channels and the diversification of producers lead to higher coordination costs, particularly for retailers whose strategy is based on a narrow assortment, such as hard discounters. Consumers may turn away from these products, not least because of inflation. In March 2022, consumer prices rose by 4.5% in France and 8.5% in the United States [LEC 22], and this trend is set to continue. This rise in prices, already present in 2021, has led to a decline in sales of organic products [PLI 22]. However, the eco-responsible approach also offers opportunities for retailers in terms of product prices and costs. First of all, green products, while more expensive, offer higher unit margins than conventional products [BEZ 13]. It is therefore in the interest of retailers to promote them in their product ranges, despite their higher price. They also help to differentiate them from competitors when some of them are offered at psychologically low prices, as in the case of Auchan, which has promoted 50 organic products at EUR 1. Second, a fine-tuned short-date strategy helps to manage known markdowns and limit wastage. Many supermarkets are setting up in-store areas dedicated to “anti-waste”. By reducing breakage costs in this way, they also limit food waste, which in France accounts for 10 billion tons of discarded products a year, of which the retail sector is responsible for 14% [MIN 23]. Finally, when coupled with local sourcing and short distribution channels, they can reduce supply costs and logistics. This diversification of producers by relying on local suppliers also increases the negotiating power of retailers.

Selling more local, organic and environmentally friendly products at reasonable prices is a challenge. But it is difficult to ask people on low incomes to change their eating habits. Even so, buying less food but of better quality is a practice that is gaining ground, and one that needs to be supported by the retailer (smaller cuts of meat, selection of products raised in a sustainable manner, etc.).

2.1.3. *Enhancing the customer experience while reducing energy waste*

Ecological considerations aside, retailers are subject to strong economic pressures. The search for value creation and sales growth often remain the company’s top priorities.

Nevertheless, consumers, associations and public authorities are speaking out against the waste of resources. This raises a number of questions. How can we continue to entice customers into a store with a window display that has no lighting? How can we attract customers without leaflets? How can we make customers dream of a memorable experience without consuming too many resources, particularly event budgets?

These are just some of the questions that retailers have to answer in a context where respect for the environment is increasingly important. Today, they are subject to a contradictory injunction that complicates their relational strategies: to do ever more for the customer with ever fewer resources. Solving this equation is far from easy.

In today’s fiercely competitive environment, the quest for retail differentiation consumes ever more energy and resources. Whether it is lighting, point-of-sale displays, animations, permanently lit digital screens or interactive kiosks, these essential elements of the customer experience are now being called into question.

The case of shop windows is particularly telling. In 2021, window lighting was the subject of negotiations in the French National Assembly as part of the Climate and Resilience Act. The prospect of giving mayors the power to ban lighting, among other things, raised a storm of protest within the retail community. This regulation was perceived as an obstacle to the freedom to enter into a relationship with the customer, and as a hindrance to city shops already affected by the growth of e-commerce. The shop window, thought of as a "customer vacuum cleaner", generates an attractiveness perceived as necessary for competitiveness. Yet, in 2022, faced with the risk of electricity shortages and soaring energy bills, retailers planned a coordinated switch-off of their storefronts. While the environmental argument may not have been enough to convince them, the economic argument carried weight.

The real question is how to produce a pleasurable customer experience within a logic of sobriety. In other words, how can sobriety be made attractive? For a long time, organic stores have been accused of being austere, very uniform in color and ultimately very dull. Merchandising can be rethought with movable, modular furniture, enabling us to reinvent product displays at little cost. L'Occitane has innovated in Japan with cardboard decorations, which are more ecological, modular and aesthetically pleasing, proving that wonder and respect for the environment can be compatible.

The human element is also key to ensuring that the experience remains rewarding. The memory of the purchasing experience is often very positively linked to social interactions at the point of sale and the words exchanged with the salesperson [FLA 17]. The authentic and human experience of the Murfy start-up appliance repairers is often praised. Beyond the fact of offering repair rather than a new purchase, which is gratifying and less expensive for the customer, the human contact and advice exchanged are part of the experience.

In short, retailers are facing major conflicts. Compromises have already been found, as the above examples demonstrate. However, there is still a long and winding road ahead to move towards a more sustainable model. Here, we propose an approach in which customers and employees are at the heart of this transformation.

2.2. Customers and employees: accelerating sustainable development in the retail sector?

Mass retailing is also characterized by the human bonds that are forged. The attitudes and behavior of customers and employees contribute to the evolution of brands toward more sustainable models. Their roles are also affected by these evolutions.

2.2.1. *The customer's voice: a gateway to new models?*

As we have just shown, the retail sector mirrors the paradoxes that tug at customers' heartstrings. Although they declare themselves to be increasingly sensitive to environmental issues, the fact remains that their consumption choices are sometimes the opposite.

The great challenge for companies is to lead consumers toward more sustainable consumption [EAG 20]. Retailers can play a central role in this transformation of consumer society. Their privileged interactions with their customers, their choice of products and their management of points of contact (store, website, application, parcel drop-off, external deliverers, etc.) are all opportunities to engage the customer alongside the company in a greener, more sustainable policy.

Increased customer attention to retailers' CSR policies is forcing the latter to commit resources to a more responsible transition. However, faced with the contradictions of customers, this is not an easy task. That is why it is essential to be very transparent in the messages sent to customers; in particular, the way in which the cost of the transition is shared by both the company and the customer. An educational approach is needed to increase consumers' willingness to pay, or to encourage them to make a greater effort.

In addition, the development of environmentally friendly processes also has an impact on the in-store customer journey and the actions customers have to carry out to do the shopping – actions commonly referred to as the customer's "work". Indeed, in service, the customer is defined as a temporary employee of the organization [MIL 86] whose activity, known as participation, is indispensable to the production of the service. This participation is one of the cornerstones of the self-service business model of mass retailing. Some retailers, such as IKEA, have amplified the customer's role by delegating tasks along the entire value chain, from product design to assembly. The customer accepts a high level of involvement because, in return, they benefit from it. Participation allows them to save money [EIG 87], as products are less expensive because they carry out some of the tasks for the company; to save time, as with self-service checkouts [CUR 07]; to feel non-dependent, as with the use of scanners [CUR 07]; or to ensure a level of quality, as they feel they can do the job better than the service provider [BIT 97]. The greening of distribution has a strong impact on customer participation and raises the question of the relevance of motivating factors. Most of the changes linked to the climate emergency are in contradiction with the notions of savings and time saving. For example, "no-packaging" requires more handling on the part of the customer, which increases the time spent in the store, and at a higher cost, as the customer assumes the cost of the container in addition to higher product prices. These are key factors in a context of accelerating lifestyles associated with the digitalization of society, and in an inflationary environment. As a result, the greening of distribution is unlikely to be very successful. Paradoxically, these new processes are proving very popular with customers, as demonstrated by the 40% growth in packaging-free sales in 2019 and 8% growth in 2020, despite the health crisis [LEC 21]. It is based on the values of the individual (respect for the environment, awareness of what is at stake for future generations) and relies on two other factors: the need to control the quantity purchased and the need to ensure a level of quality via an eco-responsible approach. These levers are particularly powerful, prompting a significant number of customers to transform their role from temporary employee to real employee of the organization. This is how *Associations pour le maintien de l'agriculture paysanne* (AMAPs, French Associations for the Preservation of Farming Agriculture) came into existence. Often stemming from organic farming, these distribution methods rely on a group of customers who handle all or part of the logistics and sales to other consumers. The volunteer customer then takes on the role of self-service employee or delivery person. These highly participatory activities raise new issues for retailers. For participation to be a source of satisfaction and productivity for the company, the customer must know how to participate, and the retailer has a responsibility to explain their role to them, even in simple processes [NIC 18]. For example, the profitability of bulk products is lower than that of ready-to-sell products, not only because of the maintenance involved, but also because of the customer's ability to properly understand their role. This is all the more true when the role becomes more complex, as is the case with AMAPs. The efforts required by customers are twofold: operational and cognitive. The customer must not only carry out more tasks, but also organize themselves more so as not to miss products that they now have to refill. It is therefore necessary for brands to train customers in these new tasks by clearly communicating the societal impacts, which are the sources of motivation.

The example of the French appliance store Boulanger shows the extent to which customer expectations can be the driving force behind changes in business models. When Boulanger asks customers what they want from their advisors, they increasingly say they want someone to advise them on how to make their products last longer. While the repair business has long been shunned in the household appliance market, it is increasingly coming to the fore, with a new business model needing to be invented to ensure profitability, even if it is lower than that of traditional sales. The retailer must truly reinvent itself: it no longer pushes products towards customers, but asks customers to bring back products so that they can be reconditioned and resold (C to B to C logic). This is a profound transformation of the retailer's business model and culture. Consumers are not the only actors who can lead retailers to commit to sustainable development. Employees are also increasingly making demands related to these issues.

2.2.2. *The voice of employees: a driving force in the transition of retailers*

Most retailers, like all major companies, are riding the wave of corporate responsibility by promoting a proactive CSR policy in the fight against global warming.

When corporate values are translated into action, they become a powerful motivating factor [BRO 06]. Employees feel buoyed by the meaning of their work for the planet, as can be seen at Marcel & Fils. This alignment between corporate values and the operational implementation of strategy is a key motivational factor. This is all the more important in the field, particularly in stores, where salaries are low and tasks are not very rewarding. A horizontal, cross-functional sustainable development policy can help to engage employees by getting them involved, which increases the meaning of their work. They become agents of change. To achieve this, decisions need to be decentralized, and local teams need to be given room to maneuver. In the food sector, the possibility of referencing local producers with simplified internal systems at the local level encourages employee involvement. Involving the whole company in CSR is doubly beneficial, boosting performance and, above all, pride in belonging. Enhancing the employer brand plays a fundamental role in recruiting the younger generation, reducing turnover and curbing the "Great Resignation" phenomenon experienced in the United States, with four million resignations in 2021. On the other hand, employees who are proud of their company are the best ambassadors for their customers. Contact staff are key to reassuring customers, who are increasingly well informed and sensitive to the sincerity of companies.

However, CSR strategy is not always consistent with a group's performance objectives, and this contradiction can be felt in stores. In fact, at the point of sale, the employees of these groups are subject to imperatives that are difficult to reconcile with the values advocated by the brand. As unit margins are low in this sector, employees are often obliged to promote star products for the customer, or those with high margins, without regard for their carbon footprint. For example, they place a well-known national brand of spread with a high palm oil content at eye level with the consumer, as it is a strong and attractive reference on the shelf. Other examples include retailers that display strong values but promote ultra-fast deliveries via precarious employment. This discrepancy between the company's declared values and those actually implemented in stores or warehouses is particularly complex to manage. Indeed, if it is perceived, it can create internal conflicts among co-workers, torn between the group's official discourse and day-to-day professional actions. This can lead to demotivation, a negative image for the company and a reduction in performance [LI 22].

Finally, the employees themselves are not free of contradictions. Although sensitive to environmental issues, they are also attentive to their personal conditions. In particular, commission-based remuneration systems push them to sell more and more. Moving from an incentive to sell more to an incentive to have equipment repaired or have the customer buy a reconditioned product would be a radical transformation for salespeople. While these injunctions are often welcomed by employees who wish to participate in the sobriety movement, giving up the bonuses associated with sales performance is clearly unacceptable. In this context, retailers seeking to embark on a profound transition must take care to adapt the way they remunerate their employees, so that the transformation does not take place at the expense of their income. Like customers, the symbolic benefits brought about by the greening of the retail sector are no substitute for the economic benefits that can be achieved in an economy of over-consumption.

In short, customers and employees are looking for more meaning in their consumption and work. The symmetry of attentions shows just how useful it is to look after your staff in order to serve your customers better. Increasingly well informed, customers and employees are pointing out the inconsistencies between what brands do and what they say, and are urging them to make progress and avoid measures that could be described as greenwashing.

2.3. Conclusion

The ecological transition is a major challenge, as it is taking place in a capitalist system where paradoxes tend to slow down change. It calls for the invention of new business models [CHA 22], which sometimes collide head-on with historical models, and this cannot be done without clashes.

Moreover, the historical role of retailing has been to serve all customers [DAU 18]. By putting everything under the same roof, supermarkets have promised to meet the needs of all customers who walk through their doors, whatever their income. However, not all customers are the same in terms of their sensitivity to environmental considerations. Nor do they all have the financial means to concern themselves with these issues, as the *Gilets jaunes* movement has reminded us. Retailers cannot ignore these differences in acculturation and access to sustainable development. This raises the question of the removal of customers with the lowest purchasing power, who would no longer be able to access the consumption to which they are entitled. The difficulties encountered by successive governments in proposing a food voucher that would provide access to healthy, environmentally friendly products attest to the complexity of the problem. In the non-food sector, the issue is identical. When a DIY company makes the conscious decision to stop selling portable heaters, which are a source of energy waste, it de facto sidelines customers for whom these products are the only means of accessing heating.

This means that retailers will have to work together to find a third way. Proposing a new model that strikes a balance between ecological and social benefits is central. In short, it is a question of bringing all employees and partners around the table to rethink, with and for the customer, a new sustainable business model.

2.4. References

[AND 16] ANDERL E., SCHUMANN J.H., KUNZ W., "Helping firms reduce complexity in multichannel online data: A new taxonomy-based approach for customer journeys", *Journal of Retailing*, vol. 92, no. 2, pp. 185–203, 2016.

[BEZ 13] BEZAWADA R., PAUWELS K., "What is special about marketing organic products? How organic assortment, price, and promotions drive retailer performance", *Journal of Marketing*, vol. 77, no. 1, pp. 31–51, 2013.

[BIT 97] BITNER M.J., FARANDA W.T., HUBBERT A.R., ZEITHAML V.A., "Customer contributions and roles in service delivery", *International Journal of Service Industry Management*, vol. 8, no. 3, pp. 193–205, 1997.

[BRA 22] BRAY F., "Des consommateurs plus responsables, mais aussi plus exigeants", *LSA Green*, available at: https://www.lsa-conso.fr/des-consommateurs-plus-responsables-mais-aussi-plus-exigeants,406816, 2022.

[BRO 06] BROCKNER J., "It's so hard to be fair", *Harvard Business Review*, vol. 84, no. 3, pp. 122–129, 2006.

[CHA 22] CHAUTARD DARDÉ T., DO VALE G., "Du business model à la culture d'entreprise : repenser l'organisation des distributeurs en profondeur", in COLLIN-LACHAUD I. (ed.), *Révolutions du commerce dans une société en transition*, EMS, 2022.

[CUR 07] CURRAN J.M., MEUTER M.L., "Encouraging existing customers to switch to self-service technologies: Put a little fun in their lives", *Journal of Marketing Theory and Practice*, vol. 15, no. 4, pp. 283–298, 2007.

[DAU 18] DAUMAS J.C., *La révolution matérielle. Une histoire de la consommation (France, XIXe-XXIe siècle)*, Flammarion, Paris, 2018.

[EAG 20] EAGLE L., DAHL S., DE PELSMACKER P., TAYLOR C.R., *The SAGE Handbook of Marketing Ethics*, Sage, Newcastle upon Tyne, 2020.

[EIG 87] EIGLIER P., LANGEARD E., *Servuction. Le marketing des services*, McGraw-Hill, Paris, 1987.

[FLA 17] FLACANDJI M., "Le souvenir de l'expérience vécue en magasin physique. Les apports de l'analyse de réseaux", *Décisions Marketing*, vol. 88, no. 4, pp. 71–87, 2017.

[LEC 21] LECLERC M., "Le vrac, une piste intéressante pour dynamiser le marché du bio", *LSA Green*, available at: https://www.lsa-conso.fr/le-vrac-promet-teur-mais-seme-d-embuches,390941, 2021.

[LEC 22] LECHEVALLIER A.-S., "Prévisions. L'insee confirme un recul du pouvoir d'achat des Français", *Libération*, available at: https://www.liberation.fr/economie/linsee-confirme-un-recul-du-pouvoir-dachat-des-francais-20220509_RA3TI3VWZFGWZOZMX63MNDGAIU/, 2022.

[LI 22] LI W., LI W., SEPPÄNEN V., KOIVUMÄKI T., "How and when does perceived greenwashing affect employees' job performance? Evidence from China", *Corporate Social Responsibility and Environmental Management*, vol. 29, no. 5, pp. 1722–1735, 2022.

[MIL 86] MILLS P.K., MORRIS J.H., "Clients as "partial" employees of service organizations: Role development in client participation", *Academy of Management Review*, vol. 11, no. 4, pp. 726–735, 1986.

[MIN 23] MINISTÈRE DE LA TRANSITION ÉCOLOGIQUE ET DE LA COHÉSION DES TERRITOIRES, MINISTÈRE DE LA TRANSITION ÉNERGÉTIQUE, Gaspillage alimentaire, available at: https://www.ecologie.gouv.fr/gaspillage-alimen-taire-0, 2023.

[MOA 09] MOATI P., "Cette crise est aussi celle de la consommation", *Les temps modernes*, vol. 4, no. 665, pp. 145–169, 2009.

[NIC 18] NICOD L., LLOSA S., "Comment former le client à son rôle de coproducteur ? Étude de l'influence de la formation et de ses caractéristiques sur les bénéfices de la coproduction", *Recherche et Applications en Marketing*, vol. 33, no. 4, pp. 50–77, 2018.

[PLI 22] PLICHON O., "Pouvoir d'achat : avec des ventes en net recul, le bio doit se réinventer", *Le Parisien*, available at: https://www.leparisien.fr/econo-mie/consommation/pouvoir-dachat-avec-des-ventes-en-net-recul-le-bio-doit-se-reinventer-20-03-2022-3PIFXRPOYVCNTDWMMC2BMO53QQ.php, 2022.

[RIA 22] RIANDITA A., "To collaborate and innovate for sustainability: Food retailers and their external partners", *Technological Forecasting and Social Change*, vol. 180, pp. 121681, 2022.

3

Corporate Social Responsibility and Loyalty

Faced with an increase in intentions for or actual behavior linked to responsible consumption and the expectations consumers have of companies in this respect, most businesses are implementing responsible actions and communicating about them. The aim is for such companies to make consumers aware of these actions so that they can improve their image, particularly in terms of responsibility [SWA 08]. Corporate social responsibility (CSR) creates intangible assets in terms of image and reputation that are difficult to copy. In this way, a company can gain a significant competitive advantage and differentiate itself in increasingly competitive markets [SWA 08]. In addition, CSR is a tool for developing and maintaining a profound relationship with consumers, thereby increasing their loyalty to a company through their identification with it [KIM 20]. This loyalty will in turn boost the company's economic and financial performance [SWA 08, KIM 20].

However, research on the influence of CSR on loyalty presents contradictory results. While some studies have shown a direct link, others have highlighted an indirect link via mediating variables [DAN 20, WAN 20]. If the link is indirect, this would mean that CSR is less a short-term, sales-generating mechanism than one that creates a deeper relationship with consumers over time, thereby building loyalty to the company [DU 07]. Managers and researchers are therefore not totally convinced of the existence of a direct relationship between CSR and loyalty (e.g. [SWA 21]).

Retailers are no exception to this phenomenon. They are particularly interesting to study, since consumers know little about the CSR actions retailers take, and when they are aware, they remain suspicious and skeptical [LAV 16]. And yet, for a

Chapter written by Didier LOUIS, Cindy LOMBART and Nathalie FLECK.

number of years now, retailers have been making CSR commitments to differentiate themselves and win the loyalty of their consumers [AIL 04].

This chapter begins with a definition of the concepts of CSR and loyalty. Next, the nature of the link between these two notions is presented according to the results of research on the influence of perceived CSR on loyalty to a company and, more specifically, to a retailer. The final section shows how concrete CSR actions (offering bulk products, on the one hand, and sponsorship, cause-related marketing or CSR-linked sponsorship on the other) can help a retailer build a relationship with its consumers, and thus win their loyalty.

3.1. Definitions of perceived CSR and loyalty

3.1.1. *Perceived CSR*

Most definitions of CSR are based on the following two major ideas [SWA 08]:

– Companies must respect the law and strive for profit, even if their obligations go beyond these legal and economic responsibilities.

– Companies are held responsible by all stakeholders in their activities, not just their shareholders.

ISO 26000 defines CSR as the:

> responsibility of an organization for the impacts of its decisions and activities on society and the environment, through transparent and ethical behavior that: contributes to sustainable development, including health and the welfare of society; takes into account the expectations of stakeholders; is in compliance with applicable law and consistent with international norms of behaviour; and is integrated throughout the organization and practised. [INT 10]

According to Helfrich et al. [HEL 19], this standard is present in 75 countries. It is recognized by institutions such as the European Union and the United Nations, and many companies refer to it in their communications or use it in their CSR initiatives. Ultimately, responsible companies are committed to minimizing or eliminating their harmful effects and maximizing their long-term beneficial impact on society [MOH 01].

CSR is generally conceptualized as a multidimensional construct [MOI 15, CHA 19]. Following their exhaustive review of the CSR literature, Chakraborty and Jha [CHA 19] emphasized that CSR has become more complex: its dimensions have evolved and their number has increased. Indeed, over time, companies have taken responsible actions in broader areas. In his meta-analysis of existing scales for measuring CSR, Moisescu [MOI 15] highlighted the following four dimensions present in numerous studies: philanthropic activities, respect for the environment, respect for consumers and respect for employees. In addition, considering the items proposed in the literature, Moisescu [MOI 15] conducted a factorial analysis of the CSR actions of companies in different sectors. The four dimensions he had identified appeared in each of the sectors studied. Chakraborty and Jha [CHA 19] also found these four founding dimensions in their literature review. In other words, these four dimensions, which correspond to responsible actions taken by companies in a very large number of sectors, including retailing, form the core of CSR.

3.1.2. *Loyalty*

Loyalty can be defined as:

> a deeply held commitment to rebuy or repatronize a preferred product/service consistently in the future, thereby causing repetitive same brand set purchasing, despite situational influences and marketing efforts having the potential to cause switching behaviour. [OLI 97]

There are several types of loyalty: transactional loyalty (based on satisfaction, which leads to a positive attitude and favorable future behavioral intention), relational loyalty (where trust is a mediating variable in the satisfaction–loyalty link) and hybrid loyalty (combining transactional and relational loyalty) [LIC 08]. In the latter case, the relational process does not replace the transactional one, but combines with it to give rise to this hybrid loyalty. Finally, there is a loyalty continuum, the ends of which are formed by transactional loyalty, on the one hand, and relational loyalty, on the other hand. Hybrid loyalty is then seen as an intermediate phase of loyalty on this continuum [DIA 17].

Now that the concepts of CSR and loyalty have been defined, the question is what is the link between the two?

3.2. The influence of perceived CSR on consumers' retailer loyalty

How does the fact that consumers perceive a company as responsible influence their loyalty to it?

There are two mechanisms that explain the impact of a company's CSR on consumer loyalty. On the one hand, when a company discloses information about its

CSR actions, it is signaling that it is responsible and acts for the well-being of consumers and society in general. In response, consumers will have more positive perceptions of the companies and become loyal to them. On the other hand, consumers concerned with ethical and moral behavior can identify themselves as members of a group that engages with a responsible company because it shares their social identity. In this way, the company's perceived CSR will help win the loyalty of these consumers.

3.2.1. *The impact of perceived CSR as a global construct on retailer loyalty*

Lombart and Louis [LOM 14] studied the impact of a retailer's perceived CSR on consumer loyalty to that retailer. The authors showed that the retailer's perceived CSR increased consumer satisfaction and trust, and improved attitudes toward it. While perceived CSR had no direct influence on future behavioral intentions toward the retailer (visiting and recommending stores or buying and recommending its private label), it did exert an indirect influence via mediating variables on these intentions. In this way, a retailer's perceived CSR creates or reinforces a hybrid loyalty between the consumer and the retailer that is both transactional and relational (Figures 3.1 and 3.2).

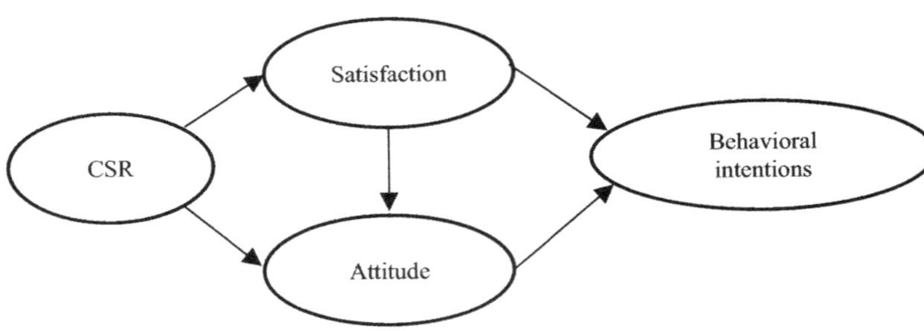

Figure 3.1. *The influence of CSR on transactional loyalty*

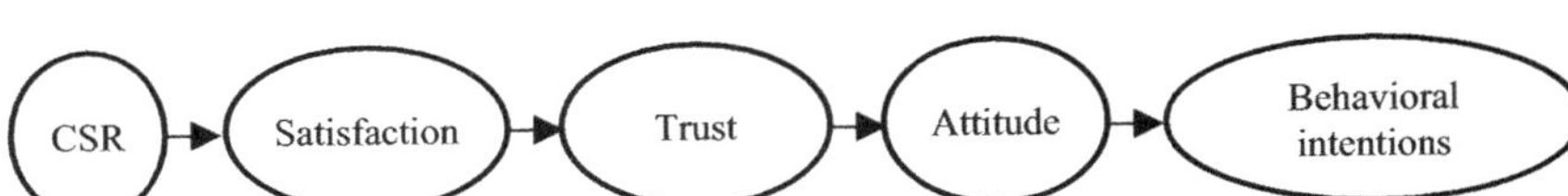

Figure 3.2. *The influence of CSR on relational loyalty*

3.2.2. *A different impact depending on CSR dimensions and consumer profiles*

Instead of studying CSR as a global construct, Louis et al. [LOU 19] considered the four dimensions of a retailer's CSR highlighted in the literature (i.e. philanthropic activities, respect for the environment, respect for consumers and respect for employees) and studied their influence on consumer loyalty to the retailer. A quantitative study was carried out with a representative sample of Quebec consumers, who were asked to choose a retailer with which they were familiar and that carried out CSR actions.

Following this study, a typological analysis was carried out highlighting three groups of consumers according to the scores obtained from individuals on the following variables: socially responsible consumption, expectations in terms of CSR, attribution of altruistic or strategic motivations to companies committed to CSR and degree of skepticism. These variables were chosen because they had either been used or mentioned as moderating variables in the literature on CSR [MOH 05, SCH 08, SWA 08, SKA 13]. Loussaïef et al. [LOU 14] reported that consumers are generally skeptical of companies committed to CSR, particularly in the retail sector, and consequently react negatively. In contrast, the attribution of altruistic motivations to responsible companies [SWA 08] by socially responsible consumers [MOH 05, SCH 08] who have high expectations of the CSR actions implemented by these companies [SWA 08] has a positive impact on their behavior toward them.

The following three groups of consumers can be identified:

– the very responsible group, who have high scores (if not the highest) in all aspects of socially responsible consumption. They have high expectations of the CSR activities implemented by companies and attribute altruistic motivations to them. While they may also attribute strategic motivations to companies engaging in CSR and be skeptical of such companies, the scores are lower than those obtained for skeptical local recyclers (whose description follows below);

– skeptical local recyclers, who have high scores in certain aspects of socially responsible consumption (e.g. recycling and consumption of local products). Although they have the highest expectations of the CSR activities implemented by companies, they are also the most skeptical of these companies, attributing strategic motivations to them;

– the least responsible, who have the lowest scores in all the variables considered to assess the socially responsible consumption of consumers (except for composting and the use of sustainable means of transport).

The statistical analyses carried out subsequently showed that for the three consumer groups identified, two CSR dimensions (respect for consumers and employees) have no influence on trust in or attitude and loyalty to the retailer. Conversely, respect for the environment increases the transactional loyalty of skeptical and less responsible local recyclers (see Table 3.1). For the very responsible, respect for the environment increases their hybrid loyalty to the retailer, both transactional and relational (Figures 3.3 and 3.4).

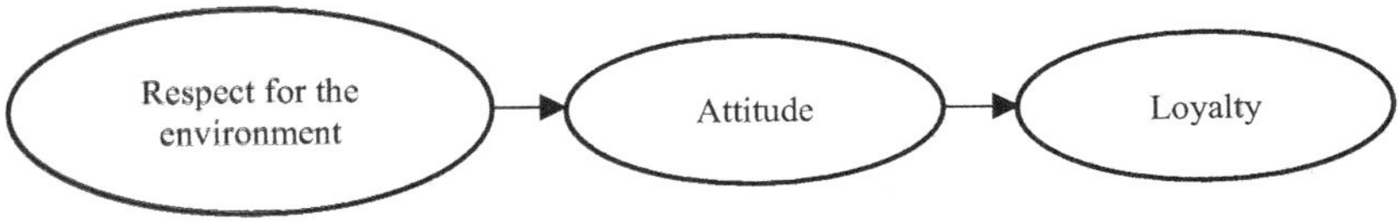

Figure 3.3. *The influence of respect for the environment on transactional retailer loyalty*

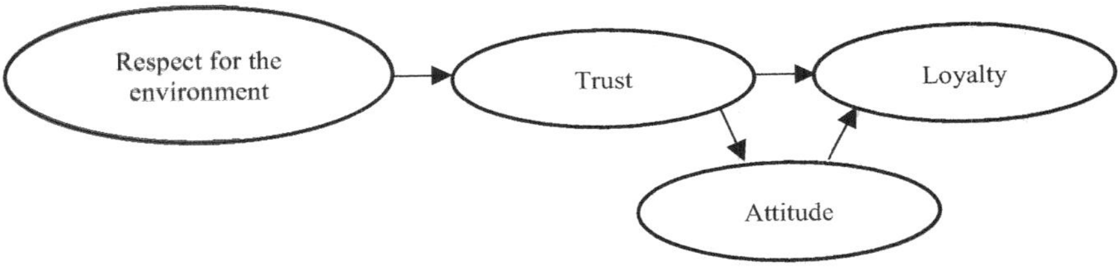

Figure 3.4. *The influence of respect for the environment on relational retailer loyalty*

While the retailer's philanthropic activities do not influence the loyalty of the less responsible, they do directly and indirectly influence that of skeptical local recyclers and the very responsible. This is called relational loyalty (Figure 3.5).

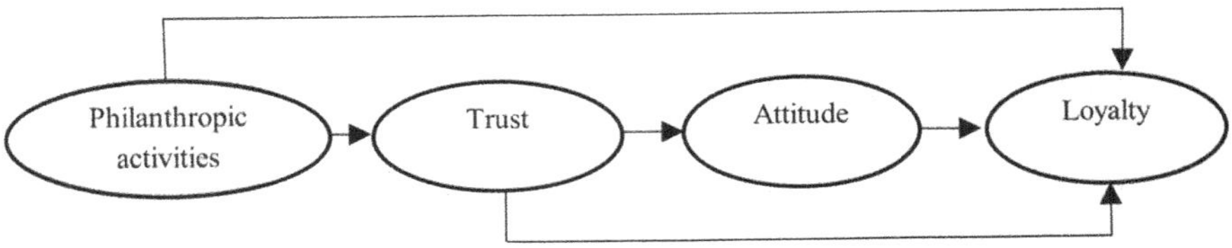

Figure 3.5. *The influence of philanthropic activities on relational retailer loyalty*

Individuals	Respect for the environment	Philanthropic activities
Very responsible	Hybrid loyalty	Relational loyalty
Skeptical local recyclers	Transactional loyalty	Relational loyalty
Less responsible	Transactional loyalty	No loyalty

Table 3.1. *Summary of results*

This research indicates to retailers which CSR actions can influence loyalty, depending on the type of loyalty sought and the individuals involved. It is important for retailers to segment their consumers. While highly responsible individuals are a prime target, skeptical local recyclers and, to a lesser extent, the less responsible should not be overlooked. Retailers should implement environmentally friendly actions and/or philanthropic activities. Regarding respect for the environment, retailers could, for example, pursue a policy of reducing or offsetting their greenhouse gas emissions, reducing their consumption of natural resources or energy, making their commercial activities more environmentally friendly and their products/services as eco-responsible as possible. Concerning philanthropic activities, retailers could invest abroad to help developing countries and support humanitarian causes, and also act locally to become involved in social, sporting and cultural activities in the regions where they operate.

3.3. Examples of concrete actions (in line with respect for the environment and philanthropic activities)

Since respect for the environment and philanthropic activities help build loyalty among all or some individuals, the results of two studies presenting levers belonging to the two specific dimensions of CSR are presented:

– The first dimension concerns the offer of bulk products by a retailer that respects the environment.

– The second dimension compares cause-related marketing, sponsorship and CSR-linked sponsorship that fall into the philanthropic category.

3.3.1. *The influence of a retailer's bulk product offer on consumer loyalty to that retailer*

Bulk is defined as "the retail sale of non-prepackaged, self-service products in the desired quantity in a reusable container" (reseauvrac.org). The bulk practice is part of the "zero waste" movement and meets environmental challenges by limiting packaging and food waste. By buying products in bulk, consumers are demonstrating their social responsibility, and offering products in bulk can be one of the actions carried out as part of a retailer's CSR policy (respect for the environment).

Louis et al. [LOU 21a] conducted a quantitative study of 1407 buyers and consumers of bulk products offered by a university cooperative in Quebec to understand the influence of the bulk product offer on relationships with and loyalty to that cooperative. These individuals were divided into three groups following a typological analysis:

– the "distrustful" of bulk products, who were the least sensitive to food waste, the least resistant to consumerism, the least socially responsible and the least price-sensitive. They had the highest scores for the barriers to buying and consuming the bulk products studied. They consumed bulk products rarely or sometimes;

– the "convinced", who were the most sensitive to food waste, the most resistant to consumerism and the most socially responsible. They had the highest scores for motivations to buy and consume bulk food. They bought in bulk often or regularly;

– the "pragmatists", who fell between the two previous groups. They were the most price-sensitive. For them, bulk was a good way to discover new products, and they were most keen to help themselves.

The statistical analyses carried out subsequently showed the bulk product offer to be a strategic tool for retailers, enabling them to create or strengthen relationships with their consumers. Indeed, bulk products create a close relationship between the consumer and the retailer, constituting the first step in the development or reinforcement of a relational chain. But what kind of proximity? Considering the literature on the subject, the following three types of proximity seem particularly relevant in the case of bulk products:

– identity proximity, which reflects the relationship between the consumer and the store or retailer, since it is perceived as a social player with values that the consumer values;

– relational proximity, which is the result of the relationships built up between the consumer and the retailer, as well as all the retailer's staff;

– process proximity, which reflects the importance attached by consumers to the store's internal operations, which guarantee the quality of the products or service they expect (product provenance or preparation and distribution methods).

Identity and process proximity for the three consumer groups, and relational proximity for the convinced and the distrustful, can then help create or reinforce a hybrid loyalty between the three consumer groups (distrustful, convinced and pragmatic) and the retailer that is both transactional (satisfaction directly influences purchasing intentions) and relational (satisfaction indirectly influences purchasing intentions via trust). Thus, if the paths vary depending on the consumer profile (from the discovery of bulk products to a well-established purchasing and consumption habit), this responsible offer makes it possible to create or strengthen hybrid loyalty, whatever the profile of the individual.

3.3.2. *Sponsorship, cause-related marketing and CSR-linked sponsorship: three CSR actions to build consumer loyalty*

Sponsorship, cause-related marketing and CSR-linked sponsorship are CSR actions that form part of philanthropic activities. In all three cases, a company would support an association or NGO. In exchange, the actions undertaken would enable the company to be perceived as responsible, and it would hope to benefit from them. What exactly do these three types of action correspond to? Sponsorship involves a company creating or supporting an event, person or group of people, association or sociocultural activity that is independent of itself, with which it associates itself through the media to achieve marketing communication objectives. Product sharing, on the other hand, corresponds to a company's offer to donate a certain sum of money to a non-profit organization or social cause each time a consumer buys a specific product in a promotion over a given period. Finally, in the case of CSR-linked sponsorship, a company associates its sponsorship action with a cause that is not directly associated with or supported by the sponsored entity (e.g. the French retailer U takes advantage of its sponsorship of FC Nantes, a football club, to make donations to *Action contre la Faim*, an anti-hunger poverty charity, even though there is no link between the club and the charity).

Louis et al. [LOU 21b] showed that sponsorship, cause-related marketing and CSR-linked sponsorship enable retailers to establish relationships with their consumers with the aim of building loyalty. Indeed, trust in a retailer plays a central role in building or reinforcing consumer loyalty. Nevertheless, the perception of a retailer's personality (e.g. its pleasant, conscientious or persuasive traits or its sophistication) and its identity proximity differ according to these three CSR actions. A ranking of these actions can be established according to their influence on the variables studied and their impact on them (see Table 3.2) as follows:

1) CSR-linked sponsorship;

2) sponsorship;

3) cause-related marketing.

Explanatory variables	Sponsorship	Cause-related marketing	CSR-linked sponsorship
Pleasant	Positive impact on identity proximity and trust	No influence	Positive impact on identity proximity and trust
Conscientious	Positive impact on identity proximity and trust	Positive impact on trust	Positive impact on identity proximity and trust
Persuasive	Negative impact on trust	Negative impact on identity proximity and trust	Negative impact on identity proximity and trust
Sophistication	No influence	Positive impact on identity proximity	Positive impact on identity proximity
Identity proximity	Positive impact on trust	Positive impact on trust	Positive impact on trust
Trust	Positive impact on loyalty	Positive impact on loyalty	Positive impact on loyalty

Table 3.2. *Paths highlighted for the three CSR actions considered*

The paths highlighted therefore differ depending on whether a company practices sponsorship or cause-related marketing. These paths are the same for CSR-linked sponsorship. In this way, sponsorship and cause-related marketing seem to complement each other for the company, which then has an interest in linking these CSR actions together.

3.4. Conclusion

Faced with an increase in responsible consumption behavior and consumer expectations, companies are implementing CSR actions and communicating these actions to appear more responsible. However, we first need to carefully segment consumers according to whether they are more or less responsible, their expectations in terms of CSR, their degree of skepticism and their perception of companies' motivations. Some consumers may become close to companies because they each share the same values (identity proximity). Others may react more or less favorably to CSR initiatives, depending on the actions implemented. Consequently, managers need to choose carefully which CSR actions they wish to commit their company to, depending on the targets they have defined and set themselves [SWA 08]. In terms of the dimensions of CSR, respect for the environment should be favored first and foremost, since it enables a company to achieve transactional or hybrid (transactional and relational) loyalty for all consumers. Note that the offer of bulk products, which is part of this dimension, helps achieve hybrid loyalty for all consumers. Second, philanthropic activities can achieve relational loyalty, but have no impact on less responsible consumers. Companies therefore need to commit to local, national and/or international causes and should, where possible, link these different causes together. For example, when U takes advantage of its sponsorship to donate to *Action contre la Faim* (an association for which U has set up a cause-related marketing operation), the retailer benefits fully from the integration of these three philanthropic actions to build consumer loyalty.

But can companies ignore their consumers, employees and suppliers? Certainly not, if they do not want to appear irresponsible. Compliance with the law is fundamental to their image. Companies should respect human rights in all the countries where they operate and respect the rights of their employees and suppliers, training them and guaranteeing their health and safety. Companies that create jobs in a given geographical area should enjoy a good image there. Similarly, companies should treat consumers with respect, guarantee their health and safety, and provide them with reliable information. In the case of bulk products, the importance of proximity to the process means that the information provided on these products can reassure consumers and remove any disincentives to consumption.

Companies should also communicate on the CSR actions they implement, albeit while avoiding greenwashing. Indeed, trust is a central variable in building hybrid and relational loyalty with consumers. Consequently, such communication should provide credible, tangible and convincing proof of the actions undertaken. All types of communication (media, non-media and digital) can be used, and retailers should also communicate in their stores. Sales staff, in particular, have an important role to play in communicating these actions by providing information and thus reinforcing the relational proximity between the retailer and the consumer.

Finally, managers need to be patient. This is because, depending on the CSR actions implemented and the individuals targeted, loyalty will build over time.

3.5. References

[AIL 04] AILAWADI K., KELLER K., "Understanding retail branding: Conceptual insights and research priorities", *Journal of Retailing*, vol. 80, pp. 331–342, 2004.

[CHA 19] CHAKRABORTY A., JHA A., "Corporate social responsibility in marketing: A review of the state-of-the art literature", *Journal of Social Marketing*, vol. 9, pp. 418–446, 2019.

[DAN 20] DANG V.T., NGUYEN N., PERVAN S., "Retailer corporate social responsibility and consumer citizenship behavior: The mediating roles of perceived consumer effectiveness and consumer trust", *Journal of Retailing and Consumer Services*, vol. 55, 2020.

[DIA 17] DIAWARA T., "La fidélité à une enseigne de déstockage physique. Une analyse de ses antécédents et processus de formation", *Revue française de gestion*, vol. 266, no. 5, pp. 127–144, 2017.

[DU 07] DU S., BHATTACHARYA C.B., SEN S., "Reaping relational rewards from corporate social responsibility: The role of competitive positioning", *International Journal of Research in Marketing*, vol. 24, no. 3, pp. 224–241, 2007.

[HEL 19] HELFRICH V., RIMAUD M.-N., DUPRÉ LA TOUR C., "Aborder la RSE avec des partenariats entreprises-associations : une approche modulaire de systèmes complexes", *Revue française de gestion*, vol. 282, pp. 77–93, 2019.

[INT 10] INTERNATIONAL ORGANIZATION FOR STANDARDIZATION, ISO 26000, Lignes directrices à la responsabilité sociétale, AFNOR NF, 2010.

[KIM 20] KIM M., YIN X., LEE G., "The effect of CSR on corporate image, customer citizenship behaviors, and customers' long-term relationship orientation", *International Journal of Hospitality Management*, vol. 88, 2020.

[LAV 16] LAVORATA L., "Perception par les consommateurs des pratiques développement durable des distributeurs", in LAVORATA L. (ed.), *Marketing et développement durable. Du distributeur au consommateur*, Economica, Paris, 2016.

[LIC 08] LICHTLE M.-C., PLICHON V., "Mieux comprendre la fidélité des consommateurs", *Recherche et Applications en Marketing*, vol. 23, pp. 121–141, 2008.

[LOM 14] LOMBART C., LOUIS D., "A study of the impact of corporate social responsibility and price image on retailer personality and consumers' reactions (satisfaction, trust and loyalty to the retailer)", *Journal of Retailing and Customer Services,* vol. 21, pp. 630–642, 2014.

[LOU 14] LOUSSAÏEF L., CACHO-ELIZONDO S., PETTERSEN I.B, TOBIASSEN A.E., "Do CSR actions in retailing really matter for young consumers? À study in France and Norway", *Journal of Retailing and Consumer Services*, vol. 21, pp. 9–17, 2014.

[LOU 19] LOUIS D., LOMBART C., DURIF F., "Impact of a retailer's CSR activities on consumers' loyalty", *International Journal of Retail & Distribution Management*, vol. 47, pp. 793–816, 2019.

[LOU 21a] LOUIS D., LOMBART C., DURIF F., "Packaging-free products: A lever of proximity and loyalty between consumers and grocery stores", *Journal of Retailing and Consumer Services*, vol. 60, 2021.

[LOU 21b] LOUIS D., LOMBART C., FLECK N., "Comparaison de l'impact de différentes actions RSE d'une enseigne sur sa relation avec ses consommateurs", *Revue Management & Avenir*, vol. 123, pp. 37–66, 2021.

[MOH 01] MOHR L.A., WEBB D.J., HARRIS K.E., "Do consumers expect companies to be socially responsible? The impact of corporate social responsibility on buying behavior", *Journal of Consumer Affairs*, vol. 35, pp. 45–72, 2001.

[MOH 05] MOHR L.A, WEBB D.J., "The effects of corporate social responsibility and price on consumer responses", *Journal of Consumer Affairs*, vol. 39, pp. 121–147, 2005.

[MOI 15] MOISESCU O.I., "Development and validation of a measurement scale for customers' perceptions of corporate social responsibility", *Management & Marketing Journal*, vol. 13, pp. 311–332, 2015.

[OLI 97] OLIVER R.L., *Satisfaction: A Behavioural Perspective on the Consumer*, McGraw-Hill International Editions, New York, 1997.

[SCH 08] SCHRAMM-KLEIN H., ZENTES J., "Corporate social responsibility of retail companies: Is it relevant for consumers' purchasing behavior?", *Colloque Etienne Thil*, La Rochelle, France, 2008.

[SKA 13] SKARMEAS D., LEONIDOU C.N., "When consumers doubt, watch out! The role of CSR skepticism", *Journal of Business Research*, vol. 66, pp. 1831–1838, 2013.

[SWA 08] SWAEN V., CHUMPITAZ C.R., "L'impact de la responsabilité sociétale de l'entreprise sur la confiance des consommateurs", *Recherche et Applications en Marketing*, vol. 23, pp. 7–35, 2008.

[SWA 21] SWAEN V., DEMOULIN N., PAUWELS-DELASSUS V., "Impact of customers perceptions regarding corporate social responsibility and irresponsibility in the grocery retailing industry: The role of corporate reputation", *Journal of Business Research*, vol. 131, pp. 709–721, 2021.

[WAN 20] WANG C.C., "Corporate social responsibility on customer behaviour: The mediating role of corporate image and customer satisfaction", *Total Quality Management and Business Excellence*, vol. 31, pp. 742–760, 2020.

4

Reinventing Loyalty Programs in the CSR Age: Moving toward Prosocial Loyalty Programs

As key features of customer relationship management, loyalty programs aim to identify, reward and retain profitable customers [CHE 21]. More than 40 years after the launch of the first loyalty program by American Airlines in 1981, they still represent a heavy investment (estimated at more than USD 8 billion by 2027[1]). Although substantial, these investments do not guarantee the success of loyalty programs. Customers are reluctant to use them: 54% do not use the loyalty programs they are subscribed to [KIM 21]. Some customers may associate these programs with the impression of a loss of freedom, leading to reactions of frustration and pressure or discomfort when using them, while others may perceive them as discriminatory and intrusive [LAN 19].

In this context, corporate social responsibility (CSR) could offer loyalty managers the opportunity to transform their programs in depth in order to renew their appeal, while overcoming some of the criticisms leveled at them. CSR has become a foundational factor in the management of many companies. It is a voluntary approach (beyond compliance with regulations imposed by law), integrating sustainable development issues into companies' strategies and the management of their day-to-day operations. Oftentimes, these issues are approached in terms of economic, environmental and social dimensions. Hence, making loyalty programs more responsible implies better consideration of environmental and social

---

Chapter written by Loubaba BELAOUD, Aïda MIMOUNI-CHAABANE and Béatrice PARGUEL.

1 Valuates Reports (2022). Global loyalty management market size, status and forecast [Online]. Available at: https://reports.valuates.com/market-reports/QYRE-Auto-20Z9073/global-loyalty-management.

impact, along with assessing economic gain. However, this idea is not widely accepted by managers, who lack a clear and inclusive framework for analysis. The aim of this chapter is to help define what a loyalty program could be in the CSR era.

After recalling the limits of traditional loyalty programs in terms of responsibility, this chapter presents how the question of responsibility in loyalty programs is posed in research and practice, defines the concept of a prosocial loyalty program and identifies its main components.

4.1. Limits of the traditional loyalty program in the CSR era

4.1.1. *A philosophy focused on purchasing behavior*

Based on the idea that it costs less to retain customers than to recruit new ones, loyalty programs are an institutionalized incentive system designed to develop customer purchasing behavior over time. Half of the academic articles devoted to loyalty programs focus on customer purchasing behavior [KIM 21]; that is, increasing quantities purchased and the frequency of visits [BEL 21].

However, looking at loyalty programs solely from the perspective of purchasing behaviors directs corporate focus to market share and profitability. Necessary to make budgetary decisions and optimize the use of resources within the company, performance indicators nonetheless divert attention from other benefits. These may include strengthening the customer's affective (e.g. attachment), cognitive (e.g. brand equity) and behavioral (e.g. activity on social networks) commitment. Moreover, collecting data is likely to improve customer knowledge and personalization of offers.

Using market share and profitability as the main performance indicators conceals effects that are "undesirable for the customer and damaging to the evolution of the relationship" [LAN 19, p. 236]. Indeed, the constant incentive to develop purchasing behavior can be experienced by the customer as unbearable pressure likely to degrade well-being [PEZ 17]. This can also lead the customer to make unreasonable purchases, taking into consideration customer views on current ecological challenges.

Finally, studying loyalty programs only from an economic viewpoint implies neglecting environmental and social impact, whether positive or negative. Beyond a philosophy centered on purchasing behavior, the very design of the loyalty program – encompassing a structure and reward system (see Figure 4.1) – raises new questions in the era of CSR.

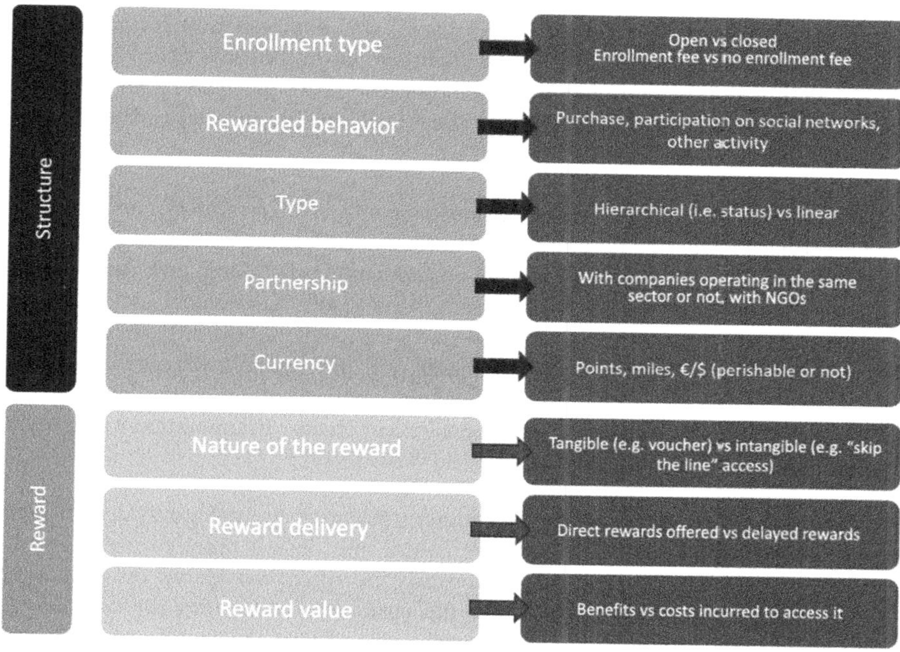

Figure 4.1. *Design components of a traditional loyalty program (adapted from [BEL 21, KIM 21])*

4.1.2. *A design that conceals environmental and social impact*

The structure of the loyalty program represents how it operates in terms of membership, rewarded behavior and reward methods (i.e. type, partnership and reward credit). Some loyalty programs may be backed by a credit function, which requires specific customer information, particularly for vulnerable customers. Loyalty programs are sometimes based on restrictive rules (e.g. no miles for the purchase of a "first-price" air ticket, no accumulation of points with a ready-to-wear promotion). This unbalances the relationship between the company and its customers, inducing a feeling of manipulation. Most programs also display an expiry date for reward credits. This can penalize customers who are not vigilant or who are unable to reach the first reward levels, and can even generate a feeling of captivity among customers who make purchases with the sole aim of prolonging the validity of their points. French deputy Patrick Hetzel opened up the debate at a political level by introducing a bill providing for an indefinite duration for benefits accumulated on loyalty cards in 2018[2]. While companies justify this expiry period for accounting reasons (in case all customers claim their loyalty points at the same time), it could be argued that it is not the customer who should bear the consequences of this practice, and that we should draw inspiration from the few companies that have chosen not to implement it (e.g. Mango and Leroy Merlin).

Hierarchical programs, which assign customers to levels or statuses according to their purchases, raise specific questions. Customers with higher status gain access to more benefits, particularly in terms of accumulation[3], breaking any principle of equality with regard to the loyalty program. As a result, hierarchical programs can generate a feeling of injustice among low-status customers [MIM 20]. They can also encourage unnecessary or irrational purchases (e.g. paying more for a train ticket to collect more status points) to preserve their hierarchical level as the date for re-evaluating status approaches. They can even create disappointment or anger among customers who have lost their status [WAG 09].

The second component of loyalty program design is the reward system, which focuses on the object of the reward, its nature, the time it takes to obtain it, its currency of exchange and its value. Rewards are often considered disappointing when compared to the efforts made by the customer. When they are difficult to achieve, they reinforce the need for redemption and thus the feeling of captivity. Whether tangible or intangible in nature, they are often customer-oriented (discount coupons on next purchase, preferential treatment, etc.), far removed from any environmental or social concerns.

Faced with the growing adoption of CSR approaches within companies, the responsibility of loyalty programs is now being questioned, both in the academic literature (see section 4.2) and in the field (see section 4.3).

4.2. The academic literature: loyalty program responsibility

To the best of our knowledge, only eight studies examine the responsibilities of loyalty programs, six of which are empirical in nature. These studies raise three types of questions which will be addressed below.

---

2 French National Assembly (2018). Proposal of law no. 1067 providing for an indefinite duration for the advantages accumulated on loyalty cards [Online]. Available at: https://www.assemblee-nationale.fr/dyn/15/textes/l15b1067_proposition-loi.

3 For example, at Air France, a Flying Blue Explorer customer earns four miles for every euro spent, while a Platinum customer earns eight.

Two purely theoretical studies consider the responsibility of loyalty programs in a general manner [NEM 10, KUM 19]. The first shows that a loyalty program that integrates a CSR approach (e.g. offering customers the opportunity to donate their points to charity or to use them to plant trees) communicates the company's CSR commitment and therefore fosters trust and engagement, as well as strong, lasting relationships with the company [NEM 10]. The second considers the integration of CSR principles into a loyalty program as a new dominant logic, which modifies the objectives assigned to the program in the sense of taking greater account of its environmental and social impact, the measure of its effectiveness, and its operation, particularly in terms of the type of reward offered [KUM 19].

Two other research projects look at loyalty programs that reward the adoption of responsible behaviors, such as reusing towels in the hotel industry or choosing more responsible products in food retail. Customers perceive companies that offer such rewards as more responsible. This perception, combined with a higher perceived value and a feeling of gratitude, leads to a better attitude toward the program and greater intention to participate [HWA 15]. In addition, these loyalty programs avoid reducing the level of satisfaction of customers who are not members and therefore do not benefit from the associated advantages [LIU 16].

Lastly, four studies focus on loyalty programs that offer the possibility of making a donation to a charitable organization as a reward. Offering customers the option of converting their loyalty points into a donation to a charity, rather than a discount coupon to be used on the next purchase, reduces the intention to participate and buy [EAS 15, HWA 20], especially when membership in the program is subject to a fee [EAS 15]. On the other hand, offering customers a choice between a personal reward or a donation fosters a sense of pride and increases customer satisfaction [GIE 16]. In addition, being able to choose the recipient association and divide the donation between several associations increases the probability of the donation and the sense of pride, which in turn improves the CSR image [MIM 21].

The initial results found in the literature help us understand customer response to the introduction of new responsibilities in loyalty programs, as well as their effectiveness in affective, cognitive and conative terms and the elements likely to influence this response. However, the literature remains theoretical, recent (the first research appeared in 2010) and divided. We therefore supplement it with an exploratory study in order to evaluate the way in which loyalty programs adapt to the new requirement of responsibility. Our exploration begins with a benchmark and continues with a qualitative study conducted with loyalty managers (see Box 4.1).

We studied 48 loyalty programs in nine different sectors: airlines, ready-to-wear apparel, cosmetics, hotels, food retail, sports equipment, coffee chains, energy and banking. To implement this study, companies from the sectors mentioned were selected for more detailed research and, using data from their corporate websites and sectorial sources, a double analysis, intra- and inter-sectoral, was applied.

To complete this benchmark, we conducted six semi-structured interviews with loyalty program experts (i.e. four program managers in the cosmetics, airline and banking industries and two loyalty consultants). The interviews started with general questions about how the loyalty programs work, why they were set up and how they are evolving. They continued with more specific questions on the possible levers for integrating the CSR approach into their management. Lasting around an hour on average, the interviews were recorded, transcribed and analyzed in the traditional way, first vertically and then horizontally.

Box 4.1. *Benchmark and qualitative study methodologies*

4.3. Benchmark study: loyalty programs

The 48 loyalty programs studied do not deviate from the philosophy of traditional loyalty programs: they all reward purchasing behavior in one way or another with tangible or intangible rewards geared toward the individual, and thus encourage (over)consumption. If we set aside the personal data initiatives made mandatory by the implementation of the GDPR, only half of the loyalty programs studied go further by incorporating initiatives reflecting the adoption of a CSR approach.

In terms of loyalty program structure, the initiatives identified reward certain "good" behaviors, such as recycling, purchasing more responsible products, adopting more responsible consumption gestures or leading a healthier lifestyle. As illustrated in Box 4.2, companies generally select the behaviors they wish to reward according to their congruence with their business (e.g. depositing unused clothes in the ready-to-wear sector, buying organic products in food retail). Such behaviors lead to the awarding of points, which are almost always, if not exclusively, intended to be converted into vouchers for a future purchase, and therefore generally result in deferred consumption.

Some programs reward the *recycling* of products no longer used by their owners. Jacadi encourages its members to exchange old pairs of shoes for a €15 voucher. Other programs reward the recycling of packaging so that it is properly recycled or reused by the owners themselves. In cosmetics, the Body Shop offers its members a fourth refill of shampoo, conditioner or shower gel in its stores equipped with a refill station.

Loyalty programs reward the *purchase of more responsible products*. H&M credits its members with one Conscious point for the purchase of a product from sustainable labels. The company sells a range of products manufactured using at least 50% organic cotton or recycled polyester. Decathlon rewards 100 loyalty points for a good deed for the planet, such as the purchase of an eco-designed or second-hand product.

The adoption of more *responsible consumption habits*, beyond the choice of product or service, can also be rewarded. For example, Etihad offers a bonus of 250 status miles to customers who travel with less than 15 kg of baggage.

With regard to adopting a *healthier lifestyle*, in the sports sector, Decathlon and Sport 2000 reward their customers' weekly exercise with loyalty points.

Box 4.2. *Examples of initiatives to reward "good" behavior*

Still in terms of loyalty program structure, the benchmark study shows that many brands now offer eco-designed, or even dematerialized, loyalty cards. This initiative has not been identified in the literature previously summarized.

In terms of the rewards systems, the possibility of converting loyalty points into donations is a common practice among the loyalty programs studied. Members of the "Mango Likes You" program can donate their "likes" in increments of 50, 200, 400 or 1000 "likes" to international organizations like the World Health Organization (WHO) or charitable organizations like Save the Children. In addition to being able to give their miles to friends, family and associations aiming to preserve the planet or promote education, members of the Flying Blue program can also donate their miles to a start-up. Yves Rocher offers its members the opportunity to plant three trees in exchange for 1000 accumulated points. These donations, whether monetary or in kind, direct (to an organization) or indirect (via the company's foundation), can generate positive feelings of pride among customers.

In addition, loyalty programs also help to reduce potential negative feelings, and in particular certain forms of guilt. Etihad, for example, offers its members the opportunity to offset the carbon footprint of their flying activities by using their miles to finance projects to combat climate change and to offset the carbon impact of their lifestyle as a whole (e.g. 3592 miles to offset six months' driving in an SUV).

Other forms of responsible rewards appeared more marginally in the benchmark study and involve the redemption of points in the form of eco-designed rewards or objects that enable more responsible behavior (e.g. a water bottle or tote bag to limit plastic consumption). For example, Engie's "*Mon Programme pour Agir*" ("My Program for Action") allows members to exchange their points for eco-responsible items, such as a smart plug or a water-saving kit. Last but not least, some programs offer discounts that contribute to more responsible consumption. For example, in the midst of the Covid-19 health crisis, Axa distributed vouchers worth €20 to its loyal customers to be used in local shops to support the local economy.

Some initiatives manage to simultaneously make use of the structure and the reward system of the loyalty program that promotes them. For example, Leclerc offers its cardholders a €0.02 donation to the Alzheimer's Research Foundation for every Leclerc leaflet returned to the store.

Our benchmark study, which was based on the analysis of company websites to understand how their loyalty programs operate, provides an interesting insight into differences in the practices observed between companies. Companies from sectors criticized for their environmental impact (e.g. air transport) or social impact (e.g. ready-to-wear) seem to integrate CSR more systematically into their loyalty programs, probably in order to improve their image. In addition, companies whose positioning and strategic ambitions have historically shown a sensitivity to societal issues have been more systematic in adapting their loyalty programs in the direction of greater responsibility. For example, in the cosmetics sector, the Body Shop offers its members the opportunity to donate their points to World and Trust, the Women's Foundation or associations that reflect the brand's long-standing commitments. Yves Rocher, which has always positioned itself in the plant-based cosmetics sector, offers the chance to plant trees. On the other hand, no initiatives tending toward greater responsibility have been identified in Sephora's loyalty program, a brand that has not historically built its positioning on the environmental or social front[4]. It therefore appears that the nature of the business sector and the positioning of the brand, variables not explored in the literature to our knowledge, act as potential facilitating factors for the adoption and implementation of greater responsibility within loyalty programs.

However, our benchmark study did not provide a detailed picture of the challenges faced by companies that choose to integrate CSR into the management of their loyalty programs. In particular, we were unable to understand the objectives of such an approach or identify the progress envisioned for the future. To answer these questions, we complemented these initial findings with interviews of experts in this field.

4 It should be noted, however, that in the United States in 2016 the company launched the "Sephora Stands" program, built around three dimensions: support for the LGBT community, support for women and support for the planet. This program has since been extended and integrated into the brand's commitments and values. See: https://www.lvmh.com/news-documents/news/sephora-stands-initiative-expands-after-successful-first-year/.

4.4. Interviews with loyalty experts

4.4.1. *Corroboration of the literature and benchmark findings*

Our interviews corroborated some of the findings from the literature and benchmark studies. According to the experts interviewed, there is an urgent need to integrate the CSR approach into the design of loyalty programs as a means for companies to increase their attractiveness: "We clearly need to establish a CSR policy in loyalty programs" (expert 1); "Today, there's a focus on sustainability" (expert 3).

However, they clearly prioritized developing purchasing behavior over the CSR effort: "You cannot do CSR, commit to the environment or a cause, if you don't make money" (expert 1); "I do not think a purely CSR program works. People are less altruistic than we would like, they need to be bribed a little, and offering them things is essential" (expert 2); "We must not delude ourselves too much either, companies are always out to make money to support their employees and obviously their shareholders too" (expert 3); "The primary objective is business" (expert 4).

In line with the literature and benchmark study, the experts spontaneously identified three main ways in which loyalty programs can be part of a CSR approach:

– Rewarding "good" behavior: "In France, [unused clothes] can be taken back to the stores, bought back from the consumer, readapted and put back into circulation, I just think that's great" (expert 1); "A program that aims to be more responsible rewards more responsible behaviors [...] at H&M, if you bring your own bag, you earn points" (expert 2).

– Offering altruistic rewards (e.g. donations to charitable organizations, funding for compensation schemes), even if they are often not redeemed in the end (expert 6): "via the loyalty system offered by the brand, you can use your reward if you wish to plant trees [...] planting trees is a gift to nature" (expert 1); "[being able to donate your points to associations] is something we're putting in place for 2022" (expert 4).

– Eco-designing and even dematerializing the loyalty card: "We have also added a 'sustainable' aspect: the card is made from recycled cardboard [...] and is also dematerialized via the application" (expert 1); "One evolution concerns the dematerialization of the loyalty card, which for a long time was a physical card" (expert 2). Expert 3, however, interpreted this trend from a technological rather than ecological perspective. Experts 4 and 5 stated that "it is not the alpha and omega": if you have got nothing else to say, and it is not integrated into a wider scheme, you can quickly be accused of greenwashing.

4.4.2. *New findings from interviews*

In addition to the lessons learned from the literature and benchmark studies, the interviews with experts provide a better understanding of the strategic thinking and operational implementation of loyalty programs.

4.4.2.1. *On a strategic level*

From a strategic standpoint, the experts shed light on the challenges of deploying more responsible loyalty programs and suggest new performance indicators to support them.

Loyalty programs which are part of a CSR approach, just like traditional programs, aim to strengthen and perpetuate the relationship with the customer by establishing a bond of trust and promoting their commitment. Moreover, they have a new strategic objective in terms of corporate branding. Experts explain that this type of program aims to anchor the company's values in the customer's mind, in order to better position the company and enhance its image: "And so Decathlon, what makes sense in their brand positioning and their product categories, is to give points to customers when they do sport […] and by doing so, they encourage people to do sport; and democratizing sport is Decathlon's motto, it proves their brand positioning" (expert 2); "[It] must respond to a problem or a positioning wish of the company" (expert 3). While all the experts agreed that loyalty programs that are part of a CSR approach have a clear objective in terms of corporate branding, expert 5 spontaneously highlighted a potential drift in the form of greenwashing: "We're going to reflect a more responsible image, but that doesn't mean that internally it creates more CSR commitment".

In line with this new objective, the experts interviewed emphasized the leading role of customer demands. According to them, the deployment of more responsible loyalty programs responds to the growth of societal concerns within the population: "This is what the consumer is asking for, we clearly no longer have a choice […] with all that is happening across the world, it has to be" (expert 1). The experts therefore suggested not failing to communicate the fact that the loyalty program contributes to the implementation of the company's values and commitments: "There are a lot of things that are done on the CSR aspect, but we don't say it enough" (expert 1).

Still on a strategic level, the deployment of more responsible loyalty programs can also be the result of a desire to align with or differentiate from competitors. Finally, on a more anecdotal level, expert 2 mentioned a public education objective, which he illustrated as follows: "If you recycle your clothes, H&M gives you extra points, so H&M tells you it's so important in our opinion to recycle and that we spend money to encourage you to bring your clothes back to us; we support you so that you do it, so that you learn. There's something about transmission, it's about teaching people to fish, rather than feeding them".

As a result of the new strategic challenges identified, new performance measurement indicators are becoming essential for loyalty managers, such as corporate image at a cognitive level or customer confidence at a more affective level. At the behavioral level, there are specific impact measures relating to the types of rewards distributed (for example, the number of trees planted, the number of donations made, etc.) or the adoption of specific behaviors: "The KPI [key performance indicator] would be the percentage of customers who convert points to an association" (expert 4); "The percentage of miles donated to associations, or the number of miles they have earned by taking responsible actions such as offsetting their flight" (expert 6). In addition, when the company is structurally committed to a CSR approach, the loyalty program contributes to the company's certification, which can then act as a performance indicator: "All the Group's subsidiaries and brands are committed to obtaining 'B Corp' certification by 2025. This certification is clearly our KPI" (expert 1).

4.4.2.2. *At the operational level*

The experts interviewed highlighted the existence of new operational levers, less visible to the customer, that can better integrate the structure and reward system of the loyalty program into the company's CSR approach.

In terms of loyalty program structure, the experts emphasized the need for a new level of digital sufficiency and readily addressed the environmental impact of the information systems serving the program. For them, the issue is as much about the energy consumed by these systems as it is about the architecture used to store the data they collect. In particular, they seemed to value the centralization of loyalty data in a limited number of data warehouses[5]: "By limiting our carbon footprint, typically in our behavior in the office, or in our storage servers" (expert 5); "Having a data warehouse to manage the loyalty program saves energy and is more responsible. Also, we ensure that the technological infrastructure linked to the loyalty program is powered by the most decarbonized energies" (expert 3). Ironically, however, expert 3 also mentioned that technology can find new applications (not neutral in terms of carbon footprint) within the framework of a more responsible loyalty program, notably through connected objects that can attest to the adoption of good behavior (e.g. exercising) and thus justify the awarding of points.

In terms of loyalty program structure, and beyond the question of eco-design or the dematerialization of loyalty cards, the experts had recommendations for communication policy. They recommended highlighting the most eco-friendly rewards or even responsible actions such as forgoing the unnecessary to avoid waste: "Anything that avoids waste. Say, we have got a gift for you, but if you are

5 A data warehouse is a database hosted on a server in a data center; in 2020, on average, a single data center consumed as much energy as a city of 40,000 inhabitants. See: https://fr.wikipedia.org/wiki/Centre_de_donn%C3%A9es.

not going to use it, do not take it, because the aim is not to have products that are thrown away. That's responsible behavior" (expert 2).

Ignoring the question of the relative ecological impact of paper versus digital communication, the experts recommended using digital channels to promote the loyalty program or, failing that, recyclable materials and labelled suppliers: "As far as communication channels are concerned, anything that is material, physical, plastic or glue should be avoided. It should be made from recycled paper" (expert 5). In terms of communication, expert 4 also mentioned the need to keep the pressure at a reasonable level.

In terms of the reward system, the experts insisted on the need to ensure that the program's reward suppliers comply with precise specifications, particularly with regard to working conditions or the use of natural resources: "We benchmark all our gift suppliers against a certain number of CSR criteria, and those who are not compliant, we take out [...] we could promote products that are more national" (expert 3); "A responsible program includes an ecosystem of partners who work for the planet" (expert 4); "We are going to choose a supplier who does not employ underage children and who does not use this or that material" (expert 5). In the same vein, the experts envisioned the adoption of more eco-friendly delivery methods for the rewards offered by the program's boutique.

Finally, for our experts, circumstances have changed: "It has changed, previously, the entire loyalty program was oriented basically around consumption and over-consumption, it was about storing points, via purchases, which then allowed you to recover either the discount or a product. For me all this was not very virtuous" (expert 1).

The deployment of more responsible loyalty programs is a major trend, regardless of the company, sector or country in which it takes place. This leads us, in the final section, to the identification of the prosocial loyalty program as the ultimate evolution of the loyalty program in the CSR era.

4.5. Toward a prosocial loyalty program

By adapting the definition of the loyalty program proposed at the beginning of this chapter [KIM 21], we can finally define the concept of the prosocial loyalty program: an institutionalized incentive system which aims, over time, to encourage responsible consumption behavior on the part of customers, that is, consumption which is respectful of the environment and positive for society.

	Frequency program	Recognition program	Community program	Prosocial program
Objectives	Retaining customers and reducing attrition	Expanding the shopping cart, personalizing the relationship and nurturing attachment to the company	Creating and strengthening social ties between customers	Having a positive impact on the environment and society
Customer value	Extrinsic, self-oriented	Extrinsic, self-oriented, etc.	Intrinsic, self- and community-oriented	Intrinsic, oriented toward society at large
Customer benefits	Utilitarian Hedonic	Utilitarian Experiential Recognition	Experiential Membership	Social (pride in engaging in altruistic behavior)
How to earn points	Repeated buying behavior (linear structure)	Repeated buying behavior (linear or hierarchical structure)	Commitment behavior (club structure)	Eco- and socio-responsible behavior (any structure possible)
Nature of rewards	Tangible and monetary rewards	Preferential treatment and value-added services	Meetings and exchanges between members	Donation, reward for responsible consumption
Key performance indicators	Volume and value of transactions	Profitability, quality of the relationship	Strength of the relationship, commitment	Trust, impact, image
Sector of activity	Weak differentiation	Symbolic consumption, including service	Strong brand identity	Image of pre-existing responsibility to be improved
Typical customer profile	New customer, low added value, highly price-sensitive	Loyal customer, high added value, not price-sensitive	Customer ambassador, regardless of value	Committed consumer-citizen

Table 4.1. *Evolution of the loyalty program over time – enrichment of the typology proposed by Mimouni Chaabane and Pez [MIM 12]*

This definition puts the emphasis more on consumption and its social dimension, oriented toward others through the consideration of environmental and social concerns, than on purchasing behavior and its mercantile, self-oriented dimension. Thus, such programs encourage their members to redeem their points for useful, eco-responsible products that they really need. The Engie example cited above is an illustration of this orientation, as opposed to a classic program that encourages members to redeem their points for discounts to increase their frequency of purchases or their purchase value. This definition does not suggest, however, that a loyalty program becomes impact-free overnight, but emphasizes the program's dynamics in terms of responsibility and its contribution to the company's CSR efforts. In other words, a loyalty program can be described as prosocial only if it continually and transparently strives to be part of a responsible consumption dynamic. To achieve the latter, it must be at the service of a genuine CSR strategy, and consistent with its principles.

After the frequency program (stage 1), the recognition program (stage 2) and the community program (stage 3), the prosocial loyalty program represents the final stage in the evolution of the loyalty program. Table 4.1 summarizes its characteristics, highlighting its objectives, values and benefits for the customer; methods of earning points; the nature of the rewards; key performance indicators; preferred sectors; and the typical profile of the targeted customer.

The prosocial loyalty program implies a change in dominant logic [KUM 19], from a philosophy centered on purchasing behavior to one driven by common sense around new environmental and social issues. From an operational point of view, its deployment raises new questions for researchers: which behaviors should be rewarded? Is it better to offer compensation or a gift? How can we design and communicate these new forms of reward to avoid greenwashing lawsuits? These new questions call on loyalty researchers to turn to new theoretical frameworks (e.g. sustainable marketing, philanthropy or donation) to renew their exploration of loyalty programs.

4.6. References

[BEL 21] BELLI A., CARRILLAT F.A., MELNYK V. et al., "40 years of loyalty programs: How effective are they? Generalizations from a meta-analysis", *Journal of the Academy of Marketing Science*, vol. 50, no. 1, pp. 1–27, 2021.

[CHE 21] CHEN Y., MANDLER T., MEYER-WAARDEN L., "Three decades of research on loyalty programs: A literature review and future research agenda", *Journal of Business Research*, vol. 124, pp. 179–197, 2021.

[EAS 15] EASON C.C., BING M.N., SMOTHERS J., "Reward me, charity, or both? The impact of fees and benefits in loyalty programs", *Journal of Retailing and Consumer Services*, vol. 25, pp. 71–80, 2015.

[GIE 16] GIEBELHAUSEN M., CHUN H.H., CRONIN J.J. et al., "Adjusting the warm-glow thermostat: How incentivizing participation in voluntary green programs moderates their impact on service satisfaction", *Journal of Marketing*, vol. 80, no. 4, pp. 56–71, 2016.

[HWA 15] HWANG J., KANDAMPULLY J., "Embracing CSR in pro-social relationship marketing program: Understanding driving forces of positive consumer responses", *Journal of Services Marketing*, vol. 29, no. 5, pp. 344–353, 2015.

[HWA 20] HWANG J., CHOI L., "Having fun while receiving rewards? Exploration of gamification in loyalty programs for consumer loyalty", *Journal of Business Research*, vol. 106, pp. 365–376, 2020.

[KIM 21] KIM J.J., PALMATIER R.W., STEINHOFF L., "An emerging theory of loyalty program dynamics", *Journal of the Academy of Marketing Science*, vol. 49, no. 1, pp. 71–95, 2021.

[KUM 19] KUMAR V., "Global implications of cause-related loyalty marketing", *International Marketing Review*, vol. 37, no. 4, pp. 747–772, 2019.

[LAN 19] LANCELOT M., MIMOUNI CHAABANE A., PEZ V., "The dark side of customer relationship management practices in the data age: Managing resistance and perceived intrusion for responsible practices", in N'GOALA G., PEZ-PÉRARD V., PRIM-ALLAZ I. (eds), *Augmented Customer Strategy: CRM in the Digital Age*, ISTE Ltd, London and John Wiley & Sons, New York, 2019.

[LIU 16] LIU S.Q., MATTILA A.S., "The influence of a "green" loyalty program on service encounter satisfaction", *Journal of Services Marketing*, vol. 30, no. 6, pp. 576–585, 2016.

[MIM 12] MIMOUNI CHAABANE A., PEZ V., "Optimiser l'efficacité des programmes de fidélité", in VOLLE, P. (ed.), *Stratégie clients. Points de vue d'experts sur la gestion de la relation client*, Pearson Education, Paris, 2012.

[MIM 20] MIMOUNI CHAABANE A., PEZ, V., "The reward gap in hierarchical loyalty programs: How to enhance bottom-tier customers' loyalty without alienating top-tier customers", *Journal of Marketing Management*, vol. 36, no. 1/2, pp. 51–77, 2020.

[MIM 21] MIMOUNI CHAABANE A., PARGUEL B., "The double warm glow effect in loyalty programs' prosocial rewards", *ANZMAC Conference*, Melbourne, 2021.

[NEM 10] NEMEC RUDEŽ H., "Integration of corporate social responsibility into loyalty programs in the tourism industry", *Tourism and Hospitality Management*, vol. 16, no. 1, pp. 101–108, 2010.

[PEZ 17] PEZ V., BUTORI R., MIMOUNI CHAABANE A., "Le côté sombre de la pression exercée sur les consommateurs par les programmes de fidélité : enjeux éthiques et pratiques", *Recherche et Applications en Marketing*, vol. 32, no. 3, pp. 76–89, 2017.

[WAG 09] WAGNER T., HENNIG-THURAU T., RUDOLPH T., "Does customer demotion jeopardize loyalty?", *Journal of Marketing*, vol. 73, no. 3, pp. 69–85, 2009.

5

Toward Greater Sufficiency in Customer Relationships

Theoretically speaking, the aim of customer management is to develop long-lasting business relationships. This can be achieved by building customer value over time [JAL 17]. By getting customers to consume more, more often and over as long a period as possible, the organization can become part of the competitive panorama and grow. With this challenge in mind, organizations encourage customers to increase their average shopping basket and/or frequency of purchase through a variety of tools, such as promotions, sales or loyalty programs. This encourages customers to consume beyond what they really need [PEZ 17]. In the current context of depleting planetary resources and the urgent need to rethink our consumption models, certain retail practices can be reexamined.

The aim of this chapter is to contribute to the debate on what future customer relationships could (or should) be based on the concept of sufficiency. Associated in everyday language with moderation and restraint, sufficiency refers – in the context of affluent societies in which the pace of production and consumption is incompatible with planetary limits – to the avoidance of over-consumption and reducing the use of natural resources and fossil fuels [GOS 22]. In other words, it is a question of going against the grain of a consumer society that calls for "faster, further, more" [SPA 19]. More specifically, this chapter:

– discusses the potential role of customer relationship practices in the systemic collapse of today's consumer society;

– invites the reader to reflect on a few customer relationship practices;

– draws up proposals for more sufficiency in customer relationships;

Chapter written by Jean-Baptiste WELTÉ, Virginie PEZ and Isabelle DABADIE.

– asks the reader about the role that customer relationships could play in the transition to a more sufficient consumption model.

Far from calling into question the validity of customer relationship practices, this chapter aims to open up avenues of reflection for more responsible practices. The aim is to strive to do "better" with "less", by systematically taking into account the environmental and ecosystemic impact of our actions. It also shows how customer relationship professionals, experts in customer engagement, can work to support the transformation toward more sufficiency in consumption practices.

5.1. The systemic collapse of consumerism

5.1.1. *The impact of marketing and customer relationship practices on the ecosystem: the anthropogenic footprint*

In a way, customer relationship practices tend to encourage (over)consumption. These practices are part of a more global phenomenon of excess specific to our current consumer societies. The postmodern paradigm [LYO 79] initially highlighted the crisis of modernity based on technical progress.

Current criticisms focus in particular on the waste of resources and its numerous consequences, the predicted collapse of the production systems on which they are based and the disruption of our ecosystem. The IPCC's reports, which combine scientific rigor with alarmist predictions, come one after another (the latest from 2022)[1]. They measure the varying degrees of impact on species extinction, water resources and food security, according to different hypotheses (of global warming). These climate change reports also highlight the correlation between different risks. For example, increasing heatwaves and droughts can reduce agricultural yields, but also labor productivity, leading to an even greater drop in harvests.

These reports illustrate the extent to which the ecological consequences of the way our societies function can only be understood in a systemic way. However, the hyper-specialized organization of our modes of production prevents a holistic consideration of these ecological issues: companies and individuals, even the most virtuous, only control at best the consequences of their own actions. They cannot understand those linked to other actors, and do not control the unsuspected consequences of their own actions.

As polemical as it may be, the term "Anthropocene" illustrates this systemic dimension. It characterizes the era in which humanity's footprint has been decisive

1 The reports can be viewed at: https://www.un.org/en/climatechange/reports.

in explaining changes in the way the Earth functions. The Anthropocene thus refutes the ontological separation that human societies make between nature and culture [DES 15, BON 22]. As a result, our actions cannot be thought of in isolation from their effects on the ecosystem. In their book *L'événement Anthropocène* [BON 16], the authors show just how closely the issues specific to the social sciences need to be blended with engineering sciences in order to understand and fully measure the effects of human actions.

Customer relationships rooted in a strictly marketing-based logic also contribute to a company's impact on its ecosystem. In addition to the waste of resources in direct marketing (a large number of prospects targeted by mailing or emailing for a low expected ROI), the logic of rewarding the customer (to reward loyalty and, more generally, maintain the relationship) encourages the over-consumption of resources. Discount coupons and cashback systems encourage customers to consume more and can lead to customers being "locked-in" to an artificial consumption cycle. These incentive systems are said to encourage consumption in excess of what is needed to satisfy needs. Gifts offered to customers in the form of material goods also lead to an unnecessary consumption of resources. The result is an accumulation of objects that are rarely used by their recipients, such as the umpteenth tote bag offered as a token of loyalty, despite the fact they are often designed as part of an eco-friendly approach to reducing disposable packaging.

Furthermore, relational strategies aimed at targeting high-value-added customers can also raise questions in the light of environmental issues. The notions of an ambassador or privileged customer sometimes suspend all rationality in the use of resources on the grounds of "disinterested" generosity. Companies are inventive when it comes to giving these customers a privileged status. The logic of status, with its associated reward levels (premium, gold, VIP, etc.), encourages the creation of systems of distinction and a spiral of rewards. These advantages can trigger a phenomenon of habituation, transforming beneficiary customers into "rightful claimants".

The customer relationship is built around mutual benefits (highly contributing customers become brand ambassadors and are remunerated for services rendered) to the detriment of the environmental ecosystem (it leads to over-consumption and the expected environmental impacts: consumption of resources, production of waste, etc.). In the banking sector, the various privilege systems associated with payment cards (e.g. Visa's "premier", "platinum", "infinite" or "premium/metal" distinctions for neo-banks like Revolut) are awarded according to customers' financial capabilities. Being able to afford, or being offered these cards acts as an important social marker. Even in largely dematerialized payment systems, possession of these cards, while not necessarily useful, is seen as a symbol of success. The many associated services (concierge services, reservations, etc.) act as an invitation to the club, at odds with everyday contingencies. The possession of these distinctive signs is a more or less conscious incentive to enjoy a status, to use the payment facilities on offer to consume to the detriment of any environmental concerns.

5.1.2. *The impact of new technologies and digital transformation on social ties: accelerating a process of disintegration*

The capitalist consumption system is based on digital transformation, the perverse effects of which are now being analyzed. The ecological impact is pernicious, since this "invisible" pollution encourages (over)consumption, which nevertheless claims to be responsible. Reading a newspaper digitally does not consume paper, but the electricity of a server; and that is without counting the multiplication of volumes consumed made possible by digital technology (we no longer read one magazine, but several, accompanied by their procession of images and videos). The impossibility of evaluating products online encourages customers to buy multiple items (the absence of a trip to the store is replaced by a double delivery: a parcel being delivered to the home, and then returned to the warehouse if the product is not kept). Finally, in the same vein, the data collected and stored by CRM programs contribute to the "dark side of digital technology", whose environmental impact is growing continuously.

In addition to the ecological problems it causes, the mobilization of digital tools in the service of customer relationships is not without social effects. As with all technologies, these tools entail an ambiguous relationship with their users [ELL 12, ELL 13]. This can lead to dispossession and dereliction, in other words, a feeling of powerlessness and abandonment. Illitch advocates user-friendly technology that can be understood and mastered by the individuals who use it [ILL 03]. The profusion of digital tools that present themselves as efficient has led to disintermediation phenomena that are supposed to serve the consumer to the detriment of former partners in the value chain.

The substitution of self-service machines for human contact is directly visible to customers. Of course, new professions have emerged, but the demand for service workers and the respect that should be due to them are also diminishing. Applied technology seems to have diminished the value of personal contact. The retailing example is illuminating in this respect. The shopkeeper could select products and act as curator. The cashiers, even if their scope of action is limited to cashing up, maintain a social link while the customer pays. In digital economies, the contact staff is often the delivery driver, whose financial remuneration is directly indexed to delivery volume. Delivery personnel are integrated into a servuction process, and technology encourages social distancing, with the telephone serving as the sole vehicle for socio-material interaction. Exchanges with the customer are thus often limited to furtive politeness on the doorstep.

The question of the added value of digital tools for the end customer is also worthy of discussion. The benefits of technology can be exploited to the point of frustration. The extra value offered by a new digital tool encourages customers to organize their practices around it, at the risk of making it essential to their existence. This is the case, for example, with applications that enable customers to buy a product with a single click, and have it delivered in record time. This makes it all the more disappointing when a gift that has been put off until the last moment cannot be found online and therefore purchased on time (precisely because technology is expected to bypass a store's closing hours).

The vicious circle of digitalization can also be seen in our relationship with time. Digital tools promise to make tasks faster. The profusion of add-on devices with specialized functionalities can create an additional mental burden. More fundamentally, digitalization is accelerating social practices [ROS 10]. Technological efficiency, measured by a reduction in the time needed to complete tasks, makes everyone more intolerant of slowness. It also accentuates the cult of urgency [AUB 18], accelerating social norms and submission to the pressure to act (the acceptable response time to emails, text messages and Instagram notifications, for example, is decreasing from a day to a second).

The ease with which content can be produced creates an abundance and intensification of fashions and formats. At the same time, consumption needs to move faster too. The multiplicity of digital content increases viewing possibilities. The emergence of issues around the attention economy and addiction to social networks reveals phenomena of control that lock consumers into a "vortex" that annihilates their cognitive capacities. Caught up in the spiral of virality, they are pushed into an incessant viewing of content, leading to saturation and dereliction. In the commercial sphere, for example, sites offering online sales for a limited period of time encourage an acceleration of consumer behavior [AYA 12].

Customer relationships also benefit from this digital acceleration. Many brands are encouraging digital virality, relying on fashion phenomena accentuated by the digital promotion of certain products. For example, rewards are offered with a time exclusivity: companies offer purchasing opportunities to their most loyal customers, offering or even urging them to buy an exclusive item. This is often a temporal exclusivity that only lasts a few minutes. They can enjoy their status (allowing them to buy) or move along. The privilege of being able to choose an envied product can thus lead to unplanned purchases that may lose their appeal once the fashion buzz dies down.

Moreover, customer relationships are eagerly embracing the possibilities offered by digital tools. Current practices consist of collecting and storing data "all over the place", sometimes without any strategic reflection or knowledge of how this information will be used in the future. In the final analysis, customer data represent very large volumes, all the more so as the technological opportunities for capturing data are becoming more refined every year, enabling us to track customer behavior in great detail (data from browsing sites, consumption and social networks, etc.). The ability of companies to collect, organize and structure customer data is unprecedented. However, collecting and storing all of these data can not only be counter-productive (the greater the volume of data collected, the more complex it is to pinpoint useful information to enable better customer service and greater value creation for the organization), but also very costly for the environment: the servers and machines that enable their storage and analysis are extremely energy-intensive.

5.1.3. *Consumption and rebound effect*

The consumerist system in which customer relationships are embedded is thus undermined in its very foundations (the resources necessary for its operation risk becoming unavailable, and downstream customers may become prisoners of a system from which they cannot escape).

Awareness of these issues is prompting marketers to consider solutions that are more respectful of the ecosystem in which they operate. Strategies integrating ecological and societal transitions are thought of under generic headings such as "sustainable development", or "social and environmental responsibility". Numerous marketing practices are attempting to become more virtuous in the constitution phase of their offer and aiming for a reduction in their environmental impact (reparability indices, eco-design, launch of low-tech products, etc.).

However, these appear to be a piecemeal response, slowing down resource depletion too slowly. More surprisingly, they can even trigger rebound effects. These phenomena are characterized by an increase in consumption, even though the proposed offer is more efficient. For example, more efficient heating systems can reach a target temperature while consuming less energy. One of the rebound effects would be an increase in the temperature chosen by residents (additional comfort for a similar consumption cost). Similarly, car-sharing schemes can encourage more people to optimize their car journeys, thereby reducing the number of journeys they make. A rebound effect may nonetheless occur, with users able to afford a vehicle whose journeys they can finance by sharing it. Contrary to the targets set, the more cars are on the road, the more journeys are made. This rebound effect can even be seen in the clothing sector, where second-hand sites such as Vinted or Vestiaire

Collective, which claim to be part of a virtuous circular economy model, are now suspected of participating in overbidding for clothing purchases. Buyers are more likely to be tempted by the ease of resale, thus contributing to the deleterious phenomenon of fast fashion.

5.2. For more sufficiency in customer relationships

These rebound effects illustrate customers' opportunistic behavior and call for more direct action on consumption practices. It is in this perspective that the concept of sufficiency is essential in the range of solutions to the challenges of social and environmental transition. Sufficiency is a concept associated with temperance and moderation, a virtuous behavior valued in ancient philosophies (Epicureanism, Stoicism, etc.), as well as in various religions. This unanimity of different doctrines brings to light an understanding of sufficiency as the capacity to enjoy in moderation. The greed of capitalist societies runs counter to these sufficient, measured and "reasonable" behaviors.

Sufficiency in the field of marketing therefore refers to a greater reflexivity on the part of the consumer concerning their practices, and more concretely to a reduction in consumption. Numerous concepts are associated with it in the field of marketing research (degrowth, voluntary simplicity, frugality, etc.). They reflect a collective or even political approach, or, on the contrary, a more individual approach that withdraws from the world. What all of these concepts have in common is the notion of commitment: sufficiency is based on a willingness on the part of the consumer. Pierre Rabhi evokes the idea of happy sufficiency as a reduction in consumption "in full awareness" that would guide towards happiness. However, these paths, which may seem logical and "self-evident", may clash with certain consumer practices, notably because they have been promoted in the context of "generous" customer relationships (e.g. unlimited packages, or point/mile accumulation programs for each act of consumption).

So how can we reconcile sufficiency practices and customer relationships? We believe there are several ways of approaching this question.

5.2.1. *Sufficiency in customer relationships: doing "less" but "better"*

Companies could adopt sufficiency in their approach to targeting customers. Mass mailings, which often end up directly in the trash can (physical or digital), are not only irrelevant for brands (low conversion rates), but also for customers, who become annoyed or even irritated by such approaches. A more virtuous approach would be for the brands to speak out less often, but more appropriately, by choosing the right message (going beyond the commercial aspect of inciting consumption to develop another form of relationship with the brand) and the right channel, taking into account all of the effects generated, not only for the customer, but also for the entire ecosystem in a holistic perspective. Such an approach, based on sufficiency, would allow for virtuous value creation, not only for the brand, but also for the customer, on whom the commercial pressure exerted would be reasoned and adapted to their wishes. Naturally, this would mean training marketing professionals in order to familiarize them with such logics and enable them to make such trade-offs. It would also mean integrating criteria of eco-friendliness into the choices made by marketing departments. For example, various ideas are being considered, such as providing brands with the technical possibility of programming an "expiry date" for commercial emails. In this way, emails would be automatically recycled on the programmed expiry date. This would reduce the environmental impact of the near-infinite storage of most commercial emails, which are likely to end up in "junk" (never consulted) or archived unnecessarily by unwary consumers.

5.2.2. *Enhancing the status of customers who practice "sufficiency"*

Customer relationships could serve to promote more sufficiency in consumption practices. First, this could be achieved by promoting the commitment of the most committed customers. The statutory definition in customer relationships is traditionally based on levels of actual purchases or presumed customer influence. These are linked to the volume of expenditure for which the customer is responsible. Customers committed to sufficiency – whose purchasing volumes are lower than those of more frugal consumers – are not valued for their convictions. Conversely, when a customer that practices sufficiency agrees to a higher expenditure (e.g. when they have chosen a more eco-friendly but more costly solution), they sometimes receive a reward that goes against their values (an object they have no use for, for example), which will harm the customer relationship (they feel misunderstood, not valued in their efforts to be a responsible consumer). A statutory classification of customer relationships based on their contribution to more responsible consumption (in general or in a particular sector) would enable recognition of these people who are individually committed to sufficiency. This population of "activists" may feel isolated in their approach, or even misunderstood by many companies. Recognizing their actions in this way could improve their perception of the brand.

Integrating sufficiency into customer relationship programs does not necessarily mean offering financial or material rewards. Symbolic valorization would function as an officialization of their role and would suffice to play the role of gratification. It does not even have to be public. In fact, it could be as simple as the brand addressing its customers in recognition of their responsible commitment to the brand. These activists would thus have an "institutional" testimonial from a major company of their beneficial role. Patagonia offers such recognition by writing to its customers when they decide to send their products in for repair: "Thank you for requesting repair of your Patagonia product! The best thing we can do for the planet is to use our stuff longer, so we're delighted you've decided to have your product repaired".

In this first scenario, the customer relationship is based on the company's statutory and distinctive functioning and serves practices that promote sufficiency. It does not transform existing practices. Those who are convinced and voluntarily and thoughtfully committed to practices that promote sufficiency represent an active minority.

This minority is certainly active, but already convinced. By enhancing their value, customer relationships integrate them back into the responsible consumption circuit (particularly for the most militant customers, who could become active resisters). This also contributes to a more general improvement in the brand's image among its influential customers.

Some brands have already adopted this approach. The Decat'Club loyalty program promises loyalty points to customers who "take care of themselves and the planet". Customers can collect loyalty points by carrying out an eco-friendly action (e.g. buying a second-hand product, buying an eco-friendly product from the range, taking part in cleaning up country paths, etc.). Similarly, Leclerc awards more points for the purchase of organic products, which are less harmful to the environment. Engie, with its "Mon Programme pour Agir" (My Program for Action) loyalty scheme, encourages reduced energy consumption and rewards "performance" with points called "KiloActs", which can then be used to order eco-friendly items, etc., with all of the limitations that this system can represent in perhaps encouraging the consumption of products that users do not really need.

However, these approaches must be tackled with subtlety, at the risk of arousing resistance from customers: the fact that a brand tries to steer their behavior in this way may be perceived as inappropriate and going beyond the relationship that customers intend to build with brands. Is it a brand's role to hand out "bonus points" to customers whose behavior it considers virtuous? How legitimate is it for the organization to judge this? These questions remind us of the delicate balance that needs to be struck when it comes to rewarding customers who adopt eco-friendly behavior without infantilizing them and giving the impression of judging their conduct.

5.2.3. *Promoting sufficiency through customer relationships*

A second approach is to engage traditional customers more directly in the sufficiency process. Customer relationships at the service of sufficiency can make customers aware of the harmful effects of excessive consumption. The company would then address all of its customers without distinction. The nature of the relationship with customers evolves in the service of raising awareness of sufficiency issues. These commitments made directly by the company could indirectly encourage customers to change their consumption practices.

Many "environmentally sensitive" companies (Patagonia, Maif) communicate their responsible practices. The idea here is to highlight the responsible behaviors that their customers could adopt. KLM is following this logic by defining its "Fly Responsibly" program in three parts: "What we do – What you can do – What the industry can do". Companies in the digital sector alert their customers to their daily or weekly screen time to get them thinking about the influence of screens on their lives and the environmental footprint of their digital practices.

The example of companies in the banking sector is instructive in this respect. A number of banks calculate their customers' carbon footprint based on their bank account spending and inform them accordingly. Some, like Onlyone, take the calculation a step further by offering customers the option of scanning their receipt for each purchase to find out its carbon footprint. Customer relationships offer a service that reflects the company's commitment, while facilitating customer involvement. More generally, it is part of a practice that decentralizes the purely commercial benefits at the heart of relationship marketing. In this case, the company assumes an educational role in raising consumer awareness. It is also the company's responsibility to check that the management of this service does not generate collateral effects in terms of environmental impact (the carbon footprint of the scan in particular).

5.2.4. *Facilitating commitment to sufficiency through customer relationships*

A third practice of promoting sufficiency through customer relations can reach beyond awareness and engage customers more directly in changing their practices. This practice is inspired by the phenomena of engagement [KIE 71] and nudge marketing [GUR 19], which aim to act directly on consumption practices without affecting values or attitudes. The principles of retribution and reward implemented by loyalty programs can thus be used to promote sufficiency.

Competitions rewarding the most virtuous practices (via bill reductions or point accumulation systems) can be launched. This gamification would use the playful dimension of customer relationships to steer customers towards a goal of reduced consumption. The reward system could include an incentive to reduce consumption. Sufficiency points would reward customer loyalty on the same principle as the amount spent. Partnership and sponsorship systems could include a sufficiency component (earning points for recommending customers who have achieved their consumption reduction targets). These consumption reduction practices could be limited to a particular business sector, with the expected risks of contradictory injunctions. In fact, rewarding the purchase of energy-efficient telephones or application systems could be in contradiction with a system that traditionally awards points according to the volume of expenditure. The points system could also be used to reward energy-saving practices outside a given company's sector of activity. To take the example of banking companies, they could integrate a bonus system into their customer relationships, rewarding a general reduction in spending. In the same way, companies could reward a change in practices initiated by other schemes (e.g. by contributing to a reward scheme for households that reduce their energy or waste bills).

Last but not least, a number of advantages combining distinction, awareness-raising and incentives to change practices could be granted to customers who choose to adopt more sufficiency in their practices; for example, in terms of means of transport. For instance, at the entrance to a store, a welcoming bicycle parking area with messages thanking users for having chosen a soft mode of transport (symbolic value), indicating the ecological benefits of this approach and its positive repercussions in terms of users' well-being (awareness), placed as close as possible to the entrance with all the facilities to shelter and secure bicycles, load shopping, etc. (incentive mechanism), would make it possible to build a customer relationship anchored in a logic of sufficiency.

Table 5.1 summarizes the three ways in which customer relationships can promote more frugal consumption behavior.

	"Symbolic" customer relationship mechanisms	**"Informative" customer relationship mechanisms**	**"Incentive" customer relationship mechanisms**
Target clientele	Followers of sufficiency	All our customers and prospects	Traditional loyal customers
Solutions in place	A response to the quest for recognition and status	Meeting the need for social compliance	Points system and gamification
Targeted strategies	Turning activists into brand ambassadors	Raising awareness and changing attitudes	Making it fun to reduce consumption

Table 5.1. *Proposed mechanisms for customer to participate in more sufficiency-based and sustainable consumption*

5.3. Conclusion

Guided by the urgent need to rethink our consumption systems in the light of the depletion of planetary resources and the rapid transition to more virtuous consumption models, this chapter advocates more responsible customer management practices, without calling into question their validity and relevance in the vast majority of cases. The aim is to do "better" while doing "less", and systematically take into account the environmental and ecosystemic impact of our actions.

A series of proposals have been put forward, promoting a form of sufficiency on the part of brands in the actions they launch and a form of sufficiency on the part of customers in their consumption of brands. The question of the role that customer relationships could play in raising awareness and engaging consumers in an approach that promotes sufficiency in terms of consumption was also discussed. Are customer relationship professionals not specialists in commitment? Perhaps they hold the key to a successful transition to a more sustainable consumption model. Their expertise and their role appear to be decisive and essential in this transition. Customer relationships, which support and shape the link with consumers, are an essential cog in the wheel!

The actions presented in this chapter are largely incentive-based and rely on the willingness of customers. Customer relationships and sufficiency finally come together thanks to incentive systems. But will these practices be enough? Are changes in practice fully effective when customers are confronted with the destruction of their consumption? Can there be such a thing as forced sufficiency? These are the new questions that undoubtedly herald an in-depth transformation of practices in the years to come.

5.4. References

[AUB 18] AUBERT N., *Le culte de l'urgence. La société malade du temps*, Flammarion, Paris, 2018.

[AYA 12] AYADI N., GIRAUD M., GONZALEZ C., "Tentations, impulsions et contrôle des consommateurs sur les sites de ventes privées", *Management & Avenir*, vol. 54, no. 4, pp. 34–52, 2012.

[BON 16] BONNEUIL C., FRESSOZ J.B., *L'événement Anthropocène*, Le Seuil, Paris, 2016.

[BON 22] BONNEUIL C., "Comment vivre l'anthropocène", *Ecorev*, vol. 52, pp. 48–68, 2022.

[DES 15] DESCOLA P., *Par-delà nature et culture*, Folio, Paris, 2015.

[ELL 12] ELLUL J., *Le bluff technologique*, Fayard/Pluriel, Paris, 2012.

[GOS 22] GOSSEN M., KROPFELD M.I., "“Choose nature. Buy less.” Exploring sufficiency-oriented marketing and consumption practices in the outdoor industry", *Sustainable Production and Consumption*, vol. 30, pp. 720–736, 2022.

[GUR 19] GURVIEZ P., RAFFIN S., *Nudge et marketing social. Clés et expériences inspirantes pour changer les comportements*, Dunod, Paris, 2019.

[ILL 03] ILLICH I., *Œuvres complètes, vol. 1 (OC1)*, Fayard, Paris, 2003.

[JAL 17] JALLAT F., PEELEN E., STEVENS E. et al., *Gestion de la relation client*, Pearson, London, 2017.

[KIE 71] KIESLER C., *The Psychology of Commitment*, Academic Press, New York, 1971.

[LYO 79] LYOTARD J.F., *La condition postmoderne*, Éditions de Minuit, Paris, 1979.

[PEZ 17] Pez V., Butori R., Mimouni-Chaabane A., "The dark side of the pressure exerted by loyalty programs on consumers: Practical and ethical issues", *Recherche et Applications En Marketing (English Edition)*, vol. 32, no. 3, pp. 71–83, 2017.

[RAB 13] RABHI P., *Vers la sobriété heureuse*, Actes Sud, Paris, 2013.

[ROS 10] ROSA H., *Accélération. Une critique sociale du temps*, La Découverte, Paris, 2010.

[SPA 19] SPANGENBERG J.H., LOREK S., "Sufficiency and consumer behaviour: From theory to policy", *Energy Policy*, vol. 129, pp. 1070–1079, 2019.

6

Metaverse Opportunities for Customer Relations

For years now, brands have been using product placement in films [HEI 07], on television or in video games such as *The Sims* or *Toca Race Driver 3* [DAS 16] to attract new customers or maintain ties with existing ones outside stores. Metaverses, a recent phenomenon, are virtual, persistent and shared universes that enable interaction with other people in avatar, 3D or 2D format. The best-known are *Decentraland*, *Roblox*, *The Sandbox*, *Meta* and *Fortnite*. They enable a variety of experiences, including meeting friends, playing games, learning, shopping and working. Brands and artists invest in them for the tremendous opportunities they represent in terms of both acquisition and loyalty. Because they offer hedonic experiences, they have a positive impact on customer relations, customer engagement, purchase intent and e-word-of-mouth [HER 19, HOG 19, HEP 20]. What precise characteristics help create unique hedonic experiences? The analysis of successful brands in the metaverse can shed light on opportunities and best practices to avoid missing out on this disruptive innovation. While the gaming industry was a forerunner, PwC reports that consumer goods and luxury goods are now involved, with events, stores, sales and engagement strategies being relocated from the real world to the metaverse: PwC estimates that the metaverse market represented EUR 47 billion in 2020, and that it will grow by 43% a year until 2025[1]. These estimates are confirmed by investment bank Morgan Stanley: the metaverse could add a further EUR 50 billion to the fashion and luxury goods industry by 2030.

Chapter written by Catherine LEJEALLE and Thierry DELÉCOLLE.

1 See: https://teknomers.com/fr/livre-blanc-de-pwc-metaverse-transforme-le-commerce-de-detail-et-lindustrie-des-biens-de-consommation/.

Interview with Stéphane Galienni, associate director of Balistikart (a digital communications agency which supports brands in their digital development)

1) What opportunities do you see for brands in the metaverse?

One of the main features of the metaverse is its immersive 360° environment, which opens up new fields of application for brands: communications and marketing, 3D product presentations, virtual stores and even brand storytelling. For example, Balenciaga chose to present its Fall Winter 2021–2022 collection in an interactive game, *Afterworld: The Age of Tomorrow*. Accessible via a simple QR code, users find themselves propelled into a futuristic world where they encounter different avatars, all stamped with the Balenciaga brand. More than a traditional fashion show, the spectator becomes both an actor and hero of the story. By incorporating the codes of gaming to create their own universe, brands are rejuvenating their image among young people.

Beyond event communication, the real challenge of the metaverse is commercial, with virtual commerce or v-commerce. Thanks to 3D modeling, brands can present their products in volume in virtual stores, offering a customer experience with all the advantages of e-commerce: online transactions, 24/7 accessibility, etc.

2) What challenges and risks do you see as a downside?

The metaverse raises fundamental questions about digital identity. How can we protect an image-based representation of ourselves when everyone can personalize their avatar in a hyper-realistic way? How can we ensure that each platform complies with the General Data Protection Regulation? One solution to these problems is probably the use of non-fungible tokens (NFTs) assigned to a digital twin[2], which authenticates the latter's virtual identity in an unfalsifiable and inimitable way. The smart contract assigned to it would ultimately protect the data provided by the user in this new digital space.

The ecological issue is a second challenge, since the platforms are based on blockchain and NFT technologies. Brands need to ensure that their initiatives are compatible with their CSR policy. The metaverse Polygon, which aims to be the first climate-positive blockchain, is a solution worth considering.

Box 6.1. *A professional's view on the opportunities and challenges of the metaverse for brands*

2 Non-fungible tokens are digital assets that grants rights in both the real and virtual world. The digital twin is a digital replica of a real good. For example, a garment worn in real life is sold with its twin, to be worn on an avatar.

6.1. An immersive, interactive and persistent universe

Metaverses are immersive, interactive and persistent 360° Web 3.0 universes. Consumers explore them with avatars or augmented or virtual reality glasses. The experience is more engaging than that of Web 2.0 with social networks. De facto, narrative formats are longer than Tweets or TikTok videos. Participation appeals to the imagination and invites people to stay for a long time, following the model of video game addiction. These functionalities open up new possibilities for brand interaction with consumers, far superior to chat and video on social networks.

Following the interruption of concerts during Covid-19, Canadian singer Justin Bieber announced his Justin World Tour 2022 that did not include Europe. To keep his audience waiting and engaged, the artist gave an interactive and immersive concert on November 18, 2021. This *Interactive Virtual Experience* combined gaming, motion capture and real-time musical performance. Participation was free and allowed fans to interact with the star and with each other. This consumer engagement maintains the customer relationship [CAR 19, HAM 21].

Brands are launching ambassadors who meet customers, interact with players and make people want to get to know the brand. The 200-year-old whisky brand Kinahan claims to be somewhere between authenticity and innovation, heritage and fiction. To celebrate Lewis Hamilton's victory at the British Grand Prix, in collaboration with Morysetta, a well-known artist in the NFT world, the company launched a Formula 1 NFT in 3D and augmented reality. The work comes with an exclusive title and can be exhibited in the metaverse. The advantage of this strategy is to link a very popular UK sporting event rooted in the real world with an extension into the metaverse. In other cases, the bridge between the two worlds consists of offering advantages in each: for example, an NFT enables you to meet a player at a soccer match or a singer at a concert in the physical world, while other NFTs enable you to dance on a rooftop at a party organized in the metaverse. At Paris Fashion Week Spring Summer 2022, several luxury brands offered NFTs to accredited guests so they could access exclusive content and augmented reality experiences. In London, Roksanda closed the show with a silhouette in the form of a limited-edition NFT that buyers could try on virtually. All these practices are a reminder that, when it comes to customer relations, hedonic and exclusive experiences in the real world are highly valued by consumers.

Whether for event communications or virtual stores, the metaverse offers an immersive experience that plunges consumers into a state of flow, conducive to customer relations and purchases. Compared with payment in cash or by bank card in-store, payment in virtual currency in a gamified environment puts the notion of money at a distance [COW 08]. The metaverse appeals to the various senses, totally absorbing the consumer into the activity and immersing them in maximum concentration. Trying on a dress in the metaverse or chatting with a virtual sales consultant from the terrace of your penthouse in *The Sandbox* is a richer experience than chatting on your mobile while on the move. Friends can be invited to give their opinion on the dress and take part in the selection process, which is easier to organize than in real life. The act of buying is simplified, staged and moved into a playful environment.

6.2. A gamified, esthetic universe

For some years now, brands have been investing in video games such as *Animal Crossing* (Givenchy) or *League of Legends* (Louis Vuitton). Now a mainstream cultural practice, video games combine competition with more sophisticated graphics than social networks. These universes are formidable breeding grounds for recruiting the younger generation via a practice rooted in everyday life and requiring conative engagement. It is not just a question of liking, but of acting in the brand's universe. After video games, the metaverse is another particularly innovative and sophisticated gamified universe.

Already chosen by Gucci and Tommy Hilfinger, *Roblox* is the metaverse Givenchy Beauty has also opted for. With more than 54 million daily active players, *Roblox* reaches young people, since 67% of players are under 16. Givenchy's adoption of *Roblox* combines tradition and innovation, as the experience features a chateau inspired by that of founder Hubert Givenchy, a garden dancefloor, a swimming pool and a metro station in the colors of L'interdit perfume. Players are invited to create looks for their avatars, purchase skins and take part in content contests to win virtual accessories. This virtual consumption of virtual clothing or accessories in the world of video games is called direct-to-avatar (D2A). In order not to tire its public, the brand varies its make-up and accessories according to the season, as in the real range. Whether brand customers or not, players spend hours in the brand's company, getting to know it and discovering its values. The bet is that they will also be tempted to buy the products for their real lives. Finally, to further engage them, as soon as 1,000 "likes" are reached, options will be unlocked. This feature maintains a high level of attention so as not to miss the arrival of new products. What is more, the consumer takes power by collectively participating in reaching the 1,000 "likes" for the product reveal. Empowerment engages by flattering the consumer's ego and increases customer satisfaction [HER 19].

Unlike *Second Life*, which was quickly abandoned by brands four years after its creation in 2007, the esthetics of the metaverse are highly sophisticated. Graphic tools and connection speeds (5G, fiber, etc.) have evolved to enable a fluid experience on mobile, tablet and computer devices alike. This quality of rendering is prompting brands to team up with artists to offer an experience more in line with cultural practices than with the commercial world. For example, on the occasion of the British Grand Prix, a Formula 1 race, the bicentenary whisky brand Kinahan issued NFTs produced by artist Morysetta. The fact that these NFTs are anchored in a hugely popular real-life event gives them a high profile. Other brands have followed suit. Selfridges has created a replica of its Birmingham store on *Decentraland*, offering an immersive augmented reality experience. In addition to purchasing the brand's products, consumers are invited to visit various art exhibitions and take part in cultural and artistic events, an investment by the brand to forget the commercial dimension and maintain the link through a gratifying experience.

6.3. A personalized world of scarcity

The value perceived by consumers encompasses several dimensions: economic, utilitarian, hedonic, social, etc. Rarity contributes to the perception of value, and uniqueness can be the ultimate grail. Luxury products fulfill some consumers' needs for uniqueness and status [KAU 18]. However, digital technology allows infinite reproduction at very low cost, driving down the value of virtual goods [MAR 18]. As they are based on a blockchain, metaverses allow goods such as land, yachts or unique clothing to be sold with a certificate of ownership. Marketing goods in the metaverse via the blockchain is a first solution for brands to bring back rarity and uniqueness. Moncler, Balenciaga and Nike market unique models of their products intended for consumer avatars. In this way, the brand can market products exclusively for virtual consumption, or digital virtual consumption, and can also market the twin of the product sold in the boutique. The virtual version is sometimes more expensive than its real twin. This is the case for the Gucci bag sold in its virtual form for some EUR 4,000, that is, four times the price of the real-life bag. More often than not, brands mix the two types of goods: Diesel, for example, markets both physical pieces to be worn in real life and unique NFT versions of the brand's clothing.

Indeed, creating NFTs is another way of increasing the value of goods sold. Also based on a blockchain, NFTs are tokens granting rights in the virtual world of the metaverse and/or in the real world. NFT clothing, jewelry or accessories can be worn by avatars, but also by consumers themselves in selfies posted on social networks or in the metaverse. In this case, they are seen as extensions of the self, allowing the wearer to show off. These NFTs can also be issued directly by stars (artists, musicians, athletes, influencers, journalists, etc.) who monetize their audience directly. While metaverses are currently less greedy than streaming or content distribution platforms and enable stars to increase their revenues, Meta has announced that it will take 50% of creators' revenues: this is a major issue in the competition between metaverses for the future.

6.4. A social and community universe

The metaverse enables brands to create virtual communities where fans can interact, exchange tips and participate in the life of the brand. They can also be used to organize events and get closer to consumers. Metaverses can be used to unite projects and raise funds in a more playful format than crowdfunding. Fervent defenders of the planet, the young founders of Aquaverse had the ambition of depolluting the oceans. They decided to invest in metaverses and launch sponges in NFT format, giving their owners governance rights. This initiative enables owners to take part in the adventure and carry out concrete actions in line with their values. The Aquaverse company won the innovation prize of the Netexplo 2022 Observatory. For users, engagement via metaverses is fun, innovative and effective. A variation was found by Elrond Trees: the model is play-to-earn, that is, the more they play, the more money they earn. This money is then invested in reforestation. A commitment to good deeds in the metaverse mobilizes young people more effectively than a cash donation. Metaverses can be used to create and animate communities of brands and interests.

In a context where inclusion and diversity are important values, the Estée Lauder group's Clinique brand is promoting a Web 3.0 that reflects diversity. With "Metaverse more like us", Clinique asked three make-up artists to create two looks, one in the physical world, the other in the metaverse for avatars. Non-fungible people (NFP), the human version of NFTs, are designed to combine the two worlds. What is more, after offering the first NFTs to loyalty card members, the brand issued 1968 NFP avatars to be won. Through this campaign, the brand is promoting its values and its fight for diversity. It also encourages consumers to join the brand with new creations and the chance to win them.

6.5. An innovative universe

Several major groups have launched recruitment campaigns using metaverses to attract young talent. Carrefour, for example, estimates that a large number of young engineers have responded to this innovative campaign, without which they would not have thought of joining the retail sector. Innovation has a positive impact on a brand's image, making people want to join. The retailer has also purchased a plot of land in *The Sandbox* for experimentation. Defending a balanced diet with five fruits and vegetables a day, and bees, Carrefour created an exclusive map in *Fortnite*. Carrefour installed an NFTBee supermarket in *The Sandbox*, where the NFTs represent fruits and vegetables pollinated by bees. The presence of garbage cans with diapers convinced Carrefour that metaverses were a sufficiently democratized living space to invest in now. The experience is both educational and fun, raising awareness about the disappearance of bees.

The P&G Group has created Beautysphere, a metaverse where the user learns about the history of Kew Gardens in the UK and explores the surrounding nature. Along the way, the user discovers five trees (aloe vera, etc.) used in the composition of P&G products, including shampoos and skincare creams. Once the five trees have been visited, the experience ends with the planting of a real tree in Veracruz, Mexico.

These innovative experiences contribute to the perceived value of the metaverse by consumers. The use of innovative and trendy technologies flatters the ego of consumers by offering others an image of someone at the cutting edge of novelty. When this use is proposed by brands, it has a positive impact on purchase intention and brand loyalty [HAM 19]. Technology adds symbolic value – linked to enhanced self-expression – and technological value to the value provided by the product itself and by the brand [HER 19]. However, given the energy-hungry nature of the blockchains on which the metaverses are based, the technology may raise ecological concerns. This concern is understood by market players, since in mid-September 2022, the leading blockchain, Ethereum, changed its operation from involving a proof of work that requires every node on the network to be active to a proof of stake that could save 99% of energy. This is a development that should be followed over time and as it spreads to other blockchains.

6.6. Conclusion

The mainstream press echoes the metaverse phenomenon, referring to a "utopian" version embodied in the science-fiction film *Ready Player One*. While the first virtual worlds, such as *Second Life*, went through a phase of disinterest, the gamified versions of these persistent universes (*Roblox*, *Fortnite* and *The Sandbox*, in particular) have attracted a population of regular members who find recreational, social and even mercantile interactions. Metaverses are already a reality. They enable brands to create their own brand worlds, sell virtual goods, launch virtual stores to sell real goods, create virtual events, offer games and rewards to be picked up in the real world in stores, or present virtual ambassadors. If we refer to the customer strategy analysis framework proposed by Pierre Volle [VOL 12], in seizing the metaverse, companies will have to answer several questions:

– Customer orientation: will companies be able to take advantage of the specific features of these new universes to offer appropriate customer relations? The experiential and playful dimension of the most popular metaverses requires an adapted proposal.

– Customer relations targets: in a context where there are not one but several metaverses, there are various relationship targets, Before even addressing their customers, brands will have to address the inhabitants of the metaverses in which they choose to establish themselves.

– Relational priorities: are metaverses a territory for acquiring new customers (notably through the intangible collections offered by NFT technology) or an experience territory designed to build customer loyalty?

– The customer experience: as experiential territory supported by video game applications, the current metaverses are obviously associated with experience. However, the question of experience refers to that of value: a trap could be that of offering a metaverse experience of being in the metaverse. The customer experience must integrate a broader dimension and design these virtual spaces to complement real spaces (multi-channel), just as the acquisition of online customers must be accompanied by offline systems.

– Relational processes and devices: in line with the previous development and the vision of metaverses as one contact point among others, customer strategy must be based on a customer's unified vision. Which phases of the relationship (initiating, selling, developing, building loyalty, retaining, etc.) have the most to gain from being transposed into a virtual universe? For example, the notion of customer sponsorship takes on a particular meaning in these playful environments, where players are invited to join groups or invite their friends. Will it be necessary to offer benefits, or will the invitation be natural, given the uniqueness of the brand experience?

The driving force behind customer intelligence lies in capturing the data on which customer strategies are based. Here, it is possible to track customer behavior within the platform. Two issues coexist here:

– the collection of data shared between the metaverse operator and the brand that has established an activity there. Metaverses are no different from current platforms (GAFAM) that concentrate data collection: the notion of privacy is not yet fully guaranteed;

– the blockchain technology which underpins the metaverse and in particular the associated ethical governance issues (i.e. decision-making rights, trust, exchange of digital assets, markets, etc.) identified by Tan and Salo [TAN 21]. By investing in private initiatives, brands are associating themselves with blockchain governance: brands will need to integrate the education of their customers regarding these issues and ensure that blockchain "practices" do not clash with the societal and environmental responsibility issues they communicate about in "real life".

The metaverse is a groundbreaking innovation in the history of the Web, marking the arrival of Web 3.0. It represents a tremendous opportunity for brands to engage young and old alike, win over and build loyalty and test innovative formats. Despite this stimulating landscape, there are a number of issues and risks that brands need to take into account. The first concerns the law, which applies both to data protection and to relationships between players (cases of rape have been reported). The second is the ecological challenge posed by the energy-hungry nature of metaverses and blockchains. While greener metaverses like *Polygon* may have emerged with a lower carbon footprint, the question remains. Lastly, for the time being and for some years to come, metaverses will be plural and unconnected. Will a consumer want to invest in a given metaverse knowing that the good is not teleportable to another metaverse if they then discover that their friends are in another metaverse? Standards are being established, uses are being built and brands are venturing out on their own, but the real paradigm shift in relation to social networks is also conditional on the arrival of interface devices such as connected glasses that are more powerful and lighter. Despite these drawbacks, it may be worthwhile for brands to embrace metaverses and launch experiments to prepare for the future of social networking. There is a stimulating future to discover, one that will redistribute the cards between timid brands and innovative brands that understand that their audience has already passed through the metaverse door and will not wait for them.

6.7. References

[BEL 88] BELK R., "Possessions and the extended self", *Journal of Consumer Research*, vol. 15, pp. 139–168, 1988.

[CAR 19] CARLSON J., WYLLIE J., RAHMAN M.M. et al., "Enhancing brand relationship performance through customer participation and value creation in social media brand communities", *Journal of Retailing and Consumer Services*, vol. 50, pp. 333–341, 2019.

[COW 08] COWLEY B., CHARLES D., BLACK M. et al., "Toward an understanding of flow in video games", *Computers in Entertainment*, vol. 2, no. 6, pp. 1–27, 2008.

[DAS 16] DA SILVA M.F., EZAN P., "Le placement de produits dans les jeux vidéo : un moyen pour revisiter la relation marque-adolescent", *Revue Française du Marketing*, vol. 1, no. 255, pp. 43–54, 2016.

[HAM 19] HAMARI J., MALIK A., KOSKI J. et al., "Uses and gratifications of Pokémon Go: Why do people play mobile location-based augmented reality games?", *International Journal of Human–Computer Interaction*, vol. 9, no. 35, pp. 804–819, 2019.

[HAM 21] HAMZAH Z.L., WAHAB H.A., WAQAS M., "Unveiling drivers and brand relationship implications of consumer engagement with social media brand posts", *Journal of Research in Interactive Marketing*, vol. 2, no. 15, pp. 336–358, 2021.

[HEI 07] HEILBRUNN B., "La publicité est dans le film. Placement de produits et stratégie de marque au cinéma, dans les chansons, dans les jeux vidéos", *Décisions Marketing*, vol. 107, no. 45, 2007.

[HEP 20] HEPOLA J., LEPPÄNIEMI M., KARJALUOTO H., "Is it all about consumer engagement? Explaining continuance intention for utilitarian and hedonic service consumption", *Journal of Retailing and Consumer Services*, vol. 57, p. 102232, 2020.

[HER 19] HERZ M., RAUSCHNABEL P.A., "Understanding the diffusion of virtual reality glasses: The role of media, fashion and technology", *Technological Forecasting and Social Change*, vol. 138, pp. 228–242, 2019.

[HOG 19] HÖGBERG J., RAMBERG M.O., GUSTAFSSON A. et al., "Creating brand engagement through in-store gamified customer experiences", *Journal of Retailing and Consumer Services*, vol. 50, pp. 122–130, 2019.

[HSI 21] HSIEH S.H., LEE C.T., TSENG T.H., "Branded app atmospherics: Examining the effect of pleasure–arousal–dominance in brand relationship building", *Journal of Retailing and Consumer Services*, vol. 60, pp. 102482, 2021.

[HSI 22] HSIEH S.H., LEE C.T., TSENG T.H., "Psychological empowerment and user satisfaction: Investigating the influences of online brand community participation", *Information & Management*, vol. 1, no. 59, pp. 103570, 2022.

[KAU 18] KAUPPINEN-RÄISÄNEN H., BJÖRK P., LÖNNSTRÖM A. et al., "How consumers' need for uniqueness, self-monitoring, and social identity affect their choices when luxury brands visually shout versus whisper", *Journal of Business Research*, no. 84, pp. 72–81, 2018.

[MAR 18] MARDON R., BELK R., "Materializing digital collecting: An extended view of digital materiality", *Marketing Theory*, vol. 18, no. 4, pp. 543–570, 2018.

[TAN 21] TAN T.M., SALO J., "Ethical marketing in the blockchain-based sharing economy: Theoretical integration and guiding insights", *Journal of Business Ethics*, doi: 10.1007/s10551-021-05015-8, 2021.

[VOL 12] VOLLE P., *Stratégie clients. Points de vue d'experts sur le management de la relation client*, Pearson, London, 2012.

7

Towards Transparent and Parsimonious Customer Data Collection

On Tuesday January 14, 2019, Justin Schuh, head of Chrome Engineering (Alphabet/Google), announced in a blog post[1] the firm's wish to phase out support for third-party cookies within the Google browser. Invented by Netscape in 1994, cookies are text files used to store information from one Web page to another.

A distinction is made between essential cookies (those enabling products to be placed in an e-commerce basket and information to be transferred from one product page to another) and third-party cookies (those deposited on the computer by a domain name other than the one visited by an Internet user). These third-party cookies make it possible to retrace an Internet user's navigation of the various websites they have visited, and thus gather information on their interests, reactions to advertising and inferred purchasing intentions, for example. They are essential to the online advertising ecosystem, enabling both finer targeting and more granular measurement of effectiveness.

Postponed at least until the second half of 2024, this decision by Mountain View's firm against third-party cookies is not a first, however, and is part of a regulatory and technological context aimed at making the Web more respectful of user privacy. Apple's Intelligent Tracking Prevention reduced cookies on Safari back in 2018, and Mozilla followed suit with Enhanced Tracking Protection on Firefox in 2019. Nevertheless, the announcement by Google will impact almost two thirds of the world's Internet users who use Chrome as their primary browser.

Chapter written by Tom VILLENET, Thierry DELÉCOLLE and Grégoire BOTHOREL.

1 See: https://blog.chromium.org/2020/01/building-more-private-web-path-towards.html.

Among the consequences of this announcement, a report[2] from the Interactive Advertising Bureau (IAB) estimates the drop in revenues for Open Internet players – who finance themselves largely through online advertising revenues – at between USD 32 and 39 billion per year by 2025. This sum would be absorbed by the Web giants: Google, Amazon, Facebook, Apple and Microsoft (GAFAM). GAFAM operate as a "walled garden": they capture data and charge companies for restricted, aggregated access (which does not allow for the kind of individualized vision possible in CRM), and they do not need third-party cookies to capture the preferences and appetencies of individuals within their (walled) environments, where people already spend most of their time online.

These technological transformations imposed unilaterally by some players in the ad tech world are having major consequences: 60.4% of data professionals in North America said they have had to invest in in-house data collection – also known as first-party data (eMarketer, July 2020).

The Covid-19 crisis was also a factor in the increased investment companies made in data collection: companies with no website, or only a small customer database, were unable to maintain relations with their customers when their stores were closed for long months.

Nonetheless, against this backdrop of accelerating data collection strategies, legislators have in recent years tightened the framework for all consumer data collection and utilization. These efforts include the General Data Protection Regulation (GDPR), which came into force in Europe in May 2018, as well as the California Consumer Privacy Act (CCPA) in the United States and its update with the California Privacy Rights Act (CPRA), which came into force on January 1, 2023. Even China has also passed legislation in this area: the Personal Information Protection Law (PIPL), which came into force on December 1, 2021, and uses the same definition of personal data, processing and data controllers.

On the consumer side, figures on the proportion of individuals using ad-blockers, those Web-browser extensions that limit the display of personalized ads, are only getting better. The latest barometers (Q3 2021), DataReportal from GWI, Hootsuite and WeAreSocial[3], reveal that on average 37% of 16- to 64-year-olds worldwide use an ad-blocker, with 34.2% in the United States and 36.2% in France.

2 The Socioeconomic Impact of Internet Tracking, February 2020. Available at: https://www.iab.com/wp-content/uploads/2020/02/The-Socio-Economic-Impact-of-Internet-Tracking.pdf.

3 See: https://www.slideshare.net/DataReportal/digital-2022-global-overview-report-january-2022-v05, page 271.

Data collection is going to have to change. Mere compliance with the various regulations will not provide a sustainable competitive advantage. Parsimony is therefore the preferred approach called for by many researchers and players. In this chapter, we show that parsimony implies less data collection and more transparency, but also more education and communication with a view to building a solid customer relationship.

7.1. Data as a means of personalizing customer relations and creating a competitive advantage

To differentiate themselves from the competition, companies have the choice of either focusing on the superiority of their product, operational excellence (optimizing production costs) or customizing their offer according to consumer needs [TRE 93]. In increasingly mature markets, disruptive innovations are becoming rarer and rarer, and cost optimization is becoming marginal beyond a certain threshold. It is therefore imperative to build customer loyalty so as not to lose customers to the competition. The third approach proposed by these authors, known as customer intimacy, presupposes knowledge of customer expectations and preferences based on the data collected.

As Beke et al. [BEK 18] remind us, collecting customer data has several uses for companies:

– monitoring and optimizing internal processes;

– improving understanding of the needs and preferences of individuals;

– delivering products and notifying customers of offer changes;

– customizing the marketing mix: product and service offering, pricing, communication, distribution and more;

– improving marketing return on investment (ROI).

Data collection is used to personalize display advertising (in the form of banners) on different sites, personalize website content, display product recommendations and optimize online customer journeys. This personalization is based not only on the sites visited, and therefore on inferred appetencies, but also on demographic data (age range, gender, socio-professional category, occupation), location data (device used, geo-location) and transaction data (past and abandoned transactions, etc.) stored in third-party cookies.

Not only does personalization enable advertisements relevant to the individual to be delivered, it also boosts the individual's receptiveness to the content of the advert, for example in job advertisements [PFI 20], which improves click-through rates [TUC 14] and increases the intention to buy the recommended products, as well as actual purchases.

Conversely, when individuals are confronted with overly personalized online banners or emails, the communications are perceived as intrusive and trigger privacy concerns (see section 7.1.1).

Individuals tend to dislike personalization when it is based on sensitive information. Early studies of recommendation systems suggest that consumers only authorize the collection of data from which they expect relevant recommendations [KNI 13]. Although the use of additional "external" data (e.g. from social networks) can improve these recommendations, individuals are reluctant to provide them [HEI 15].

The personalization of prices and promotions, in addition to the ethical aspects linked to discrimination between customers, naturally does not meet with unanimous approval when consumers are questioned. Individuals reject price discrimination when they are unable to understand why they pay more than other customers, and perceive these personalized prices as "unfair" [FEI 02]: this personalization is based on the inference of propensity to pay rather than on factual data.

7.1.1. *Risks in terms of breaches of privacy for the consumer*

As identified by Martin et al. [MAR 17b], "when a company collects, stores and uses consumer data, it increases the risk of harm and therefore the sense of vulnerability". Data vulnerability is the first risk identified; that is, consumers' perception of the likelihood of harm arising from the use of their data (e.g. access to personal data and the risk of profiling, but also the risk of information being shared between companies, or the risk of data leakage). This risk affects not only the company that holds the personal data, but also its competitors, because if data are lost, it reinforces the belief that a data leak is possible for other companies (negative spillover effect). The greatest risk is when data are misappropriated and used for the wrong purposes: fraudulent activities increase the danger from risks of harm to proven harm (financial, identity theft, social).

The second risk stems from the nature of the data collected and can be illustrated in the context of the U.S. Supreme Court's 2022 repeal of the Roe versus Wade case law that de facto guaranteed the right to abortion. States are now free to prohibit this practice[4]. Numerous digital traces left by Internet users could be used by judicial

4 See: https://www.nytimes.com/2022/07/13/technology/personaltech/abortion-privacy-roe-surveillance.html.

authorities. For example, the website Motherboard[5] revealed that data broker SafeGraph was selling data of women who had passed through the door of a family planning agency for USD 160, so that anti-abortion activists could send messages urging them to stop having an abortion.

The third risk lies in data matching. A piece of data, taken in isolation by one player, may have no value. But when aggregated and supplemented by other players, it can provide a great deal of information. By providing an anonymized email address to a data broker – a company that does not collect data, but aggregates them at the level of the individual, such as Acxiom-Liveramp, Experian, Nielsen, etc. – it is possible to retrieve the individual's appetency according to the sites visited, socio-demographic data or other information enabling the individual to be reidentified: personal identifiable information (PII) data.

Faced with data aggregation, Kosinski et al. [KOS 13] have shown, for example, that it is possible to infer sexual orientation, ethnicity, religion, skin color, happiness, substance use, parental divorce, age, gender, personality traits and intelligence from Facebook likes. These psychology researchers have compared these inferences with surveys, achieving predictive accuracy rates ranging from 60% for parental divorce to 95% for skin color, and close to standardized test accuracy for personality traits. The authors showed that although the 58,466 individuals had 68 median "likes", a single "like" already enabled inferences to be made. Youhou et al. [YOU 15] went further and showed, by cross-referencing the "likes" of 70,520 individuals with their Facebook psychometric test results (personality tests), that it was possible to infer an individual's personality more accurately by algorithm than by the judgment of colleagues with 10 "likes" for the individual, friends with 70 "likes", a family member with 150 "likes" or even a spouse with 300 "likes". Sweeney [SWE 02] showed how easy it was to identify 87% of Americans by cross-referencing three pieces of data: zip code, date of birth and gender. According to the author, a higher proportion of French and English people could be identified due to smaller populations and larger zip codes.

More generally, researchers use the concept of privacy concerns in order to measure the importance attached to the consumer's privacy and explain the refusal of consent [MAL 04]. Perceived risks on the consumer side can lead to various consequences, including a form of reaction. Martin et al. [MAR 17b] have identified four behaviors that stem from consumers' vulnerability to data collection:

– avoiding company content;

– providing false information;

5 See: https://www.vice.com/en/article/m7vzjb/location-data-abortion-clinics-safegraph-planned-parenthood.

– expressing negative word-of-mouth;

– switching to a competitor.

Thus, people's concerns about the use of their data can lead them to lie, which degrades the value of the database and reduces the effectiveness of the resulting actions.

7.1.2. *Risks in terms of strategic dependencies for companies*

Beyond the negative reactions of their customers and negative effects on their prospects, which can result in a loss of customers and therefore sales, and ultimately a reduction in the company's share price [MAR 17a], another risk concerns partnerships between companies.

A distinction according to data type and property identifies three types of data:

– first-party data, which belong to the company and are specific to it. They therefore provide a competitive advantage and, as the American Marketing Association points out[6], are often more accurate and therefore require fewer resources to clean up and remove the noise. These data come from CRM databases or any other information provided with consent (e.g. customer data platforms, which store cookies and site browsing behavior);

– data belonging to other companies that coexist alongside these data:

- second-party data are the first-party data of partner companies, which can be used to enrich their own first-party data;

- third-party data are data collected from different sources and made available in aggregate form, so that they cannot be tracked at the level of the individual and therefore of the customer relationship.

This distinction poses a risk for companies that have no first-party data and the bulk of whose digital marketing strategy is carried out via the social networks and channels controlled by GAFAM. These platforms collect customer data and provide access to them, but only within their own ecosystem, without enabling them to manage measurement, segmentation, targeting, attribution and capping (maximum number of ads) outside their "walled garden". These platforms appeal to corporate clients because of their ease of use, the quality of their

---

6 See: https://www.ama.org/pages/california-consumer-privacy-protection-act-what-you-need-to-know/.

segmentation (aggregation of all individual behaviors, further enhanced by data brokers) and their high reach (i.e. the ability to reach a large number of consumers). However, this aggregated vision does not give companies a people-based view of the individual, monitored on all their other channels, in order to achieve customer intimacy. GAFAM only provide aggregated key performance indicators (KPIs) for all individuals and figures that do not come from a trusted, independent third party.

This risk of dependency can also have commercial repercussions. An investigation by the *Wall Street Journal*[7] revealed, for example, that Amazon uses the information collected on the back of companies that rely on Amazon to distribute their products to identify opportunities for private-label products, whether in terms of characteristics to be imitated, price or even growth segments in which to launch.

7.2. The new connected consumers and their multiple perceptions of different data collection methods

Martin and Murphy [MAR 17a] argue that it is no longer a question of whether consumers are willing to provide their personal information, but how they react now that their data are accessible and available to marketers and interested parties. Indeed, individuals are becoming increasingly familiar with the value of personal data for marketers.

More recently, Morewedge et al. [MOR 21] have put forward the concept of psychological ownership to explain the evolution of the relationship between ownership and data. Ownership is a dual concept, with both a legal and a psychological dimension. Although legal ownership is based on legal rights and is recognized by others, psychological ownership is an attitude toward an object that the individual considers to be "theirs", without this recognition necessarily being acknowledged by others. According to these authors, the challenge for companies when it comes to data collection is to reduce psychological ownership of data so as to limit the number of compensations they have to grant.

While data may have been static in the past, today they are frequently collected continuously. Morewedge et al. [MOR 21] cite heart rate and blood pressure, for example, which are often collected continuously and displayed in real time on wearable devices or via application dashboards with animation, audio and gamification [KOI 19]. The experiential and/or gamification aspects of these applications, which draw on codes from the world of video games, are likely to

---

7 See: https://www.wsj.com/articles/amazon-scooped-up-data-from-its-own-sellers-to-launch-competing-products-11587650015.

threaten the psychological property of consumers. Not only do they complicate the evaluation of the extent of data collection, but they also make it more difficult to control the data.

The immaterial aspect of data also complicates the sense of psychological ownership. Who owns the data? Who owns the data collected by a connected fridge? The consumer? The company that designed the collection device? The company that provides the interface application? Or the company that owns the servers on which the data are stored? Cloud-hosted data are less tangible than a paper file. The risk arising from this loss of psychological ownership lies in the search for responsibility in the event of a data security incident. Individuals are more likely to blame the company rather than themselves.

A paradox has been identified by researchers: when individuals are asked about the importance of their privacy and the intention to provide personal information, they declare that they are attached to it. On the other hand, when their actual behavior is analyzed, individuals do nothing to protect their privacy. This paradox is referred to as the privacy paradox [AGU 15].

Another persuasive practice is the use of dark patterns in data collection. In France, the CNIL's recommendations of September 17, 2020, on cookie banners require consent in order for companies to deposit such cookies in the individual's Web browser. To obtain this consent, some companies use techniques that aim to manipulate individuals into adopting behavior that is not in their best interest: dark patterns. In the field of privacy, the practice in terms of user experience (UX) design can consist of playing with colors, formulas, fonts and the placement of elements to maximize consent. For example, a customer thinking they are accepting only legitimate cookies may click on a validation button entitled "accept all cookies", as the "legitimate cookies" button is grayed out whereas the one clicked is "green" (we refer the reader interested in patterns and manipulation to Chapter 8 of this book).

7.3. Why authorize the collection and use of personal data?

A first explanation comes from the nature of the relationship itself.

In marketing, trust is defined as the customer's perception of the service provider's reliability, skills and expertise, enabling them to anticipate the ability to effectively meet expectations (credibility). It is also the perception of the company's sincerity and honesty, and the perception that the company cares about preserving the relationship and seeking common profit rather than its own interests (integrity). Finally, it is the perception that the company renews its products and services by taking into account advances in research and listens to its consumers in order to evolve its offering (benevolence).

Trust, in addition to being a fundamental variable in customer–company relations, is the key variable enabling data collection [MAR 17a]. Antecedent to privacy concerns, when trust is not present, there is a negative impact on the willingness to provide data. Conversely, consumers are more inclined to provide their personal information in the context of strong relationships with companies, with the exception of truly private and embarrassing information, which is kept private.

Benefits	Definition for data collection
Utilitarian value	The product's physical and practical performance is derived from its tangible, concrete attributes. Gouthier et al. [GOU 22] have shown that personalization is seen as a primary benefit in return for the data collected, increasing the relevance of content, but that the level of personalization has an impact on the feeling of invasion of privacy
Knowledge value	Sense of mastery and competence in the product category. E.g. Mint profiles its customers based on transactional data collected within the application, and resells these profiles only to partners who help Mint customers save money. This gives customers better information on how to optimize their personal finances
Experiential stimulation	The ability of the experience to stimulate the individual's senses and absorb them to the point of making them forget their direct physical environment and feel a sense of well-being. This is the experiential potential of gamifying connected objects (refrigerators, washing machines) and systems (electricity, water) that continuously collect people's activity
Social bond	The role of the product/service as an aid to social interaction. As Morewedge et al. remind us [MOR 21], one way for companies to facilitate collection, particularly among digital natives, extroverts and narcissists, may be to encourage the sharing of positive social signals, that is, the sharing of knowledge, experience or status
Self-expression	The ability of a product or service to reflect personality. E.g. The American company Stitch Fix has its customers fill in a 15-minute questionnaire to access the personal shopper service. Based on the results of this survey, the company sends out clothing that matches the individual's budget on a monthly basis. The company monitors the success of its recommendation algorithm according to the return rate
Spiritual value	The ability to reflect on the meaning of life

Table 7.1. *Data collection and potential values for customers*

Trust in the company, and consequently acceptance of information gathering and use, depends greatly on past experience with the company [CHE 05].

The social exchange theory provides an explanation with the concept of privacy calculus: individuals calculate costs and benefits and compare alternatives prior to exchange. The theory assumes a two-way relationship in which both parties are mutually enriched by either a transaction or an exchange. In this framework, consumers reveal their personal information when the perceived benefits outweigh the perceived costs.

Companies have two levers to use to enable collection: increasing benefits or reducing costs. As summarized by Aurier et al. [AUR 04], there are six types of benefits: utilitarian value, knowledge, experiential stimulation, social bond, self-expression and spiritual value (see Table 7.1).

Individuals value their personal data differently depending on the type of data and the type of collection, and expect something in return [MOR 15].

Thus, individuals place little value on voluntarily provided data (email addresses, employment, education, age, gender), a little more value on digital traces (geolocation data, browsing history on smartphones, desktops or other connected technologies) and a lot on profiling data (personalized profiles used to predict individuals' interests and behaviors, obtained by combining voluntarily communicated data, digital traces and other data).

The more sensitive the data are perceived to be, the more individuals expect in return. Health data, for example, are more highly valued than energy consumption data. Moreover, this expected value also increases as the main benefit derived from the use of data passes from the consumer (through product improvements) to the company (through revenues from the resale of data).

7.4. How can we encourage parsimonious data collection?

With a view to forging a solid, lasting relationship with consumers, researchers [PAL 19] advocate respecting the privacy of individuals by minimizing the data collected to the strict minimum required in order to offer an optimal experience, and by empowering consumers through transparency and the provision of control tools.

Article 5 of the GDPR introduces the principle of proportionality, stipulating that the collection and processing of data will be limited to data that are "adequate, relevant and limited to what is necessary in relation to the purposes for which they are processed".

Since the GDPR came into force, it has no longer been possible to collect all of an individual's personal data in order to process just a few pieces. Their retention over time must be proportional to the processing (in principle, 36 months for marketing data with the possibility of going beyond this provided it can be justified; for example, for longer purchasing cycles, such as real estate or automobiles, a duration beyond 36 months is allowed by the CNIL in France).

In this section, we look at ways of going beyond the law to stand out from the competition.

7.4.1. *Minimizing data collection*

Simple compliance with Article 5 of the GDPR already requires minimizing data collection. Two avenues are worth mentioning: the quantity of data collected, but also no longer collecting data, but developing partnerships between companies with data sharing to avoid redundant collections.

The R Project association – an open-source statistical analysis and visualization software program – offers mailing list subscriptions to keep its users up to date with the latest updates, community questions and news according to centers of interest. Subscription involves an initial opt-in, providing an email address and selecting the subscription lists. An email is then sent requesting confirmation of subscription requests (second opt-in). Every month, an email summarizing the various subscriptions is sent, allowing the user to unsubscribe with a single click (triple opt-in).

For companies, this means retaining only the most receptive consumers, which has a positive impact on the quality of their relationship with customers and prospects. On the consumer side, it provides the certainty of not being overwhelmed by content, and for companies, it provides a way of giving power back to the individual and thus avoiding relationship fatigue or reactance/rejection.

This practice also has a positive impact on email deliverability: inbox placement depends in particular on the individual's past opening and clicking behavior, but also on the behavior of all email recipients. The greater the proportion of targeted individuals who open emails, the more likely internet service providers (ISPs) are to place content sent by the company in the inbox. Otherwise, the content is sent to a sub-folder, like Gmail's "Promotions" or "Social Networks" folders, which are opened less frequently than the inbox.

Another advantage of multiple opt-in is a reduction in routing costs. Variable sending costs (i.e. an email costs around EUR 0.0033 to send) can represent substantial savings, depending on the size of the database.

It should be noted, however, that the practice of double opt-in can be more or less complicated to implement, depending on the company's context and customer orientation. Some companies continue to give priority to the number of individuals "stored" (i.e. in their database) rather than the quality of the database (and its associated measures: deliverability, opening and reactivity rates).

Collecting data represents a cost for companies. However, not all companies necessarily have access to end consumers, as in the case of companies that work through a distributor. These companies are historically data-poor. Other companies may have access to data on transactions with their consumers, but arouse little interest among consumers (who do not feel sufficiently involved in the product category to share their information). For all these companies, collecting customer data presents a greater difficulty or cost in terms of motivating individuals to share their information.

From the point of view of parsimonious data collection, there is another way forward: the implementation of coopetition strategies between companies through the sharing of second-party data and the development of data cleaning rooms and safe havens. These are digital environments that enable two partners (very often an advertiser and a retailer) to share data on their users, securely and anonymously. More specifically, this enables the advertiser to enrich its first-party data with data collected by its advertising partner (Ads Data Hub, Amazon Marketing Cloud, Snowflake, Habu, etc.) to improve its advertising and marketing strategy. Each company can determine the level of data permission access.

Rather than collecting data, the use here is based on sharing data already collected in search of synergies.

This ecosystem is made up of four players:

– the brand wishing to run the campaign, often "poor" in data;

– distributors who monetize their data;

– the technology partner who hosts the distributor's data;

– a trusted third party that analyzes the data, creates segments and uses these data to activate them via marketing campaigns.

Advantages are present throughout the customer relationship:

– acquisition, through the ability to identify buyer profiles in the category, and thus optimize the acquisition of new customers;

– loyalty, by retaining customer profiles with the highest lifetime value (customer lifetime value);

– development of customer value by identifying levers in relation to the share of the wallet, while optimizing CRM expenditure by measuring the impact of marketing campaigns on incremental sales generated in the retailer's store.

Finally, some players have sought to pool data collection. For example, IAB Europe developed the Transparency and Consent Framework, so that authorization to place advertising cookies would be collected only once to facilitate real-time bidding (RTB) advertising – automated online auctions of user profiles for advertising. This standard would be made possible by recording user preferences in a consent platform. Collected only once, consent would be shared securely and anonymously in an appropriate advertising ecosystem. However, the Belgian data protection authority ruled in early 2022 that this protocol violated the GDPR.

7.4.2. *Relying on transparency when collecting data*

Transparency refers to efforts to explain the collection, use, storage, protection and extent of consumer control [PAL 19].

Transparency has three dimensions [POR 20]: objectivity (clarity, impartiality and sincerity of information provided), clearness (precision of information) and openness (collaboration between the company and the consumer and between consumers themselves). A company is thus transparent if it publishes intelligible (clear, concise and relevant) information in a visible (easily accessible and prioritized) and contextualized (if necessary) way; if it provides objective (comparable and not manipulated) information, negative as well as positive consumer viewpoints, and the possibility of collecting feedback from customers (with a chat, for example); or if it is open-minded in that it allows its customers to contact it instantaneously (automatic call-back, WhatsApp conversation, etc.) on all channels (social networks, email, telephone, etc.). The items used to measure clarity deal specifically with data collection, its purpose, the type of data collected, the collection channel and the storage of these data.

The value of transparency is rooted in social contract theory [BEK 18]: it improves relations between consumers and the company by guaranteeing a fair exchange of information, and reduces the feeling of intrusion into private life. It also increases purchasing intentions and makes people more willing to share information.

When companies explain their data collection practices, consumers are less likely to regret their consent to data collection, storage or use, because their intentions match their behavior. The mere presence of a privacy policy is enough to increase trust in the company intention to share data and even purchase intention [ALJ 10].

The GDPR insists upon this principle of transparency because it specifies that the company must communicate "in a concise, transparent, intelligible and easily accessible form, using clear and plain language" to its customers various forms of information:

– whether the person is the subject of data collection;

– the purpose of the processing and its legal basis;

– the data retention period;

– how to request access to data and withdraw consent if processing is based on it, the right to portability;

– the existence, where applicable, of automated decision-making;

– whether there is an intention to carry out further processing for a purpose other than that for which the personal data were collected;

– if the data have not been collected directly from the data subject and its source;

– appeal procedures.

Recital 60 of the text, moreover, mentions the possibility for marketers to accompany information "with standardized icons in order to provide a good, easily visible, comprehensible and clearly legible overview of the intended processing".

The Guardian's initiative to create videos to explain its privacy policy, in addition to articles showing how data are collected and used, and even how to protect ourselves on the Internet, is a good example.

The key to a good charter seems to lie in presenting first the costs (e.g. collection reduces anonymity) and then the benefits in a concise, easy-to-read way.

It is your choice.

When we make the Guardian available to you online, we use cookies and similar technologies to help us to do this. Some are necessary to help our website work properly and cannot be switched off, and some are optional, but support the Guardian and your experience in other ways.

For instance, we and our partners may store cookies and other similar technologies to access personal data, including page visits and your IP address. We use this information about you, your devices and your online interactions with us to provide, analyse and improve our services. This may include personalising content or advertising for you.

We use cookies and similar technologies for the following purposes:

– store and/or access information on a device;

– personalized ads and content, ad and content measurement, audience insights and product development.

You can find out more in our privacy policy and cookie policy and manage the choices available to you at any time by going to "Privacy settings" at the bottom of any page.

Are you happy to accept cookies?

To manage your cookie choices now, including how to opt out where our partners rely on legitimate interests to use your information, click on Manage my cookies.

Yes, I'm happy Manage my cookies

Box 7.1. The Guardian*'s consent pop-up*

Morey et al. [MOR 15] mention the case of Disneyland, which uses visitor profiling based on data collected with its MagicBand wristband to enhance customer experiences in its theme parks and hotels and better target its marketing efforts. Using their MagicBand with sensors at Disney facilities, guests can access the parks, book attractions, open their hotel rooms and record their food consumption and purchases. Users transmit a great deal of data in this way, but they get a service and feel they have privileged access in return. Consumers know exactly what they are getting into, because Disney clearly communicates its data collection policy during the online registration process for its MagicBands, pointing distinctly to the FAQ area, as well as to other information relating to privacy and security information.

7.4.3. *Giving consumers control*

Giving people back control over how their data is used enables a fair exchange of information between consumer and company [MAR 17, BEK 18, PAL 19]. This control enables individuals to feel more confident and less vulnerable, be more invested in the relationship with the company, and be more inclined to provide their personal data to obtain personalized service. Giving control to individuals reduces the number of acts of falsification of information [CLO 22]: when individuals are able to access their settings and manage the information collected and used on Facebook, they feel less vulnerable and provide less erroneous information.

In addition to these relational benefits, consumers may be concerned about the veracity or inaccuracy of information held by companies, all the more so when it stems from erroneous inferences or past statements. While the GDPR provides for a right to rectification in Article 16, companies can provide interfaces enabling access to information to directly correct potential errors. For example, Google offers to inform you about your appetencies and centers of interest inferred from your browsing, your Gmail account and information provided by its partners, and provides the ability to deactivate these personalization criteria in one click. The advantage for the company is to have more refined advertising profiles and be able to sell more effective ads to advertisers, and the advantage for the consumer is to have more targeted, relevant ads.

Here are two examples of control systems:

– Ahead of the future ePrivacy regulation, the CNIL published its September 17, 2020, recommendation on cookie banners, applicable from April 1, 2021. The purposes of the various cookies must be described, and the possibility of accepting or refusing them must be left open, one case at a time. Prior to this recommendation, it was accepted that continued browsing constituted "tacit" consent.

– Since April 2021, consent has been explicit, that is, consent must result from a clear act. In order to give individuals control, it must also be as easy to accept cookies with one click as it is to refuse them. Pre-ticked boxes and the burying of "Refuse" boxes at the bottom of explanatory pages are therefore illegal. It should be stressed that a consent management platform is not compulsory, as companies are responsible for proving the consent of individuals and the legality of the consent collection mechanism, whatever the tool used.

7.5. Conclusion: finally, what is the value of data?

Thinking in terms of transparent and parsimonious data collection means thinking beyond simple compliance with the law (minimizing the data collected and ensuring transparency of collection). Such thinking must take place in a turbulent market context characterized by:

– heavy dependence on US giants;

– disparities according to the actors and the places where data are collected and processed;

– expectations of consumers who are increasingly well-informed, but also paradoxical: the issue is no longer compliance with the law, but the value provided by the company and therefore the benefits granted to facilitate consent.

"Acting in favor of privacy is not a short-term approach designed to reap quick profits" [MOR 15]. The foundation of a solid relationship takes time. This strategy implies doing it authentically, that is, for the company as a whole and not in a cosmetic way: involving the consumer, informing them transparently about the data collected and how they are used, and giving them real control over their data, but also providing a counterpart in exchange for these data.

Palmatier and Martin [PAL 19] have argued in favor of sharing the profits generated according to the contribution of the data provided, and thus of monetizing consumer data. For these authors, offering free services is a "short-term crutch", all the more so as, in the event of data loss or leakage, it is the customer who sees their information revealed and who therefore suffers the greatest harm.

On the business side, collecting data is expensive, and while some companies in direct contact with consumers are in a strong position to collect data, this is not the case for all companies. Partnerships between companies are therefore possible, provided that the right players are identified, and can help to achieve greater parsimony in terms of data collection.

7.6. References

[AGU 15] AGUIRRE E., MAHR D., GREWAL D. et al., "Unraveling the personalization paradox: The effect of information collection and trust-building strategies on online advertisement effectiveness", *Journal of Retailing*, vol. 91, no. 1, pp. 34–49, 2015.

[ALJ 10] ALJUKHADAR M., SENECAL S., OUELLETTE D., "Can the media richness of a privacy disclosure enhance outcome? A multifaceted view of trust in rich media environments", *International Journal of Electronic Commerce*, vol. 14, no. 4, pp. 103–126, 2010.

[AUR 04] AURIER P., EVRARD Y., N'GOALA G., "Comprendre et mesurer la valeur du point de vue du consommateur", *Recherche et Applications en Marketing (French Edition)*, vol. 19, no. 3, pp. 1–20, 2004.

[BEK 18] BEKE F.T., EGGERS F., VERHOEF P.C., "Consumer informational privacy: Current knowledge and research directions", *Foundations and Trends in Marketing*, vol. 11, no. 1, pp. 1–71, 2018.

[CHE 05] CHELLAPPA R.K., SIN R.G., "Personalization versus privacy: An empirical examination of the online consumer's dilemma", *Information Technology and Management*, vol. 6, pp. 181–202, 2005.

[CLO 22] CLOAREC J., "Privacy controls as an information source to reduce data poisoning in artificial intelligence-powered personalization", *Journal of Business Research*, vol. 152, pp. 144–153, 2022.

[HEI 15] HEIMBACH I., KOSTYRA D.S., HINZ O., "Marketing automation", *Business & Information Systems Engineering*, vol. 57, pp. 129–133, 2015.

[KNI 13] KNIJNENBURG B.P., KOBSA A., "Making decisions about privacy: Information disclosure in context-aware recommender systems", *ACM Transactions on Interactive Intelligent Systems (TiiS)*, vol. 3, no. 3, pp. 1–23, 2013.

[KOI 19] KOIVISTO J., HAMARI J., "The rise of motivational information systems: A review of gamification research", *International Journal of Information Management*, vol. 45, pp. 191–210, 2019.

[KOS 13] KOSINSKI M., STILLWELL D., GRAEPEL T., "Private traits and attributes are predictable from digital records of human behavior", *Proceedings of the National Academy of Sciences*, vol. 110, no. 15, pp. 5802–5805, 2013.

[MAL 04] MALHOTRA N.K., KIM S.S., AGARWAL J., "Internet users information privacy concerns (IUIPC): The construct, the scale, and a causal model", *Information Systems Research*, vol. 15, no. 4, pp. 336–355, 2004.

[MAR 17a] MARTIN K.D., MURPHY P.E., "The role of data privacy in marketing", *Journal of the Academy of Marketing Science*, vol. 45, no. 2, pp. 135–155, 2017.

[MAR 17b] MARTIN K.D., BORAH A., PALMATIER R.W., "Data privacy: Effects on customer and firm performance", *Journal of Marketing*, vol. 81, no. 1, pp. 36–58, 2017.

[MOR 15] MOREY T., FORBATH T., SCHOOP A., "Customer data: Designing for transparency and trust", *Harvard Business Review*, vol. 93, no. 5, pp. 96–105, 2015.

[MOR 21] MOREWEDGE C.K., MONGA A., PALMATIER R.W. et al., "Evolution of consumption: A psychological ownership framework", *Journal of Marketing*, vol. 85, no. 1, pp. 196–218, 2021.

[PAL 19] PALMATIER R.W., MARTIN K.D., *The Intelligent Marketer's Guide to Data Privacy: The Impact of Big Data on Customer Trust*, Springer International Publishing, Cham, 2019.

[PFI 20] PFIFFELMANN J., DENS N., SOULEZ S., "Personalized advertisements with integration of names and photographs: an eye-tracking experiment", *Journal of Business Research*, vol. 111, pp. 196–207, 2020.

[POR 20] PORTES A., N'GOALA G., CASES A.S., "Digital transparency: Dimensions, antecedents and consequences on the quality of customer relationships", *Recherche et Applications en Marketing (English Edition)*, vol. 35, no. 4, pp. 72–98, 2020.

[SWE 02] SWEENEY L., "k-anonymity: A model for protecting privacy", *International Journal of Uncertainty, Fuzziness and Knowledge-Based Systems*, vol. 10, no. 5, pp. 557–570, 2002.

[TRE 93] TREACY M., WIERSEMA F., "Customer intimacy and other value disciplines", *Harvard Business Review*, vol. 71, no. 1, pp. 84–93, 1993.

[TUC 14] TUCKER C.E., "Social networks, personalized advertising, and privacy controls", *Journal of Marketing Research*, vol. 51, no. 5, pp. 546–562, 2014.

[YOU 15] YOUYOU W., KOSINSKI M., STILLWELL D., "Computer-based personality judgments are more accurate than those made by humans", *Proceedings of the National Academy of Sciences*, vol. 112, no. 4, pp. 1036–1040, 2015.

8

From Persuasion to Customer Manipulation: The Role of Dark Patterns

With the boom in the digital economy, we are witnessing the development of business models based on free access and the monetization of attention. These digital business models take the form of two- or multi-sided platforms [ROC 03, DEJ 10], where Internet users' connection time has an impact on the platforms' advertising revenues, enabling some of them to become market leaders. These business models can be found in a variety of forms (advertising models, freemium models or classic transactional models and all their derivatives, such as the "premium" model, of which Amazon is a good example) and in many sectors (digital social networks, the press, e-commerce, sports betting, online pornography, music and video streaming). Attention, and the free access to content, finds its financial interest in the rise of targeted advertising and the need to collect large volumes of data, which can also be used to make commercial recommendations in e-commerce or resold to data brokers.

Internet user behavioral data are becoming a key strategic factor in sales development, feeding into research marketing to target Internet users, strategic marketing to assess target market volumes and operational marketing to help define value-added functions, test digital service formulas and monitor marketing actions. In this way, the race to collect, store and process customer data is being transformed into a race to capture the Internet user's attention via Web pages and/or applications on smartphones and tablets.

Captology, defined as the way in which digital interfaces can incite users to behave in certain ways, was developed by one of the fathers of human–machine interaction

---

Chapter written by Florence JACOB, Jeoffrey DROUARD, Séverine ERHEL, Marianne LUMEAU and Raphaël SUIRE.

(HMI) in 1998: Brian J. Fogg[1]. He developed a whole arsenal of techniques to get users to perform actions: persuasive methods. He explains that:

> as computers have migrated from research labs onto desktops and into everyday life, they have become more persuasive by design. Today computers are taking on a variety of roles as persuaders, including roles of influence that traditionally were filled by teachers, coaches, clergy, therapists, doctors, and salespeople, among others [FOG 03].

The generation trained in HMI by Fogg and his disciples developed a science of captology, cataloguing interfaces and digital designs developed to make the Internet user act in a certain way. Designers of digital platforms use their knowledge of human behavior to exploit cognitive biases, decision heuristics and hidden information to develop hundreds of graphic and textual techniques [GRA 18].

Examples of these dark patterns are legion. For example, when an accommodation booking site indicates that there are only three rooms available in a hotel, it activates the scarcity bias [CIA 16], or when the general conditions of use of a site or application encourage the individual to click on the "I accept" button, by highlighting it with a darker color and shade, this button benefits from a highlighting effect and becomes the default option. This practice is not new, as Schüll [SCH 12] shows that the design of slot machines and the interior architecture of Las Vegas casinos encourage players to gamble more and more, capturing their attention and leading to addiction by design. Where then is the line between commercial persuasion, as it is known in marketing, and manipulation of customers and Internet users, using their cognitive, psychological and social biases to get them to consume more products or advertising by capturing their attention?

To address this question, we are going to take a look at research into dark patterns, and how digital platforms tend to aim to manipulate their customers in order to maximize their connection time. In the first section of the chapter, we present some definitions of dark patterns. Then, in the second section, we show how these designs modify marketing practices. In section 8.3, we link these designs to the problematic uses of the Internet by Internet users. Finally, we look at ways of combating misleading designs.

8.1. Dark pattern definitions and typologies

To understand what a dark pattern is, we must first understand what an HMI pattern is. For Alexander [ALE 77], a pattern is an individual entity that:

1 See Figure 8.2 in the Appendix.

– describes a recurring problem with its environment;

– describes a repetitive solution to this recurring problem;

– maintains the uniqueness of the solution despite repetition;

– follows the same pattern.

According to Seidel [SEI 17], to describe a pattern we need: a name, a problem to be solved (= initial state), a context, a description of the solution, examples, the resulting state, the pattern's professional strength(s) (= managerial objective) and finally, the hidden mechanics (= the theoretical rule that enables the pattern to function).

Since 2010 and the first work of designer Harry Brignull [BRI 11], many definitions of darks patterns have emerged, but we prefer the one by Gray et al. [GRA 18]:

> We use the term dark patterns to define instances where designers use their knowledge of human behaviour (e.g., psychology) and the desires of end users to implement persuasive functionality that is not in the user's best interest.

A dark pattern is therefore perceived as a function that is undesirable for the Web user and which is not designed in their own interest (but in that of the service that implements it). The authors therefore consider that the deceptive, dark side can only be assessed according to moral and legal considerations based on "local" codes (visions linked to a particular society), which are therefore based in essence on a value judgment.

In its IP no. 6, the LINC association supports this idea:

> It could be considered that abusive or misleading design [...] on digital services may give rise to various disorders of consent, of a sufficiently objective and demonstrable nature for it to result in the invalidity of the individual. [...] Abusive or misleading design could also be considered as a willingness on the part of the controller to inappropriately influence the individual.

Dark patterns can be different in nature and play on different behavioral dimensions. A typology is presented in Table 8.1. It is the most commonly used, as it presents the dark patterns through the prism of the resulting state for the consumer.

However, what differentiates these dark patterns from dubious commercial techniques described long ago [COC 10], such as the deceptive display of start-up costs in the 1990s with the explosion in computer purchases (which can be likened to sneaking), the use of yellow colors or even the technique of truncating prices at "0.99" to achieve framing effects (which can be likened to the misdirection technique)?

What changes researchers' vision today, compared with Fogg's work, is first that the possession of big data and the development of artificial intelligence, coupled with the platformization of the economy (based on powerful network effects), create a much greater sounding board effect. As a result, big data are making it possible to gain more detailed knowledge of the online behavior of Internet users, and, thanks to advanced statistical analysis:

– the patterns to which each Internet user is most sensitive;

– the behaviors associated with each pattern;

– the profiles of Web users sensitive to each pattern;

– models for anticipating the future behavior of (new) Internet users.

In this way, data-marketing takes advantage of the rise of big data in order to offer versions and signals closer to the revealed or anticipated preferences of each Internet user [RAN 20]. A description of this phenomenon can be found in the October 2021 hearing of whistle-blower Frances Haugen, a former Facebook employee, before the U.S. Senate, revealing that Instagram's design would lead to a drastic increase in connection time on this social network and, for a significant number of teenagers, to behavioral disorders or problematic Internet use. This example shows that the platform's design is created to maximize advertising revenues by keeping users (and their attention) for as long as possible, creating negative externalities for them. In other words, the design is intended to enhance the platform's well-being at the expense of the users.

Second, marketing draws on cognitive science, psychology and the social sciences, following the example of the nudge movement, in order to use these mechanisms to create incentive designs that are both structured and documented. Although the designer of a nudge (e.g. a public decision maker) will seek to modify the architecture of choice of individuals to lead them to significantly modify their behavior to increase their well-being, the Web interface designer seeks to promote the well-being of the company for which they work. In order to maximize their profits, platforms therefore have an interest in implementing mechanisms to retain Web users for as long as possible, lock their use within the platform or ecosystem of services and encourage their engagement within a path marked out by dark patterns.

	The resulting state	Theoretical mechanics	Example
Sneaking	Adding an unwanted expense or transmission of information	Creation of a very late billing line addition to increase the purchase amount, or non-visibility of information transmission = hidden information	Discovery of additional fees, hidden subscriptions, or hidden conditions that allow the platform to obtain all of the user's data
Urgency	Creating a sense of urgency	Creating a sense of urgency in users to speed up decision-making: FOMO's[2] psychological bias	"Please turn on notifications: know right away when people follow you or like and comment on your post"
Misdirecting	Diverting attention	Use of visuals, language or emotional reactions to push users toward one choice rather than another: cognitive biases of colors and shapes, framing biases, highlighting effects, etc.	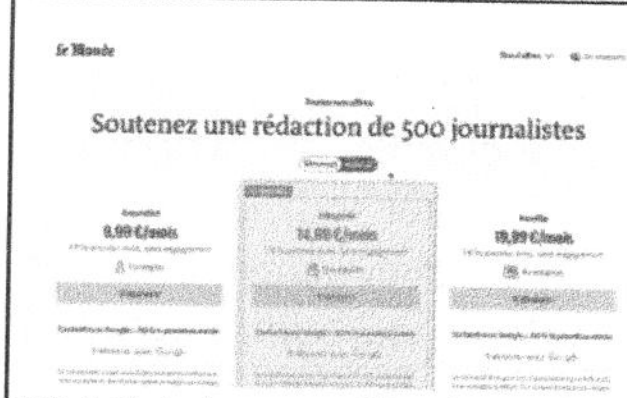 Highlighting an offer through pink framing in relation to others
Social proof	Exercising social pressure	Social conformity bias	Indicating on a social network the names of contacts who have already liked a post to encourage them to like it too
Scarcity	Giving the impression of rarity	Signaling limited quantities or high demand for a product to increase its perceived value and desirability	On an e-commerce site, the words: "Only X products left"
Obstruction	Creating a more difficult process that discourages continuation	Aiming to make it harder than necessary to perform certain actions in order to discourage the user from carrying them out	Unsubscribing requiring 10 clicks and seven operations for a user account

2 Fear of missing out. This fear is linked to social anxiety, reflecting a constant worry about missing an important piece of news or an event providing an opportunity for social interaction.

	The resulting state	Theoretical mechanics	Example
Forced action	Forcing users to take action to get what they want	Patterns forcing the user to perform an additional action in order to complete the task initially undertaken: the escalation bias commitment	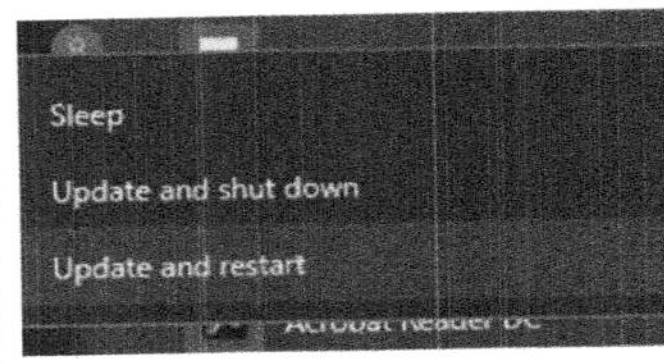

Table 8.1. *First typology of dark patterns (from [MAT 19]). For a color version of this table, see www.iste.co.uk/delecolle/newfrontiers.zip*

8.2. Marketing as usual?

To understand the benefits of dark patterns, we also need to understand their place in the user journey. In one of the most recent research articles on the subject, showing the mechanisms at work to build loyalty and engage the Internet user [SIE 20], the authors explain the need to create loyalty loops and involvement spirals, as shown in Figure 8.1.

The authors conducted qualitative research based on observations, interviews and documents concerning the practice of three digital services (Tinder, CrossFit and Pokémon Go) in order to conceptualize what an alternative to a fluid, loyalty-building journey may look like. As shown in Figure 8.1, this requires several service design ingredients (in red), such as rapid entry into the spiral, streamlining, endless variation and the events represented by dots, such as re-triggering or curiosity. All these customer relations mechanisms may seem harmless in persuading Web users to remain loyal and involved if they did not have, as a mirror image, persuasive designs whose roles are to trigger purchases and capture attention to create a current of capture or create novelty.

Moreover, the authors brush aside the question of the negative consequences of such mechanisms for Internet users, even though the question of addiction comes up in many of the selected interview quotations:

> It's very addictive […] I would spend a lot of time […] It was like an addictive game, so in order to stop using it, at some point, I just deleted it, and it worked fine […] If I don't want to do something, I'm trying not to have sirens around me. (Sophia, former Tinder user)

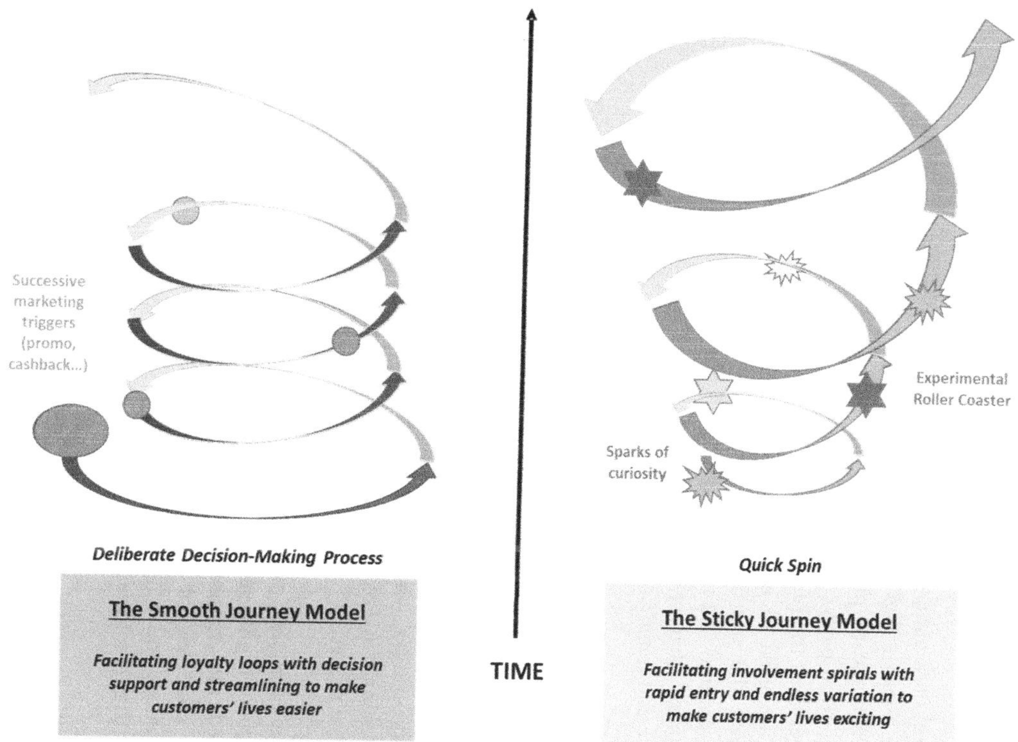

Figure 8.1. *The dynamics behind the creation of the loyalty loop (smooth journey) and the involvement spiral (sticky model) (taken from [SIE 20, p. 50]). For a color version of this figure, see www.iste.co.uk/delecolle/newfrontiers.zip*

Based on the most in-depth work on dark patterns [GRA 18, MAT 19], we can classify these different mechanisms into two categories: on the one hand, structural dark patterns that exist for all Internet users at precise moments in the journey, such as entry into the course or exit solutions; on the other hand, conjunctural dark patterns that only appear as a function of conditional activity on the part of the Internet user (if [behavior] then appearance of [dark pattern]), which are programmed by computer algorithms.

For structural dark patterns, we can see that some of them are patterns placed at the entrance to a user's digital journey on a platform to create a quick entry point, such as the technique of proposing to use our Facebook login and password to connect to a third-party website, without showing the conditions of data transmission between the two sites (sneaking dark pattern). Similarly, a number of dark patterns are used to obstruct the exit route, such as the forced continuity technique, where the site continues to bill the user after the service they have purchased has expired. As users do not check the expiry dates of the service, the company "assumes" that when the service expires, the user wishes to continue with the paid service and remain a subscriber.

However, dark patterns are conjunctural, that is, they appear when a user performs a specific sequence of actions or no longer connects to the platform. Examples include the activity stream, which is a series of broadcasts or notifications illustrating recent events and which uses the powerful psychological bias of FOMO [ELH 20], encouraging the user to reconnect, or video games, where the leaderboard is a technique that places the user among a list of players, chosen according to one or more specific criteria, who will be called by other players in case of need at any time (raid mechanics in Pokémon Go, for example), with non-response sometimes downgrading the player.

From these examples, we suspect that there is therefore a link between the business models of digital service platforms which seek to capture and keep Internet users connected, the ergonomics of the sites/applications of these brands, and the processing in real time of behavioral data using statistical models powered by behavioral sciences and adaptive designs, which present the Internet user with the most tempting digital interface to keep them connected.

Although this assertion is often made (e.g. in an article in *Le Monde*[3]), it has not been scientifically proven. This would require two virtually impossible links: the effect of persuasive design on problematic Internet use and the managerial willingness of digital platforms to knowingly deceive, using morally dubious

3 See: https://www.lemonde.fr/idees/article/2018/06/22/comment-nous-rend-on-accros-a-nos-applis_5319323_3232.html.

techniques aimed at exploiting the cognitive/psychological or social vulnerability of Internet users by exposing them to precisely the technique to which they react best.

8.3. Problematic Internet use due to dark patterns?

In psychology, we do not speak of Internet addiction in the same way as alcohol or drug addiction, but as problematic use of the Internet. This view stems from the fact that the brain has the capacity to return to a 100% non-problematic state without any after-effects, which is not the case with alcohol or narcotics. Problematic use of the Internet is first and foremost a behavioral disorder based on compulsive and excessive use of the Internet. This use interferes with daily activities. For Kuss and Griffiths [KUS 17], this disorder is accompanied by the following symptoms:

– the prominence of Internet activities, which become increasingly important for the individual;

– a change in mood following Internet activity;

– an increase in tolerance, leading people to engage more and more in Internet activities to achieve the same feelings or state of mind;

– the presence of a psychological or even physiological deficiency, which occurs when the individual is deprived of the use of the network;

– rapid reinstatement of problematic behavior;

– the presence of conflicts in relation to addictive behaviors, which may be intrapsychic (loss of control, loss of self-esteem) or interpersonal (school or work environment).

A number of studies are attempting to understand the origins of these problematic uses based in particular on biopsychosocial models: biological, psychological and socio-economic dispositions that explain why certain individuals are more at risk of developing those problematic uses.

Moreover, the prevalence of this disorder is not uniform across the world's population. A meta-analysis [CHE 17] integrating data from 31 countries with 89,281 individuals shows that 6% of this sample had it: 2.6% of the population in Northern Europe, 7.1% of the Asian population, up to 8% in North America and 10.6% in Middle Eastern countries (Lebanon, Turkey, Israel, Iran). A study by Banyai et al. [BÁN 17] conducted on 5,961 Hungarian adolescents showed that 4.5% demonstrated problematic use. Another study of students in France showed that almost 6.5% had it [LOP 13].

The I-PACE theoretical model [BRA 16] takes individual psychological predispositions and adds situational factors linked to digital business models, such as the type of content (games, pornography, online shopping and social networking) and the types of addictive mechanisms used in captology for the construction of information on the Internet (gratification, use of cognitive biases, use of affective responses, coping, flow, etc.). This model has not been tested, but it compiles the results from the literature concerning a set of predictors of problematic use of the Internet.

The Internet users affected would only represent the fringe of the population whose daily lives are affected, but this does not take into account the ordinary problematic uses linked to the difficulties of parting with our smartphones. Thus, the measurement of the effects on Internet users and the action of dark patterns cannot be carried out due to a lack of a simple model and available data, as they are held by the platforms themselves, which refuse to allow researchers to access these data[4].

It is also worth looking at the creation of service designs to see how impossible it is to observe.

8.4. Impossible to observe and yet combatable

In order to assess the effects of dark patterns, we need to be able to observe them in vivo and carry out experiments to link the presence of dark patterns with the problematic Internet use of consumers of digital platforms that have an interest in capturing their attention. A number of research articles have simply attempted to count the appearance of dark patterns using several techniques:

– qualitative hand coding of patterns on some e-commerce sites [GRA 18] or gaming sites [KIN 19], with an attempt to rate subjective dangerousness [PIN 21];

– scraping then automated processing by an indexing robot to search for dark patterns from the first three clicks of 100 e-commerce sites [MAT 19];

– experimentation (A/B testing with or without exposure) in the health field, with spot testing of three dark patterns [CAP 21];

4 Researchers petition to make Meta data open. See: https://www.businessinsider.co.za/mark-zuckerberg-meta-open-letter-kids-mental-health-300-scientists-2021-12. The Digital Service Act (adopted in July 2022 by the European Parliament) allows researchers to have access to platform data on request. It remains to be seen how this will work in practice.

– qualitative behavioral work (filling in logs of behavioral events over one month) in the field of social networks [ORJ 18];

– internal smartphone tracking from a healthcare application [SIT 20];

– observation and counting by hundreds of volunteers or recording and database compilation by volunteers from the activist DP project.

All these techniques, however laudable, fail to take into account the two decisive elements for adequate observation of the appearance of these persuasive designs and their effects on problematic use of the Internet: the long connection times needed to set up the loops and spirals shown in Figure 8.1, and the actual observation of problematic Internet use (e.g. by means of repeated questionnaires) in order to assess the deterioration in psychological state and the connection times in relation to the person's schedule. In addition, we need to be able to identify the appearance of dark patterns that are only triggered in the event of certain behaviors, or access the programming algorithms that reveal the dark patterns of the platforms. The causal link is difficult to demonstrate scientifically, but there are concordant indications of proof [ROW 22].

To combat this suspicion of manipulation, several voices have proposed solutions. On the one hand, designers have proposed to develop manipulation literacy [ZAG 13] by training individuals to recognize manipulative actions by design[5]. On the other hand, legal experts are questioning the Constitution and the protection afforded to the collection and processing of Internet users' data, as well as the need for transparency in algorithms [KOE 19] in order to create safeguards. The United States and Europe are currently conducting major audit campaigns to strengthen consumer protection laws. Some even imagine using interface design to reinforce consent with legal design [COR 21].

Finally, one approach would be to consider that the individual is capable of evaluating the ethical conduct of the platform [HUN 19]. To do this, the user must be able to make, on the one hand, deontological evaluations by assessing the rightness or wrongness of the company's actions in relation to a set of pre-determined deontological standards and, on the other hand, teleological evaluations, that is, assessing the perceived consequences of this behavior by considering the probability of a negative consequence, as well as the desirability or otherwise of other consequences (consumption of a free service such

5 For instance, see, in no particular order, https://persuasive-patterns.herokuapp.com/ or https://twiter.com/dark-patterns.

as a social network). For ethical evaluation, manipulation literacy can be a powerful lever; for teleological evaluation, the value added by the free access platform seems to be far more powerful than the risk perceived by Internet users.

Dark patterns belong, within customer strategy, to a broader trend: dark CRM [NGU 22]. Nguyen et al. [NGU 22] have shown that one of the practices of dark CRM is customer journey tracing. In this way, platforms use the tracing of Internet behavior as a means of discovering the most powerful cognitive/psychological/social biases for each user, in order to make them consume more advertising and/or products, and thus open up an asymmetrical relationship in which the company uses its strong asymmetry of information about the surfer to manipulate them.

As early as 2016, these researchers concluded that, by its very nature, CRM encourages and reinforces the consumption of the most profitable customers, and thus potentially leads to addiction. It will take many strong shocks to push platforms to reduce their use of dark patterns.

The European Union's Digital Service Act (DSA) prohibits, as of January 2023, the use of dark patterns, which are defined as "deceptive interfaces designed to mislead users or cause them to make a decision they would not otherwise have made". The DSA aims to regulate the use of these dark patterns so that users are protected from deceptive and unscrupulous practices.

The Digital Market Act (DMA) also provides penalties for companies that break the rules on the use of dark patterns. These penalties can range up to a fine of 10% of the company's worldwide annual sales, which can be very significant for large companies. In addition, the use of dark patterns could lead to criminal prosecution of the companies concerned. The DMA also aims to encourage companies to be transparent and offer users clear and precise information on the products and services they offer, particularly with regard to general terms and conditions of sale/use.

Observers doubt, however, that the DSA and DMA can be easily applied to all dark patterns, and in particular conjunctural dark patterns. It is hopeful, however, that this legislation will encourage platform designers to adopt more virtuous developments for mental health based on well-being by design. In this sense, design teams should no longer rely solely on IT developers, marketing, user experience (UX) and cognitive psychology specialists [VAS 21], but should also include ethics specialists.

8.5. Appendix

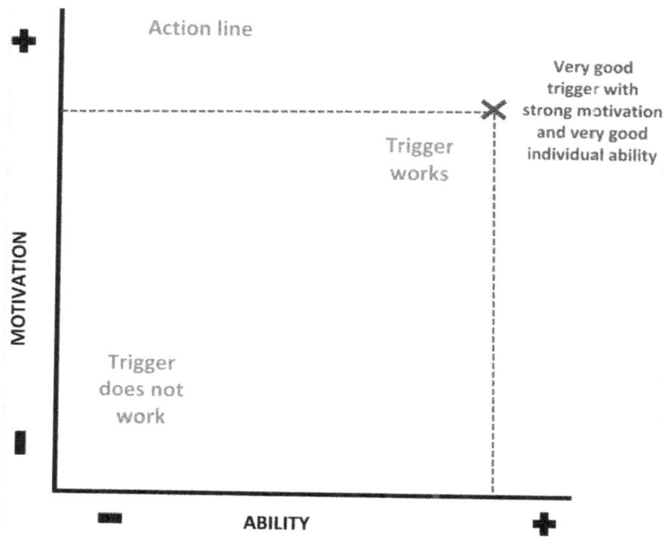

Figure 8.2. *Behavioral model developed by Fogg (2002)*

8.6. References

[ALE 77] ALEXANDER C., *A Pattern Language: Towns, Buildings, Construction*, Oxford University Press, Oxford, 1977.

[BÁN 17] BÁNYAI F., ZSILA Á., KIRÁLY O. et al., "Problematic social media use: Results from a large-scale nationally representative adolescent sample", *PLoS ONE*, vol. 12, no. 1, 2017.

[BRA 16] BRAND M., YOUNG K.S., LAIER C. et al., "Integrating psychological and neurobiological considerations regarding the development and maintenance of specific Internet-use disorders: An Interaction of Person-Affect-Cognition-Execution (I-PACE) model", *Neuroscience & Biobehavioral Reviews*, vol. 71, pp. 252–266, 2016.

[BRI 11] BRIGNULL H., "Dark patterns: Deception vs. honesty in UI design", *Interaction Design, Usability*, vol. 338, pp. 2–4, 2011.

[CAP 21] CAPURRO D., VELLOSO E., "Dark patterns, electronic medical records, and the opioid epidemic", arXiv preprint, 2021.

[CHE 17] CHEN C., ZHANG K.Z.K., GONG X. et al., "Understanding compulsive smartphone use: An empirical test of a flow-based model", *International Journal of Information Management*, vol. 37, no. 5, pp. 438–454, 2017.

[CIA 16] CIALDINI R., *Persuasion: A Revolutionary Way to Influence and Persuade*, Simon and Schuster, New York, 2016.

[COC 10] COCHOY F., *Une histoire du marketing : discipliner l'économie de marché*, La Découverte, Paris, 2010.

[COR 21] CORRALES COMPAGNUCCI M., HAAPIO H. et al. (eds), *Legal Design: Integrating Business, Design and Legal Thinking with Technology*, Edward Elgar Publishing, Cheltenham, 2021.

[DEJ 10] DEJEAN S., PÉNARD T., SUIRE R., "La gratuité est-elle une fatalité sur les marchés numériques ? Une étude sur le consentement à payer pour des offres de contenus audiovisuels sur internet", *Économie prévision*, vol. 194, no. 3, pp. 15–32, 2010.

[ELH 20] ELHAI J.D., GALLINARI E.F., ROZGONJUK D. et al., "Depression, anxiety and fear of missing out as correlates of social, non-social and problematic smartphone use", *Addictive Behaviors*, vol. 105, pp. 106–135, 2020.

[FOG 03] FOGG B.J., "How to motivate & persuade users", *CHI 2003 New Horizons*, 2003.

[GRA 18] GRAY C.M., KOU Y., BATTLES B. et al., "The dark (patterns) side of UX design", *Proceedings of the 2018 CHI Conference on Human Factors in Computing Systems*, Montreal, pp. 1–14, 2018.

[HUN 19] HUNT S.D., "The ethics of branding, customer-brand relationships, brand-equity strategy, and branding as a societal institution", *Journal of Business Research*, vol. 95, pp. 408–416, 2019.

[KIN 19] KING D.L., DELFABBRO P.H., GAINSBURY S. et al. "Unfair play? Video games as exploitative monetized services: An examination of game patents from a consumer protection perspective", *Computers in Human Behavior*, vol. 101, pp. 131–143, 2019.

[KOE 19] KOENE A., CLIFTON C., HATADA Y. et al., A governance framework for algorithmic accountability and transparency, Report, European Parliamentary Research Service Panel for the Future of Science and Technology, 2019.

[KUS 17] KUSS D.J., GRIFFITHS M.D., "Social networking sites and addiction: Ten lessons learned", *International Journal of Environmental Research and Public Health*, vol. 14, no. 3, pp. 311–339, 2017.

[LOP 13] LOPEZ-FERNANDEZ O., FREIXA-BLANXART M., HONRUBIA-SERRANO M.L., "The problematic internet entertainment use scale for adolescents: prevalence of problem internet use in Spanish high school students", *CyberPsychology, Behavior, and Social Networking*, vol. 16, pp. 108–118, 2013.

[MAT 19] MATHUR A., ACAR G., FRIEDMAN M.J. et al., "Dark patterns at scale: Findings from a crawl of 11K shopping websites", *Proceedings of the ACM on Human–Computer Interaction 3. CSCW*, vol. 81, pp. 1–32, 2019.

[NGU 22] NGUYEN B., JABER F., SIMKIN L., "A systematic review of the dark side of CRM: The need for a new research agenda", *Journal of Strategic Marketing*, vol. 30, no. 1, pp. 93–111, 2022.

[ORJ 18] ORJI R., MOFFATT K., "Persuasive technology for health and wellness: State-of-the-art and emerging trends", *Health Informatics Journal*, vol. 24, no. 1, pp. 66–91, 2018.

[PIN 21] PINEAU K., FABRE A., "Évaluer la captologie et le design persuasif des services numériques", *I2D – Information, données documents*, vol. 2, no. 2, pp. 151–173, 2021.

[RAN 20] RANGASWAMY A., MOCH N., FELTEN C. et al., "The role of marketing in digital business platforms", *Journal of Interactive Marketing*, vol. 51, no. 1, pp. 72–90, 2020.

[ROC 03] ROCHET J.C., TIROLE J., "Platform competition in two-sided markets", *Journal of the European Economic Association*, vol. 1, no. 4, pp. 990–1029, 2003.

[ROW 22] ROWE F., MARKUS M.L., "Taking the measure of digital giants: Amazon and the social welfare computing research agenda", *Electronic Markets*, vol. 32, no. 2, pp. 437–446, 2022.

[SCH 12] SCHÜLL N.D., *Addiction by Design*, Princeton University Press, Princeton, 2012.

[SEI 17] SEIDEL N., "Empirical evaluation methods for pattern languages: Sketches, classification, and network analysis", *Proceedings of the 22nd European Conference on Pattern Languages of Programs*, New York, 2017.

[SIE 20] SIEBERT A., GOPALDAS A., LINDRIDGE A. et al., "Customer experience journeys: Loyalty loops versus involvement spirals", *Journal of Marketing*, vol. 84, no. 4, pp. 45–66, 2020.

[SIT 20] SITTIG S., FRANKLIN A.L., "Persuasive technology: designing mobile health triggers to impact health behaviour", *AMCIS Proceedings Conference*, 2020.

[VAS 21] VASAN N., JOHANSEN S., "A psychiatrist's perspective on social media algorithms and mental health", Stanford University Seminar, 2021.

[ZAG 13] ZAGAL J.P., BJÖRK S., LEWIS C., "Dark patterns in the design of games", *Foundations of Digital Games*, Chania, 2013.

9

Digital Consumption and Inclusion

9.1. Introduction: when the digitalization of customer journeys raises challenges

The digital journey has become a real growth driver for organizations. According to McKinsey [MCK 20], the Covid-19 crisis has accelerated the digitization of interactions between organizations and users by several years. We are witnessing a massive digital transformation of journeys and relationships [MOR 17, FOR 18], whether in the public domain, where 83% of the 250 most used procedures were already dematerialized by 2022[1], or in the private sector, where global spending on digital transformation is expected to reach USD 2.8 trillion by 2025[2]. This makes it more urgent than ever to turn digital journeys into real strategic assets for organizations by (re)thinking the place of the user within them.

Indeed, this new digital structuring of service journeys has implications for the role of the user, value creation and construction of the user experience. This phenomenon is leading to a new managerial priority for organizations to encourage the participation of all users during the digital journey for fast, efficient and satisfying value creation. Yet, in a highly digital environment, interaction as a source of value is de facto a digital interaction, in other words, an interaction between the user and a digital resource – devices, connected objects, websites, etc. – which implies a link between the individual and digital technology.

However, not all users are equal when faced with digital technology, and the journeys are not always suitable for everyone [WÜN 20]. For the United Nations:

Chapter written by Léa CAUCHARD.

1 See: https://www.happysilvers.fr/numerique-ce-qui-va-changer-en-2022/.

2 See: https://www-statista-com.ezpum.scdi-montpellier.fr/statistics/870924/worldwide-digital-transformation-market-size/.

> The accelerated pace of digital transformation risks increasing the social exclusion of already vulnerable groups who are not digitally literate or connected[3].

For this reason, the social responsibility of organizations is engaged. New managerial perspectives are opening up, ensuring that all users, regardless of their profile and initial relationship with digital technology, can participate in digital journeys and enjoy a satisfying experience. We speak of *digital inclusion*.

This chapter provides insights for organizations wishing to anchor themselves in a more inclusive digital perspective. Why is it necessary to develop journeys that are both digital and inclusive? How is an inclusive digital process defined? Are current actions in favor of digital inclusion effective enough to deliver satisfactory digital journeys for all? To answer these questions, we look back at the issues and consequences of digitizing journeys, present the limits of current digital inclusion initiatives and propose a new definition of digital inclusion that focuses on user perceptions.

9.2. Consequences of the digitization of customer journeys

9.2.1. *A transformation of the user's role during the journey*

Massive deployment of digital technology in customer journeys is transforming the user's role. For Cova and Cova [COV 09], collaborative marketing arose from the increase in new technologies and the increasingly large-scale use of digital technology in customer journeys. The foundations of Vargo and Lusch's Service Dominant Logic [VAR 04] echo this situation: value must be co-created to offer real benefits:

> It's no longer a question of marketing to users (market to), but of marketing with users (market with). [COV 09, p. 87]

Digital technology is thus shaping a new user, more informed and demanding, but also more robust and autonomous when faced with organizations. The user is "put to work" [DUJ 08], they become an actor in the relationship and a co-creator of value [LIE 18]. Value creation is thus linked to the quality of interaction between the user and the digital journey.

3 United Nations, February 17, 2021, UN/DESA Policy Brief #92: Leveraging digital technologies for social inclusion. See: https://www.un.org/development/desa/dpad/publication/un-desa-policy-brief-92-leveraging-digital-technologies-for-social-inclusion/ [Accessed November 23, 2021].

9.2.2. *Interaction at the heart of the value creation process*

For the most part, using a service means submitting to social interaction [BRA 12]. However, digital technology modifies – or even interrupts – original service scripts and transforms interaction by replacing, on the organizational side, human with digital interfaces. This transformation of interaction can strengthen or weaken overall service evaluations, depending on the valence of the encounter. In other words, it can strengthen or weaken the user's perceived value of the service [MEN 14, FEE 17]. The active participation of the user during a digital journey therefore calls for particular questioning on the valuing of interactivity and its impact on the quality of the user's experience.

9.2.3. *User participation*

> Every service requires a greater or lesser degree of customer participation for its consumption to be a source of value. [VER 12, p. 5]

Participation is defined as the role(s) assumed by the user during the journey, that is, their physical or mental involvement [CAD 13], characterized by the efforts they make to interact with digital interfaces. Yi and Gong [YI 13] identify two types of behavior for the co-creation of value: participation behaviour, which groups together the actions that the user must produce for the service to be realized, and citizen behavior, which echoes the set of actions that the user can perform. These behaviors are closed to intra-roles and extra-roles [MIF 15]: intra-roles correspond to the set of behaviors expected for the realization of the service and to the set of efforts to be made for its proper performance. The extra-role goes further, for example, helping others or cooperating with the institution's stakeholders. More precisely:

> The intra-role is what the customer has to do to make the service happen, such as browsing the shelves in a store, placing an order in a restaurant, etc. The extra-role covers activities that are not obligatory for the service to be produced, but which the customer can possibly perform as part of the service, such as helping other customers or employees, or generating word-of-mouth about the store. [NIC 13, p. 4]

However, when it comes to digital technology, we cannot deny that the intensity of participation is not the same for all users, whether voluntary (lack of interest) or involuntary (lack of access or capabilities). Users therefore develop their own level of participation during the digital journey, which determines the singularity of their behavioral responses. These depend both on the user's relationship with digital technology and the level of complexity of the journey encountered. Indeed, when faced with a multi-channel experience (online and offline, for example), the user experience is built up through a series of micro-experiences that follow one another and combine. These more complex and fragmented journeys make it more difficult to create a quality user experience [BAD 13].

9.2.4. *A complex user experience*

Over the last few decades, organizational strategies have evolved from offering product-centric to solution-centric strategies to the user – through the user journey. The aim is to improve the experience by offering a multitude of points of contact with the organization (omnichannel approach). As stated above, however, the deployment of these omnichannel journeys makes understanding the user experience more complex.

Organizational strategies – multi-channel, cross-channel and omnichannel – can be understood through the prism of the organization or the user [BEC 15]. The organization offers an experiential context, and the user decides what actions to carry out within it [COL 15]. They articulate the different channels proposed according to their expectations and the situation. The user's experience is thus structured according to the experiential context and their interactions within it [ROE 12]. However, understanding these interactions can prove complex during an omnichannel journey. The sequential logic encountered during these journeys takes the form of "successive and simultaneous micro-experiences" that create experiences specific to the user [ANT 13]. We are thus witnessing a "fragmentation of the lived experience" between the different channels. Faced with this fragmentation:

– Organizations seek to recreate a seamless, fluid experience – a single experience that allows users to limit their efforts throughout the journey. If this is the case, users feel no fragmentation of the experience, and they participate effectively and enjoy the experience.

– Users themselves seek to "stitch together" these micro-experiences to create a personalized and satisfying experience.

Nevertheless, to "bring together" these micro-experiences, users need to interact with numerous digital channels, which is necessarily dependent on their relationship with digital technology. This is where *digital inclusion* plays a crucial role. The aim of digital inclusion is to enable every user, regardless of their initial relationship with digital technology, to participate effectively during the digital journey, to have a fluid experience, and to create value despite the complexity of the journeys.

9.3. New managerial challenges arising from the digitization of journeys

9.3.1. *Improving users' relationships with digital technology*

Digital inclusion has become a top-priority socioeconomic issue for organizations intent on fighting digital inequalities. Vendramin and Valenduc [VEN 06] define the objectives of digital inclusion as the reduction of digital inequalities, the exploitation of digital opportunities and the involvement and expression of all in society (via self-expression, social participation and autonomy). To limit the risks of exclusion, users must meet the following conditions [BRO 09]:

– have the cognitive and digital skills they need to achieve their goals, and be aware of their own capabilities;

– perceive the benefits and utility of using digital technologies and resources, and be able to count on social support in case of difficulty.

These areas of development relate to users' human capital[4]. By strengthening this capital in a digital context, users' relationship with the digital world improves, thereby limiting the risks of inequality participation during digital journeys. This participation is then beneficial for organizations (market share, quality of interaction and value creation), as well as for users, who aspire for more satisfying experiences.

9.3.2. *Still insufficient digital inclusion initiatives*

The digital transformation of services creates a new kind of pressure among users: to be equipped and have the digital skills to take advantage of it [BRO 19]. This dual requirement feeds the risk of a digital divide, that is, inequalities between users who can meet these demands and those who cannot [MAZ 19].

Actions to promote digital inclusion (Table 9.1) aim to improve access to digital resources for all users, while enhancing their digital skills, in other words, their level of digital literacy. By focusing on these strategic axes, organizations are taking users' previously underestimated digital struggles into account [WÜN 20].

4 "Human capital represents the knowledge and skills that people accumulate such as education, training, and work experience (Becker 1964)" [MET 22, p. 123].

The Conseil national du numérique (French Digital National Council) defines digital literacy as "the ability to understand and use digital technology in everyday life, at home, at work and in the community, in order to achieve personal goals and extend our skills and abilities".

This refers to all the cognitive processes put in place by users to adapt, evolve and interact within their digital environment. All this is undertaken to achieve a satisfying, high-quality digital experience.

Box 9.1. *Definition of digital literacy*

Nevertheless, is strengthening human capital sufficient to progress toward digital inclusion and the effective participation of all users? In a digital context, designing inclusive offers remains difficult [BRO 19].

Faced with digital profile diversity, organizations focus on certain exclusion factors instead of others, risking developing exclusive services: "Service exclusion occurs when services (service providers or service systems) deliberately or unintentionally fail to include or adequately serve customers in an equitable manner" [FIS 18, p. 835].

Actions	Objectives
Beginning in 2021 and for a period of two years, the French government is funding the training and deployment of 4,000 "France Services digital advisors" to enable them to run introductory digital workshops for the 13 million French people far removed from digital technology[5]	Facilitate access to digital support services
In 2019, the French government deployed digital passes (books of vouchers to be used with structures qualified to provide digital support services). Between 10,000 and 20,000 people are said to have benefited from this scheme[6]	
The French "Aidants Connect" scheme aims to secure the work of mediators forced to take steps on behalf of the users concerned	Secure and protect digital support
The "France Services" program was set up in response to the dematerialization of public services: the "Banque des Territoires" operationalizes France Services structures to help citizens with their administrative formalities as close to home as possible	Facilitate access to digital support services Facilitate access to essential public services

5 See: https://www.blogdumoderateur.com/exclusion-numerique-publics-emmaus-connect/.

6 Défenseurs des droits, 2022, "Dématérialisation des services publics : trois ans après, où en est-on ?"

Actions	Objectives
Since 2014, the Orange Foundation has been offering a number of digital mediation initiatives aimed at young people and women, among others (fondationorange.com)	Facilitate access to digital tools Develop digital skills
Between December 2020 and March 2021, the Don de Giga operation launched by Bouygues Telecom in partnership with the French Red Cross collected more than 240,000 gigabytes, distributing nearly 20,000 rate plans and 10,000 smartphones to populations in need[7]. The operation was repeated in October 2022	Facilitate access to digital tools
The SFR is working with Emmaüs Connect and WeTechCare on accessibility and digital autonomy (sfr.fr/options/option-solidaire)	
The PIX certification was developed in 2016 (France). It supports public and private organizations in the training of their employees, pupils and students	Assess, develop and certify digital skills

Table 9.1. *Examples of digital inclusion initiatives in France*

This trend is confirmed when we analyze the digital inclusion actions promoted. They all focus on concrete issues of digital access and training in order to strengthen users' human capital and encourage digital use. However, digital access and digital literacy alone cannot justify the nature of the user's relationship with digital technology and their behavioral responses.

9.3.3. *Moving beyond a focus on digital uses*

Not using digital technology is not always involuntary or synonymous with digital exclusion [JAU 12]. Not using digital technology can be a choice, for example, among users who are not in favour of the digital transformation of society.

Regular digital use does not always imply digital inclusion, as uses can be passive, that is, involve the user very little in the process of co-creating value. For example, digital natives are not exempt from the digital divide. According to INSEE and the Laboratoire d'analyse et de décryptage du numérique (2021), 3% of 15- to 29-year-olds have digital difficulties, as a result of digital under-equipment or regular but very limited digital use. Highlighting these realities encourages us to adopt a new semantic perspective: we refer to "differentiation in digital use" [PET 06] rather than inequalities in digital use. These considerations make it difficult to understand and reduce digital inequalities, as everyone adopts digital innovations and devices at their own speed, according to their own preferences and

7 See: https://rhinocc.fr/blog/.

needs. This suggests the creation of more complex digital divides, which depend above all on users' relationships with digital technology and the roles they associate with it, but also on their personal background, past experiences and motivations with regard to digital technology.

In view of these factors, the process of digital inclusion requires being part of the social field to understand the psychological and social mechanisms at play when the user is faced with digital journeys. Indeed, perceptions strongly guide the user's behavioral responses and shape their experiences [PAT 21]. As a result, the user's responses to digital journeys (abandonment, discouragement, request for help, self-learning, etc.) are based more on their perceptions, imbued with multiple cognitive and emotional biases, than on objective realities of use or mastery of digital technology (access or frequency and intensity of digital use, for example).

9.4. Defining the digital inclusion process

9.4.1. *The role of perceptions in the inclusion process*

Hartung et al. [HAR 15] suggest that social inclusion perceived by the user has more impact than real social inclusion. For Metz et al. [MET 22], social capital factors[8] are at the origin of the individual's inclusion experiences, not human capital factors.

Patrick and Hollenbeck [PAT 21], for their part, draw on theories of evaluation and social inclusion to define inclusive design as a means leading to a "diminishing degree of mismatch between the user and the design object" [PAT 21, p. 1].

Their DARE framework – Design, Appraisal, Response, Experience – breaks down the user's cognitive mechanisms: the journey sends signs of inclusion/exclusion to the user, who evaluates them and determines a greater or lesser mismatch between their identity and the characteristics of the journey encountered. Depending on the degree of perceived mismatch, the user defines the quality of the experience.

9.4.2. *Adopting a two-level approach to the digital inclusion process*

A smart customer journey is one that provides users with a variety of channels – and therefore alternatives for participation – to encourage the creation of a satisfying experience. A journey becomes inclusive if it enables every user, whatever their relationship with digital technology, to create an experience where there is no distance between them and digital channels.

---

8 "Social capital is "the ability of actors to secure benefits by virtue of membership in social networks or other social structures" (Portes 1998, p. 6)" [MET 22, p. 123].

To achieve this objective, two levels of action need to be considered: the level of the design of the digital channel and the level of the user perceptions.

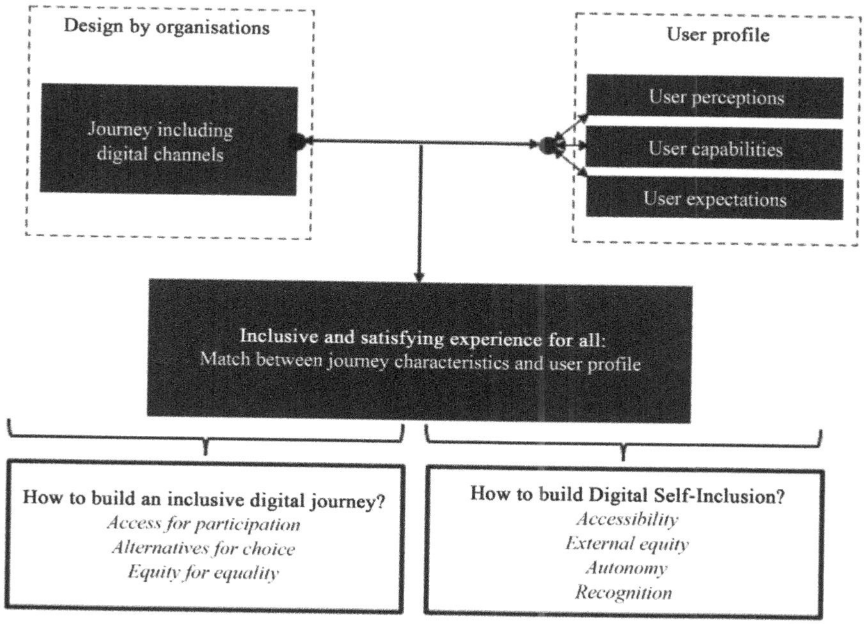

Figure 9.1. *Toward an inclusive digital experience*

9.4.2.1. *Designing more inclusive digital journeys*

To design an inclusive service, the literature recommends working on the dimensions of accessibility, equity and empowerment – via the fluidity of the journey and the freedom of choice offered to the user.

Vanderheiden and Tobias [VAN 00] identify four points of reflection for the design of more inclusive products: accessibility versus usability, independence versus codependence, effectiveness versus urgency and ease of implementation.

Fisk et al. [FIS 22] identify four pillars for building inclusive services: empowering users by giving them access to the service in order to co-create value through its use; giving users a choice between several different service offerings (while leaving them the choice not to benefit from them if they so wish); providing equitable access to essential services (basic needs and rights); and fostering happiness by creating positive interactions. More precisely, the authors define service inclusion as "an egalitarian system that provides customers (e.g. consumers, clients, patrons, citizens, patients and guests) with fair access to a service, fair treatment during a service and fair opportunity to exit a service" [FIS 18, p. 835].

Patrick and Hollenbeck [PAT 21] define three main steps in designing an inclusive process: providing accessibility, creating equitable experiences to support user participation and creating fluid experiences to support user autonomy.

9.4.2.2. *Integrating user perceptions of inclusion*

As part of the doctoral work carried out by the author[9], an exploratory qualitative study was conducted with professionals in the digital inclusion value chain (12 interviews) and individuals (13 interviews) in order to analyze users' representations and perceptions in a digital context. This study and the related literature review enable us to propose a four-dimensional conceptualization of digital inclusion as perceived by users.

Digital self-inclusion is then defined as the way in which users perceive their ease of access to digital resources (accessibility) and how they use their skills to adapt to the digital journey while remaining consistent with their identity and values (autonomy), but also the way in which they feel they are treated in relation to other users (equity) and how they ensure that their digital uses are valued and recognized by the organization, society and those around them (recognition). This self-evaluation allows the user to extract from digital resources the value enabling them to satisfy their expectations and evaluate the adequacy of the journey with their identity and expectations. In the long term, digital inclusion perceived by the user promotes user engagement and greater well-being.

Accessibility refers to ease of access to the digital resources available in the environment evaluated by the user to achieve the expected value.

Autonomy refers to the level of autonomy felt by the users during the journey. Do they have the necessary skills? Can they act freely and independently?

External equity refers to whether treatment is felt to be fair by the users. Are they treated fairly in relation to other users? Are digital devices designed for everyone?

Recognition refers to recognition by those around us, by organizations and by society in general.

Box 9.2. *Conceptualizing digital inclusion as perceived by the individual*

Nevertheless, the effectiveness of a digital journey also depends on users' perceptions and their evaluation of the journey. Patrick and Hollenbeck [PAT 21] define an inclusive offer as one that reduces the distance between the user and the

9 Still in progress at the time of writing.

digital journey. Metz et al. [MET 22] stress the importance of addressing the user's perception of inclusion, considering that it contributes to the creation of a more or less satisfying experience.

The evaluation of the quality of an experience results from the user's interpretation of particular stimuli according to their perceptions [BEC 20].

9.4.3. *From inclusion to digital inclusion as perceived by the user*

Table 9.2 provides a summary of the definitions of digital inclusion according to the level of action recommended.

	Definition	**Dimensions**
Digital inclusion	Process grouping together all the interdisciplinary actions implemented within the "living together" program, aiming to bring an individual X closer to digital uses, so that they can participate fully in the economic, social and cultural life of the digital society, enjoy all their rights and claim a better quality of life, all by using digital technology	Access Participation Digital usage
Digital inclusion, marketing and organizational approach	Process grouping together all the interdisciplinary actions implemented by the organization to bring all users, regardless of their relationship to digital technology, closer to digital interactions during a digital journey, in order to offer them a satisfying experience. In other words, to enable them to participate effectively (intra-role and extra-role), access the maximum value offered by the organization (value co-creation) and make a lasting commitment to the organization	Access Participation Digital usage Creating value Quality of experience
Digital inclusion, marketing and individual approach	A process that brings together all the perceptions that users mobilize to assess how well the digital journey matches their identity and expectations It is about how the user assesses their ease of access to digital resources during the process and uses their skills to adapt to the digital journey while remaining consistent with their identity and values, but also how they assess their treatment in relation to other users, and how they act to be valued and recognized by the organization, society, and those around them. This self-assessment enables users to extract value from digital resources, enabling them to satisfy their expectations and position themselves within the digital society. In the long term, digital self-inclusion promotes a better quality of life	Accessibility External equity Autonomy Recognition

Table 9.2. *The digital inclusion process by action level*

Digital self-inclusion identifies the perceptions mobilized by the user to assess their position in relation to the digital journey encountered. The greater the degree of digital inclusion, the less distance there will be between the user and the digital journey, and the more value will be created by their behavioral responses.

9.5. Conclusion: toward digital consumption for all

In 2020, Euromonitor International identified "inclusion for all" as one of the fastest-growing and emerging trends. The United Nations defines "leaving no one behind" as a sustainable development goal. Designing more inclusive services in a highly digital environment is a top priority for organizations. Adopting a more inclusive digital perspective allows them to increase their market share by reaching users who have until now been left behind and guarantee more effective participation of all users during digital journeys – participation is synonymous with value creation, satisfying experience and engagement.

Digital inclusion can then occur at two levels:

– Organizations need to think about the design of their digital journeys. These journeys need to be accessible, fair and full of alternatives in order to empower users. But they must also be structured in such a way as not to leave the user without guidance and support at the risk of destroying value.

– The evaluation of users' digital and inclusive experience depends on their appreciation of the characteristics of the digital journey, and more specifically their influence on their perception of accessibility, external equity, autonomy and recognition. Understanding the cognitive and social mechanisms involved in the user's inclusion process and their evaluation of digital experiences is a critical issue. As a result, organizations need to consider the digital inclusion and its dimensions as essential levers of value creation during digital journeys (participation). The design of digital journeys must be thought through hand-in-hand with all users, whether close to or far from digital uses, to ensure the construction of digital journeys in line with user perceptions, vectors of qualitative digital interactions and value creation. In this respect, Table 9.3 suggests strategic axes for organizations to cultivate an inclusive design mindset.

By adopting this more empathetic approach, organizations reduce the risk of designing digital journeys that are stigmatizing or excluding, because they are specific to a segment of the population. They also ensure the sustainability of their digital strategies and increased user satisfaction.

Strategic priorities	Objectives
Finding a pace of innovation that ensures the continuous improvement of digital devices, while reducing barriers to entry. To achieve this goal, organizations need to reduce the obsolescence of digital devices, a vector of inequality of access. They can, for example, avoid offering mobile applications that are only compatible with latest-generation smartphones, at the risk of excluding some users *Ensuring continuity in the chronology of journeys and in the ergonomics of their contact points*. The failure of the SNCF Connect application launch with the general public shows that organizations sometimes have to prioritize the stability of user habits over the evolution of their offers, at the risk of generating negative behavioral responses	Stimulating the user's perceived accessibility
Emphasizing user choice, so that the user feels in control during the journey. For example, on organization websites, users could be offered decision support. This would take the form of personalized recommendations presenting the different points of contact to be prioritized according to the user's individual preferences: online booking, in-store appointment, telephone contact, etc. *Offering learning resources*: it is important to offer learning resources (documentation, tutorials, e-learning, etc.) to help users understand the courses offered to them. These resources must be simple, clear and accessible to all	Stimulating the user's perceived autonomy
Highlighting their commitment to greater social and digital justice. For example, in its "The Greatest" advert at the end of 2022, Apple demonstrated that its products are accessible to everyone, regardless of ability *Offering a fun, collaborative approach to design*. Through its "Build for real" campaign, Lego invited people with disabilities to use Lego to design projects adapted to their needs, in order to improve their quality of life. This type of action could be implemented by urban and mobility players, for example, during the design phases of their offers	Stimulating the user's perceived external equity
Involving users in company decisions to reinforce their sense of belonging. Many companies have already set up systems to integrate their employees into corporate governance: Patagonia has created a voting system so that employees decide how profits are used. Zappos has adopted a "holacracy" system where employees are consulted to validate the company's strategic decisions. They are also involved in the creation of new products. It would be wise to see this type of involvement develop at user level, so as to integrate them more concretely (beyond brainstorming) into the design of the customer journey *Encouraging participation from users who like to feel involved and valued*. PIX has implemented messages of encouragement and congratulations throughout their training programs. Valuation systems could thus be designed at each critical stage identified during digital journeys	Stimulating the user's perceived recognition

Table 9.3. *Proposed strategic axes for digital inclusion perceived by the user*

9.6. References

[ANT 13] ANTEBLIAN B., FILSER M., ROEDERER C., "L'expérience du consommateur dans le commerce de détail. Une revue de littérature", *Recherche et Applications en Marketing*, vol. 28, pp. 84–113, 2013.

[BAD 13] BADOT O., LEMOINE J.-F., "Du paradigme dichotomique de l'expérience d'achat au paradigme ubiquitaire", *Recherche et Applications en Marketing (French Edition)*, vol. 28, no. 3, pp. 3–13, 2013.

[BEC 15] BECK N., RYGL D., "Categorization of multiple channel retailing in multi-, cross-, and omni-channel retailing for retailers and retailing", *Journal of Retailing and Consumer Services*, vol. 27, pp. 170–178, 2015.

[BEC 20] BECKER L., JAAKKOLA E., "Customer experience: fundamental premises and implications for research", *Journal of the Academy of Marketing Science*, vol. 48, no. 4, pp. 630–648, 2020.

[BRA 12] BRADY M., VOORHEES C., BRUSCO M., "Service sweethearting: Its antecedents and customer consequences", *Journal of Marketing*, vol. 76, pp. 81–98, 2012.

[BRO 09] BROTCORNE P., VALENDUC G., "Les compétences numériques et les inégalités dans les usages d'internet", *Les Cahiers du numérique*, vol. 5, no. 1, pp. 45–68, 2009.

[BRO 19] BROTCORNE P., BONNETIER C., VENDRAMIN P., "Une numérisation des services d'intérêt général qui peine à inclure et à émanciper tous les usagers", *Terminal. Technologie de l'information, culture & société*, pp. 125–126, 2019.

[CAD 13] CADENAT S., BONNEMAIZON A., BENOIT-MOREAU F. et al., "Regards sur la co-production du client : comment les entreprises nous font-elles participer ?", *Décisions Marketing*, vol. 70, pp. 9–24, 2013.

[COV 09] COVA B., COVA V., "Les figures du nouveau consommateur : une genèse de la gouvernementalité du consommateur", *Recherche et Applications en Marketing*, vol. 24, pp. 81–100, 2009.

[FEE 17] FEENSTRA F., GLÉRANT-GLIKSON A., "Identifier et comprendre les sources de valeur dans l'interaction avec les SSIT (Self-Service Information Technologies) en magasin", *Décisions Marketing*, vol. 86, pp. 47–66, 2017.

[FIS 22] FISK R.P., GALLAN A.S., JOUBERT A.M. et al., "Healing the digital divide with digital inclusion: Enabling human capabilities", *Journal of Service Research*, vol. 26, no. 4, pp. 542–559, 2022.

[FOR 18] FORNERINO M., RIVET C., REGHEM J., "Explorer l'expérience de shopping dans un magasin phygital", *Décisions Marketing*, vol. 91, pp. 45–60, 2018.

[HAR 15] HARTUNG F.-M., SPROESSER G., RENNER B., "Being and feeling liked by others: How social inclusion impacts health", *Psychology & Health*, vol. 30, no. 9, pp. 1103–1115, 2015.

[JAU 12] JAURÉGUIBERRY F., "Retour sur les théories du non-usage des technologies de communication", in KLEIN S.P., KLEIN A. (eds), *Connexions : communication numérique et lien social*, Presses universitaires de Namur, Namur, 2012.

[LIE 18] LIEFOOGHE C., "Les tiers-lieux à l'ère du numérique : diffusion spatiale d'une utopie socio-économique", *Géographie, économie, société*, vol. 20, vo. 1, pp. 33–61, 2018.

[MAZ 19] MAZET P., "Vers l'État plateforme", *La Vie des Idées*, available at: https://laviedesidees.fr/Vers-l-Etat-plateforme, 2019.

[MEN 14] MENCARELLI R., RIVIÈRE A., "La participation du client dans un contexte de self-service technologies. Une approche par la valeur perçue", *Revue française de gestion*, vol. 40, no. 241, pp. 13–30, 2014.

[MET 22] METZ I., STAMPER C.L., NG E., "Feeling included and excluded in organizations: The role of human and social capital", *Journal of Business Research*, vol. 142, pp. 122–137, 2022.

[MIF 15] MIFSUD M., CASES A.-S., N'GOALA G., "Service appropriation: How do customers make the service their own?", *Journal of Service Management*, vol. 26, pp. 706–725, 2015.

[MOE 10] MOELLER S., "Characteristics of services – a new approach uncovers their value", *Journal of Services Marketing*, vol. 24, no. 5, pp. 359–368, 2010.

[MOR 17] MORAVCIKOVA D., KLIESTIKOVA J., "Brand building with using phygital marketing communication", *Journal of Economics, Business and Management*, vol. 5, no. 3, pp. 148–153, 2017.

[PAT 21] PATRICK V.M., HOLLENBECK C.R., "Designing for all: Consumer response to inclusive design", *Journal of Consumer Psychology*, vol. 31, no. 2, pp. 360–381, 2021.

[PET 06] PETER J., VALKENBURG P.M., "Adolescents' Internet use: Testing the "disappearing digital divide" versus the "emerging digital differentiation" approach", *Poetics*, vol. 34, no. 4, pp. 293–305, 2006.

[ROE 12] ROEDERER C., "Contribution à la conceptualisation de l'expérience de consommation : émergence des dimensions de l'expérience au travers de récits de vie", *Recherche et Applications en Marketing (French Edition)*, 2012.

[VAN 00] VANDERHEIDEN G., TOBIAS J., "Universal design of consumer products: Current industry practice and perceptions", *Proceedings of the Human Factors and Ergonomics Society Annual Meeting*, vol. 44, no. 32, pp. 6–19, 2000.

[VAR 04] VARGO S., LUSCH R., "Evolving to a new dominant logic", *Journal of Marketing*, vol. 68, pp. 1–17, 2004.

[VEN 06] VENDRAMIN P., VALENDUC G., "Fractures numériques, inégalités sociales et processus d'appropriation des innovations", *Terminal*, vol. 137, pp. 137–154, 2006.

[WÜN 20] WÜNDERLICH N.V., HOGREVE J., CHOWDHURY I.N. et al., "Overcoming vulnerability: Channel design strategies to alleviate vulnerability perceptions in customer journeys", *Journal of Business Research*, vol. 116, pp. 377–386, 2020.

[YI 13] YI Y., GONG T., "Customer value co-creation behavior: Scale development and validation", *Journal of Business Research*, vol. 66, pp. 1279–1284, 2013.

10

Improving Effective Accessibility of Products and Services for Vulnerable Customers

Improving the effective accessibility of products and services by reducing the effort required of customers is as much an operational challenge as it is a great business opportunity. Indeed, the more accessible the offers are, the more sales increase. What is more, thanks to greater accessibility, customers are more satisfied, more loyal and more likely to recommend the company to new prospects.

However, improving accessibility is also an issue of social responsibility when it comes to vulnerable customers, a subject that is still not taken into account much by organizations.

In fact, most of these organizations need to improve the accessibility of their offerings by deploying methodologies that reduce the effort required of customers, thereby enhancing their experience.

After clarifying the notion of effective accessibility and highlighting the specific difficulties encountered by vulnerable customers, we present two methodologies for improving accessibility.

Chapter written by Pierre VOLLE and Sylvie LLOSA.

The authors would like to thank Louise Goral, a graduate of the Master's program in Marketing and Strategy at Paris Dauphine University ("Consulting and Research" course), for her contribution to the conclusion, based on a dozen interviews with professionals

10.1. Effective accessibility of products and services, a challenge for organizations

10.1.1. *Definition of effective accessibility*

Organizations (e.g. companies, associations and public services) are faced with the challenge of the "effective accessibility" of their products and services for all customers, in particular for vulnerable customers who face specific difficulties (see Box 10.1). It is a question of allowing everyone to easily access the interfaces that provide access to products and services, what we call here the "points of contact" (e.g. toll-free numbers, websites, chatbots and conversational agents, mobile applications and points of sales). Thus, it is a question of allowing "access to access points", so that the customer can not only access the resource (e.g. an ATM and a store) but also mobilize it to co-produce the service (e.g. withdrawing cash from an ATM, shopping at a retail store).

Effective accessibility contributes to the inclusion of each and every person, including the most vulnerable users such as people with disabilities and, more generally, all those who may face difficulties due to a lack of resources (such as owning a car) or skills (such as reading), whether permanent or temporary. This form of accessibility is underpinned by an ideology of corporate social responsibility, of values of empathy and benevolence, and manifests itself in the ambition to leave no one behind. In a way, the figure of the consumer – thus that of the simple passive beneficiary – is gradually giving way to that of the proactive actor, the contributor. This evolution is all the more remarkable given that today's customers are being increasingly called upon. Their participation is growing. Nowadays, customers scan products in-store on their cell phones, modify their plane tickets on their apps, participate in innovations by giving their opinions, and decipher video games by proposing comprehensive guides on forums.

The technological developments of recent years, the quest for productivity and the shift of the economy toward services have led to an increase in the power of the customer and a heavy demand on their resources [BIT 97, LAR 17]. The customer is becoming a free part-time employee for the company. However, the extra effort required of the customer is only positive and feasible for the company if two conditions are met:

– The customer must find value in it. For example, it is possible to shop at 2 a.m. (i.e. time flexibility), from the comfort of your own sofa (i.e. convenience), from pre-established shopping lists (i.e. time savings) and with home delivery (i.e. convenience).

– The customer must be able to perform the tasks required to access the product or manufacture the service.

At a time when customers are being asked to do more, the challenge is to reduce costs. This is an exciting paradox facing companies, associations and public services today.

10.1.2. *Effective accessibility: a challenge for organizations?*

While most organizations go to great lengths for their customers, customers also go to great lengths to compare and choose, to buy and use the products and services offered by companies. These efforts are probably even on the increase due to the growing sophistication of offers, the increasing complexity of customer journeys, the multiplication of contact points and the company's desire to transfer the tasks that used to be carried out by contact personnel to the customer in order to increase profitability.

The efforts required by companies from their customers are manifold: financial efforts, of course, but also physical efforts (e.g. walking, carrying and handling), cognitive efforts (e.g. comparing, memorizing, interacting with a machine and calculating), socio-affective efforts (e.g. taking it upon oneself, accepting that one may make mistakes, lose money or be ridiculed) and relational efforts (e.g. sharing personal information, signing up for a program, contacting the company in case of concern). In addition to money and time, the efforts required sometimes involve resources or capabilities that the customer does not have (e.g. the use of a computer).

In general, the more effort the company requires from the customer, the less the offer will be valued [LUK 18] and the less satisfied the customer will be with their experience.

Fully aware of this, some companies innovate to reduce the level of effort required of customers. Unfortunately, they rarely consider the problem in its entirety. They often focus on reducing the effort linked to the product or service itself (easy opening of packaging, for example), but often ignore the effort required of the customer at all contact points. Many companies are short-sighted in the sense that they focus on improving the "core" experience – that of the basic product or service – and largely ignore what happens before and after [VOO 17].

On the other hand, when effort is considered in its entirety, across all contact points and at all moments of the experience, companies do not always know how to concretely reduce effort beyond the product/service itself. In fact, the design of the offering is the area in which they have the most expertise, and on which R&D resources and capabilities are concentrated. It is time to make companies aware of this notion of "complete" effort required of customers and to offer them methodologies to reduce this effort, especially the most vulnerable customers.

10.2. The challenges of effective accessibility for vulnerable customers

10.2.1. *How do you define a vulnerable customer?*

The notion of vulnerability is a tricky one to handle for marketing professionals [BRE 98]. Like Wunderlich et al. [WUN 20], we believe that customer vulnerability occurs when a person is unable to realize the maximum value of a service without the help of the service provider or a third party.

Following the work of Baker et al. [BAK 05], in particular, we adopt a situational conception of vulnerability, which leads us to consider as vulnerable those individuals who lack the necessary skills to make the right decisions – those that maximize their utility or well-being – in a given context[1].

This difficulty in making good decisions results from an inability to know one's own preferences and/or an inability to act on one's preferences due to a lack of knowledge, a skills deficit or reduced freedom. This is the loss of autonomy in optimal decision-making. For example, recent research shows that pregnant women can find themselves in a vulnerable situation due to a lack of knowledge about the possible toxicity of certain cosmetic products [ANI 20]. They do not all have the capacity to carry out the sophisticated information research required (e.g. cross-referencing available information, following groups on social networks, attending online courses and using technical data sheets published by health professionals).

According to this situational approach, vulnerability depends jointly on the customer's characteristics (e.g. physical or cognitive abilities) and the situation they have to face (e.g. discrimination, stigmatization and time pressure). For example, a visually impaired customer is not necessarily vulnerable because of their disability. They become vulnerable when the situation in which they find themselves requires them to use their vision to make the right decision, and when their visual impairment leads them to make a decision that is not good for them.

Wunderlich et al. [WUN 20] note that vulnerability may arise during access to the service (e.g. no Internet connection, lack of stairs or buses) or in the processing of resources (e.g. illiteracy, language unknown to the customer or impossible physical effort). The causes of vulnerability are linked to the customer's individual characteristics (e.g. disability, age, minority status, obesity), to a transient individual state (e.g. bereavement, which makes rapid decisions worrying) or to external conditions (e.g. lack of transport or dismissive staff).

---

1 Another "hybrid" conception of vulnerability has been proposed in the literature [COM 08], which consists of distinguishing between a "group" component (linked to age, for example), identical for all individuals in the group, and an individual component, specific to each individual.

Vulnerability is not mechanically and systematically the result of the customer's objective characteristics: it is socially constructed and subjectively experienced by the customer. In other words, vulnerability is an experience that affects the individual's personal and social identity (the way others see us). This highly topical view sees vulnerability as an experience, a process rather than a state.

Vulnerability can also be more or less temporary. When the customer is momentarily emotionally upset – for example, when organizing the funeral of a loved one [REV 15] – we may prefer to speak of fragility rather than vulnerability.

It should be noted that the development of digital services is certainly not a panacea insofar as technologies produce specific exclusionary effects, such as "illectronism" [VAL 20]. Once again, a paradox emerges. New technologies make access easier for some people (e.g. being able to consult a doctor by videoconferencing when physical travel is difficult or when the doctor is too far away) and disqualify those who have not mastered them, making them dependent on the assistance of a relative. This loss of autonomy brought about by the closure of certain channels (such as the gradual disappearance of physical points of contact) is hard for many customers[2].

10.2.2. *Reduced effective accessibility for vulnerable customers?*

The efforts required of companies are sometimes such that certain products and services become inaccessible to these vulnerable customers who face specific difficulties (see Box 10.1).

> Vulnerable customers encounter numerous difficulties in exercising their day-to-day rights as consumers, customers and users. They are then led to implement specific strategies in an attempt to partially circumvent these difficulties. For example, the study by Beudaert et al. [BEU 17] shows that consumers with hidden hearing difficulties (such as hyperacuity) may feel excluded when visiting shopping malls (excessively high sensory stimulation, difficulties in interacting with staff, etc.). These consumers are then prompted to change their behavior: avoiding certain places, preferring electronic touchpoints or asking their loved ones for help.

2 The digitization of public services and the closure of physical touchpoints are posing real problems for some French people, who may become dependent on a third party to do their tax returns, for example. The French government has recently come to grips with this issue, and in some departments is now opening "Maisons France Service", which seem like a good idea, provided the staff are competent and friendly. See the annual reports of the French Ombudsmen on this subject.

Other studies focus on visual disability. In particular, the study by Falchetti et al. [FAL 16] shows that visually impaired or blind individuals have painful experiences in terms of well-being and acceptance, self-esteem, anxiety, even depression and prejudice. The study shows, however, that reactions are highly contrasted according to the individual's "mental schema", with some experiencing significant distress while others cope with their condition with greater ease.

Replacing personal interfaces with digital/automated interfaces sometimes requires an unpleasant cognitive effort on the part of some customers unfamiliar with the technology. Automated check-in at airports, where customers have to queue in front of a machine, check-in following a sometimes complex procedure, retrieve their luggage tag and then queue a second time to place it on a conveyor belt, is designed solely in the interests of the company, not the customer. The proof is in the pudding: lucky holders of a high-status loyalty card can check in with "real" staff, etc. Just like before! These practices discourage some customers, for whom the airport journey seems too complex. They sometimes prefer to travel by train, a simpler route in their eyes.

Consumers with disabilities encounter multiple difficulties in accessing digital services, difficulties which lead them to make much more limited use of these services than other people [CI 09]. When vulnerable people do make online purchases, their experience remains marked by difficulties that lead to partial disengagement and a feeling of isolation [ELM 12] and dependence [BAK 01].

Box 10.1. *Difficulties encountered by vulnerable customers*

As the quality of experience of vulnerable customers is lower than that of the average customer, it is up to companies to take active steps to reduce the effort required of customers before, during and after the transaction and/or to give vulnerable customers the skills they need to have a fully satisfactory experience. As companies are depriving themselves of business opportunities, because what makes life easier for vulnerable people often makes life easier for everyone – but above all because they are not meeting the challenges of responsibility – it is important for them to reduce the effort required of vulnerable customers and make their offers more accessible.

10.3. Ways to improve the effective accessibility of products and services for vulnerable customers

While the notion of vulnerability is complex, the company's approach to the issue is even more so. What position should be adopted? What can be done?

10.3.1. *How should we respond to the challenge of effective accessibility for vulnerable customers?*

Some companies ignore the issue of vulnerable customers, either through a lack of awareness or deliberately, for example, by arguing that all customers should be treated equally for legal or ideological reasons.

Some companies choose to limit – or even avoid – marketing to vulnerable customers. As Brenkert [BRE 98], one of the first to address the issue of vulnerability, points out, "not marketing to the vulnerable is not the solution". For him, while circumvention is not the solution, denying the difficulties encountered by vulnerable customers is morally unjustifiable.

The right approach is not to ignore the specific problems faced by vulnerable customers, but to avoid the naive tendency to treat them differently. Even with the best of intentions, actions that focus on vulnerable customers often have the unintentional effect of stigmatizing them. In fact, a number of studies have shown that vulnerable customers are uncomfortable when they are seen as vulnerable individuals before they are seen as customers [BAK 07], particularly when staff are overly eager to offer help.

The right approach is to consider vulnerable customers as capable without being capable of everything. This posture leads the organization to recognize vulnerable customers' capacity for agency, independence, resilience, creativity, commitment, etc., provided they receive specific support.

Some studies have identified ways of improving customer experience – particularly in the retail sector [EDW 18] – but these studies discuss the customer experience at a very general level, and do not generally mobilize the notion of the customer journey.

As an extension of the principles outlined above, we present how and to what extent journey modeling and experience design – two now classic approaches to customer experience management – can be deployed for the vulnerable customer population.

10.3.2. *How can we rethink journeys to improve accessibility for vulnerable customers?*

Journey modeling is at the heart of customer experience management [LEM 16, HOM 17]. Although the first customer journey models date back to the 1960s and 1970s, as an extension of the service blueprint [SHO 84], the popularity of these techniques began to assert itself in the 2010s, notably with the mobilization of design thinking [JAC 15, JAC 21].

The application of these experiential journey modeling techniques to vulnerable customers is considered exceptional by both academics and practitioners[3]. The health sector is an exception.

The study by Crosier and Handford [CRO 12] highlights the difficulties encountered by blind people living in Lincoln in the UK, when they wish to go shopping in the city center. Based on individual interviews with eight respondents, the study identifies 16 critical moments in the shopping journey, 10 of which are associated with strong negative emotions. The study, which was presented to all stakeholders (representatives of the public transport company, city center retailers, the municipality, etc.), enables us to identify the areas we need to work on to reduce the strain on vulnerable customers and enable them to shop in better conditions.

In addition to this case study, which to our knowledge is the only empirical study of vulnerable customer journeys, Wünderlich et al. [WUN 20] identify three key strategies for improving the experience of vulnerable customers:

– flexibility: the company must offer several alternative channels for delivering the same services (information, order, complaint, etc.) through several channels. Customers are free to choose the channel that is most convenient for them. However, this approach can be complex and costly for most companies;

– guidance: the company limits the number of channels used to deliver a given service at a particular stage of the customer journey but, if necessary, supports vulnerable customers with special devices. The aim is to offer simplicity through restricted channels with a high degree of customer guidance. This strategy requires a thorough understanding of the uses and expectations of vulnerable customers and a detailed analysis of customer journeys in light of their vulnerability;

– initiative: the company takes the initiative and initiates interactions with vulnerable customers so as to provide them with specific support. This costly strategy presupposes upstream collection of individual data on vulnerable customers, which can be difficult. This approach encourages the company to take the lead through notifications on a mobile application or by approaching the customer in-store before they ask, etc.

In any case, whatever the strategy adopted, we recommend that companies design the journeys followed by vulnerable customers. Ultimately, this does not

3 By way of illustration, a Google search conducted at the end of 2020 using the keywords "vulnerable customer experience" and "disabled customer experience" identified only a handful of cases, most of them British and in the financial services, energy or utilities sectors.

necessarily mean proposing specific journeys for vulnerable customers (this option is discussed below), but first asking about the possible consequences of vulnerability for the effective accessibility of contact points and the effective seamlessness of the journeys for vulnerable customers.

To this end, we propose a seven-step approach to meeting this challenge:

– diagnose, for each stage of the customer journey, the level of effort required of vulnerable customers, then deduce the total level of effort, the components of this effort and the difficulties encountered;

– analyze the skills of vulnerable customers, both those they have and those they may not have. It should be noted that vulnerable clients may have skills available to them through their entourage, which means going beyond an understanding of the client-individual;

– identify gaps between the effort required and the skills of vulnerable customers;

– develop a program to close these gaps, while drawing on the specific skills of vulnerable customers. Note that the gap can be bridged by reducing the effort required and/or by providing vulnerable customers with the necessary resources and capabilities;

– test and deploy the program;

– analyze the program's success and continuously improve it;

– draw lessons from this approach for all customers.

This approach must include vulnerable customers from the outset in order to identify the components of the effort required of them, understand the difficulties they face, identify the skills they can draw on and determine their specific needs for additional resources or capabilities.

At step four of the method described above, the company may be faced with a dilemma: whether to improve existing journeys to take into account the specific needs of vulnerable customers or to propose specific journeys.

By default, we often prefer the first option, to limit costs and avoid stigmatization. If this option is chosen, it is then possible to modify the method to integrate vulnerability as an additional dimension of each journey.

Many questions remain unanswered, including the following:

– How can a customer's vulnerability be identified (or even anticipated)?

– How can we acknowledge the real and varied obstacles posed by each channel according to the type of vulnerability without categorizing (or prioritizing) one disability as more valid than another?

– How can we direct vulnerable customers to the most appropriate channels without stigmatizing them?

– What concrete help can we provide beyond digital technologies? More technology? More human contact? What is the best solution for each situation?

– How can we mobilize employees and all stakeholders around this important but complex issue?

– How can we align the ambition to treat vulnerable customers better with brand strategy?

– How can we enrich or even create delight in certain journeys (or certain moments of truth in a few well-chosen journeys), given that the experiential promise is often much richer than a "simple" reduction in effort?

– How can we integrate the presence of other customers, who may represent obstacles or support, into this specific approach to vulnerable customers?

– Should we encourage help from co-clients present during the experiment [CAM 13], or rather from collaborators?

Despite the difficulty, some companies are tackling this issue head-on (see Box 10.2).

SNCF is very concerned about vulnerable customers, who are particularly hard hit when traveling by train. Even if the task is far from complete, they are tackling the issue through a wide range of actions. These include efforts to improve physical support (floor guidance, automatic doors, adapted seats, etc.), the creation of a "reduced mobility" guide to anticipate the journey, the Andilien app, sign language training for employees, reception and assistance in stations, a visual assistant to take over the audio announcements and a host of free or paid services to support the customer from one end of the journey to the other, from the journey preparation phase, booking and ticket exchange, to the journey itself and baggage handling. The company works in collaboration with federations representing various vulnerable groups (customers with physical and mental disabilities, older customers, etc.) and consumer associations.

In response to the recent pandemic, several supermarket chains have offered to help the most vulnerable populations with their shopping. These include the elderly, but also immune-compromised individuals, those with diabetes, patients suffering from respiratory insufficiency and others. Local initiatives have been set up, with morning slots reserved exclusively for these customers, to avoid close contact with other people and limit the risk of contamination. In Paris and the Paris region, for example, Franprix and Monoprix offered home delivery of emergency baskets containing food and hygiene products to keep people fed for a few days. The baskets were delivered free of charge to the home via a toll-free number[4]. The challenge, however, is to perpetuate these initiatives and transform these ad hoc approaches into a genuine accessibility strategy for vulnerable customers.

Box 10.2. *Some remarkable initiatives to support vulnerable customers at different points of contact*

10.4. Conclusion

The market for vulnerable people is substantial, whether they are permanently or temporarily vulnerable. At some point in our lives, we will all be in a situation where our skills and ability to act are overwhelmed by the complexity of the situation. While the economic and ethical stakes are high, most companies and public organizations have yet to take up the subject in a proactive, strategic way. In particular, we encourage them to adopt design methods applicable to customer journeys to take into account the specificities of vulnerable customers and make their daily lives easier.

In addition to providing resources, the support offered by companies to vulnerable customers must include an emotional dimension (reassuring, valuing and encouraging vulnerable customers). The addition of a few kind words significantly enhances customer participation whenever possible. The timing of customer training/assistance is also an important characteristic to take into account.

Until now, in the absence of a clear strategy or legal obligation, companies have tended to focus on reactive assistance, for example, having an employee simply come to the aid of a customer who has lost their way. A complementary, more proactive vision is possible, where the customer can prepare, anticipate and understand their role upstream. In this way, even before encountering any difficulties, vulnerable customers can understand the tasks they have to perform, decide for themselves whether or not help from the company is necessary, and choose the help that best suits them [NIC 20].

At the same time, employees need to be made aware of the issue. It is a safe bet that this will not be a major difficulty, as the staff in contact with customers are often willing to take part in these actions, which make them proud of their company. Working on customer vulnerability is a win–win situation: the customer is more

4 LSA, published March 17, 2020. Available at: https://www.lsa-conso.fr/coronavirus-multiplication-des-dispositifs-de-courses-pour-aider-les-clients-ages-et-fragiles,342955.

satisfied, the employees are more committed and the managers see the market open up to new audiences.

10.5. References

[ANI 20] ANIN C., GUIZANI H., "L'expérience de la grossesse entre résistance et vulnérabilité du consommateur", *Actes du congrès de l'Association Française du Marketing*, Biarritz, 2020.

[BAK 01] BAKER S.-M., STEPHENS D.-L., HILL R.-P., "Marketplace experiences of consumers with visual impairments: Beyond the Americans with Disability Act", *Journal of Public Policy and Marketing*, vol. 20, no. 2, pp. 215–224, 2001.

[BAK 05] BAKER S.-M., GENTRY J.-W., RITTENBURG T.-L., "Building understanding of the domain of consumer vulnerability", *Journal of Macromarketing*, vol. 25, no. 2, pp. 128–139, 2005.

[BAK 07] BAKER S.-M., HOLLAND J., KAUFMAN-SCARBOROUGH C., "How consumers with disabilities perceive "welcome" in retail servicescapes: A critical incident study", *Journal of Services Marketing*, vol. 21, no. 3, pp. 160–173, 2007.

[BEU 17] BEUDAERT A., GORGE H., HERBERT M., "An exploration of servicescapes' exclusion and coping strategies of consumers with "hidden" auditory disorders", *Journal of Services Marketing*, vol. 31, no. 4/5, pp. 326–338, 2017.

[BIT 97] BITNER M.-J., FARANDA W.-T., HUBBERT A.-R. et al., "Customer contributions and roles in service delivery", *International Journal of Service Industry Management*, vol. 8, no. 3, pp. 193–205, 1997.

[BRE 98] BRENKERT G.-B., "Marketing and the vulnerable", *Business Ethics Quarterly*, vol. 8, pp. 7–20, 1998.

[COM 08] COMMURI S., EKICI A., "An enlargement of the notion of consumer vulnerability", *Journal of Macromarketing*, vol. 28, no. 2, pp. 183–186, 2008.

[CRO 12] CROSIER A., HANDFORD A., "Customer journey mapping as an advocacy tool for disabled people: A case study", *Social Marketing Quarterly*, vol. 18, no. 1, pp. 67–76, 2012.

[EDW 18] EDWARDS K., ROSENBAUM M.-S., BROSDAHL D. et al., "Designing retail spaces for inclusion", *Journal of Retailing and Consumer Services*, vol. 44, pp. 182–190, 2018.

[ELM 12] ELMS J., TINSON J., "Consumer vulnerability and the transformative potential of Internet shopping: An exploratory case study", *Journal of Marketing Management*, vol. 28, no. 11/12, pp. 1354–1376, 2012.

[FAL 16] FALCHETTI C., CANNIATTI PONCHIO M., POLI BOTELHO N.-L., "Understanding the vulnerability of blind consumers: Adaptation in the marketplace, personal traits and coping strategies", *Journal of Marketing Management*, vol. 32, no. 3/4, pp. 313–334, 2016.

[HOM 17] HOMBURG C., JOZIC D., KUEHNL C., "Customer experience management: Toward implementing an evolving marketing concept", *Journal of the Academy of Marketing Science*, vol. 45, pp. 377–401, 2017.

[JAC 15] JACOB F., VOLLE P., "Conception de parcours client cross-canaux dans le commerce : préoccupations des managers et pratiques de design thinking", *Actes du congrès de l'Association Française du Marketing*, Marrakech, 2015.

[JAC 21] JACOB F., PEZ V., VOLLE P., "Principes, modalités, apports et limites de la Design Science Research en marketing – application illustrative au pilotage des parcours clients", *Recherche et Applications en Marketing*, vols. 37–2, pp. 1–30, 2021.

[LAR 17] LARIVIÈRE B., BOWEN D., ANDREASSEN T.-W. et al., "Service encounter 2.0: An investigation into the roles of technology, employees and customers", *Journal of Business Research*, vol. 79, pp. 238–246, 2017.

[LEM 16] LEMON K.-N., VERHOEF P.-C., "Understanding customer experience throughout the customer journey", *Journal of Marketing*, vol. 80, pp. 69–96, 2016.

[LUK 18] LUK S.-T., LIU B.-S., LI E.-L., "Effect of multilevel trust on effort-in-use and service co-design behavior", *Journal of Services Marketing*, vol. 32, no. 4, pp. 505–519, 2018.

[NIC 20] NICOD L., LLOSA S., BOWEN D., "Customer proactive training vs customer reactive training in retail store settings: Effects on script proficiency, customer satisfaction, and sales volume", *Journal of Retailing and Consumer Services*, vol. 55, pp. 102–136, 2020.

[REV 15] REVAT R., ROEDERER C., "Expérience extrême et vulnérabilité du consommateur : l'organisation des obsèques d'un proche", *Actes du congrès de l'Association Française du Marketing*, Marrakech, 2015.

[SHO 84] SHOSTACK L., "Designing services that deliver", *Harvard Business Review*, vol. 1, pp. 133–139, 1984.

[VAL 20] VALL M.-R., "Rapport d'information fait au nom de la mission d'information sur la lutte contre l'illectronisme et pour l'inclusion numérique", *SÉNAT*, no. 711, 2020.

[VOO 17] VOORHEES C.-M., FOMBELLE P.-W., GREGOIRE Y. et al., "Service encounters, experiences and the customer journey: Defining the field and a call to expand our lens", *Journal of Business Research*, vol. 79, pp. 269–280, 2017.

[WUN 20] WÜNDERLICH N.-V., HOGREVE J., CHOWDHURY I.-N. et al., "Overcoming vulnerability: Channel design strategies to alleviate vulnerability perceptions in customer journeys", *Journal of Business Research*, vol. 116, pp. 377–386, 2020.

11

The Patient Experience

Customer experience has been the subject of growing interest over the last decade among researchers and practitioners in strategy and marketing, for whom understanding the customer experience has become a major objective [BEC 20]. From the in-store experience to the tourist experience via the digital experience, the customer experience raises many questions about the experience lived by consumers and how it is valued. However, not much research has addressed the question of patient experience.

The usefulness and legitimacy of transposing the principles and concepts of marketing to the healthcare field, where marketing has long been dismissed for its mercantile connotations, are now recognized by healthcare organizations and developed both in terms of academic research and operationalization in the field. In particular, the health democracy movement, which is developing in France and aspires to strengthen patients' rights and develop their autonomy, is leading healthcare organizations to rethink patients' healthcare journeys and to think about programs aimed at making patients more autonomous in managing their disease (disease management). While the theoretical framework of Service Dominant Logic[1] can be mobilized to provide a better understanding of the patient-oriented service [COU 16], we need to shed new light on the analysis of patient behavior from an experiential perspective, taking into account the cognitive, affective, symbolic and social dimensions of the patient's experience. A new framework for analyzing patient behavior is proposed, using a holistic approach based on patient experience, in the light of the experiential model of Holbrook and Hirschman [HOL 82].

Chapter written by Stéphanie VERFAY.

1 The Service Dominant Logic approach considers the offer not in the form of products associated with services, but in the form of a global service in which the product is merely a facilitating element that enables the overall service offering to be built up [COU 16].

This chapter is part of transformative service research (TSR), which studies the emergence and development of services designed to improve the well-being of individuals, society and ecosystems in general [AND 18]. The ability of a service to achieve the well-being objectives illustrated by TSR depends on the quality of the service's conception, particularly in health services [AND 18].

11.1. From the health service to the patient experience

11.1.1. *Patient satisfaction as a starting point*

The patient is a user of the health service who benefits from a range of services, the basic service of which is care, with the aim of preventing, treating or maintaining their health [BEN 17]. Taking patient satisfaction into account is an essential legal requirement for French hospitals (article L.710.1.1 of order no. 96-346 of April 24, 1996, which stipulates that all healthcare establishments must carry out regular satisfaction assessments), and is mainly based on a comparative evaluation of the performance of the various attributes of the healthcare offering [MER 09].

Satisfaction was conceptualized by Oliver [OLI 81] as an assessment based on the expectations confirmation/disconfirmation model. A major determinant of satisfaction lies in the quality of service, the assessment of which is based on the comparison of service perceptions with service expectations. This is essentially a cognitive assessment. The patient subjectively assesses service quality on the basis of their expectations. The assessment of patient satisfaction, in the context of a hospitalization experience, can thus result from a process of evaluating the perceived quality of interpersonal relations with staff, the physical environment, procedures and the technical quality of care [MER 09]. Satisfaction survey-type tools provide global or partial information on patient satisfaction, and complementary approaches, such as Llosa's tetra-class model [LLO 97], provide a more managerial analysis of the levers for action to improve patient satisfaction, specifying the extent to which each element of the service contributes to satisfaction and dissatisfaction [LLO 97].

However, Oliver [OLI 97] points out that it can be difficult, if not impossible, to assess the quality of a service that has a strong technical dimension, or that the user may not wish to evaluate it so as not to have to face a situation of cognitive dissonance in the event of a result contrary to expectations. In the context of a healthcare service, it may be difficult for the patient to assess negatively a service on which their health depends. Similarly, assessing satisfaction can prove complex when emotions are predominant, as satisfaction measurement tools are generally based on a cognitive assessment of satisfaction. However, unlike service quality, which is based on an essentially cognitive assessment, satisfaction is more experiential, both cognitive and affective [GAB 14].

In particular, when it comes to evaluating a long consumption experience or repeated experiences over time, a dynamic approach to satisfaction shows that satisfaction evolves over time, and that the relative weight of affective attributes decreases with cumulative experience, in favor of cognitive attributes of satisfaction [WHI 10]. In addition, global assessments of patient satisfaction are prone to bias and difficult to interpret; it would be preferable to adopt measures focused on the patient experience such as the Consumer Assessment of Healthcare Providers and Systems (CAHPS) developed in the United States.

This calls for a rethink of the tools used to measure patient satisfaction within healthcare establishments, and to approach this measurement differently, by looking at the patient's experience and adopting a more experiential approach to satisfaction. Today, it is essential to understand patient experience as a whole, across all its dimensions – cognitive, affective, sensory, social and symbolic – and to integrate it into a patient-centered management approach with a dual objective. The first can improve patient care by better listening to and understanding the patient's experience. The second can guide the patient's decision-making process; the patient cannot be forced to undergo medical follow-up or treatment or stay in a care facility, and there must be free consent for the healthcare pathway best suited to them. The aim is to trigger a genuine organizational transition in healthcare establishments, through action plans designed for and with the patient, and guided by the patient experience.

11.1.2. *The patient from an experiential perspective*

In the experiential approach conceptualized by Holbrook and Hirschman [HOL 82] or Pine and Gilmore [PIN 98], experience is seen as a subjective perception by the consumer [BEC 20]. In their original work, Holbrook and Hirschman [HOL 82] mobilized a "fantasies–feelings–fun" analytical framework to study consumer behavior toward products or services that are sources of sensory pleasure and emotion, in the context of a search for hedonic experiences. This analytical framework has led to a focus on gratifying experiences and their hedonic benefits, but the scope of the experiential approach can be extended to other types of experience, notably in the social field, and more generally to all experiences that form part of the consumer's daily life, including more trivial experiences that are likely to be evaluated negatively [GAB 14].

The experiential approach thus makes it possible to go beyond the purely functional benefits of the patient experience and take into account the symbolic and affective dimensions of this emotionally charged experience, which is all the more significant as it directly affects the individual's health [BEN 17]. Healthcare services generate intimate experiences strongly linked to emotions, which can be marked by uncertainty, vulnerability and powerlessness due to the patient's lack of medical knowledge [AND 18]. The patient can be considered as a consumer, a user of the healthcare service, living a consumption experience that has the particularity of not stemming from a desire to consume but from the obligation to treat or maintain good health [BEN 17].

The patient experience takes the patient's perspective to better understand the patient's reality and feelings by integrating the emotions felt throughout the healthcare journey. Instead of the term "care journey", which refers to clinical actions, we prefer the notion of "health journey", which integrates a broader scope of actions to contribute to a positive state of health [MIN 18]. The patient experience is therefore not limited to a stay in a healthcare facility, and can be viewed from a longitudinal perspective, as proposed by Arnould et al. [ARN 02]: anticipatory experience (e.g. information seeking), purchasing experience (e.g. choice of practitioner or healthcare facility), lived experience (e.g. hospitalization) and recall experience (e.g. memories evoked during a discussion or recalled when approaching a new period of hospitalization).

11.1.3. *Designing a meaningful experience*

Patients, as consumers of healthcare, are no longer seen as passive users of healthcare services, but as active co-creators of their healthcare experience in a patient-centered approach. The co-creation of value with patients has been the focus of recent work in TSR, which studies the relationship between service and well-being to create value that generates inspiring change, with the aim of improving the well-being of individuals, communities and the ecosystem through interactions between service providers and consumers [AND 18]. In particular, research is investigating how patients can take control of their experience of healthcare services and develop co-production behaviors over time, especially for treatment compliance [SPA 15].

However, in the specific context of healthcare services, patients need to be helped and guided, and the ability of a health service to achieve the well-being outcomes illustrated by TSR depends on the quality of the design of the service experience [AND 18]. It is a question of (re)thinking and designing the patient experience to enable healthcare services to improve the mutual well-being of all participants in the healthcare system – patients, carers and caregivers [AND 18].

The co-production of the patient experience can be envisaged in a managerial approach through a strategic approach to *experiential design* [PIN 98]. In fact, experience is created in the patient's mind in particular through the impressions formed from the cues around them, which contribute to creating an experience perceived as pleasant or unpleasant by the patient. The strategy of adding an experiential touch/design to the patient's environment can thus help to create a meaningful experience throughout the patient journey. This patient journey must be designed by identifying the key moments that generate strong emotions in the patient. The success of an experiential strategy, particularly for ordinary utilitarian or functional consumer experiences, lies in the ability of organizations to take into account the practices of individuals and "produce" experiential contexts capable of delivering an experience that creates meaning and value [FIL 22].

The patient experience must create value. A perceived value approach, based on patient experience, can therefore shed new light on the value that patients can derive from the experience resulting from their interaction with healthcare services. From a managerial point of view, it is an interesting analytical tool for identifying levers for action.

11.2. Enhancing the value of the patient experience

11.2.1. *The perceived value of the patient experience*

The notion of perceived value of experience emerges naturally from the experiential approach, which considers experience as a subjective perception [BEC 20]. A better understanding of the patient's lived experience and how the patient can value this experience is essential for the design and production of an optimal and meaningful patient experience.

In the marketing literature, there are two main approaches to perceived value: purchase value, which is formed before the acquisition of a good, and consumption value, which is formed during and after consumption [RIV 12]. Purchase value is based on a utilitarian aggregate approach based on a cost/benefit trade-off, while consumption value is based on an experiential analytical approach in terms of sources of perceived value. A mixed approach to perceived value has been developed from these two conceptualizations, combining the cost/benefit trade-off of purchase value with components of consumption value [RIV 12]. The mixed approach is particularly interesting in the healthcare field to define and measure the perceived value of actions or programs implemented with patients, such as a therapeutic patient education program which can be valued through perceived benefits (cognitive, utilitarian, psychological and relational benefits) and associated perceived costs (psychological and emotional costs) [LAB 21].

The multi-dimensional analytical approach nevertheless remains relevant for identifying and defining the dimensions of perceived value generated by the patient experience offered by healthcare services. The value of the patient experience corresponds to the value resulting from the experience that patients derive from their interaction with healthcare services. Holbrook's experiential analytical approach [HOL 94] proposes a typology of the perceived value resulting from a consumer experience based on combinations of three distinctions (self-oriented/other-oriented value; extrinsic/intrinsic value; active/reactive value):

– self-oriented value (the consumption experience is valued for the personal interest and benefits it can bring to oneself) versus other-oriented value (the consumption experience is valued for the benefits it can bring to others);

– extrinsic value (the consumer experience is a means to an end, external to itself) versus intrinsic value (the consumer experience is valued for its own sake and is an end in itself);

– active value (the consumer actively participates in the consumption experience) versus reactive value (the consumer responds passively to the consumption experience).

In their managerial approach, Pine and Gilmore [PIN 98] focus on the self-oriented experience and propose a typology of experience based on two dimensions very similar to Holbrook's extrinsic/intrinsic and active/reactive dimensions [HOL 94]: the consumer's connection with the experience (absorption versus immersion) and the consumer's participation in the experience (passive versus active). The experience can thus be valued by the consumer as an entertainment experience (absorption/passive), an educational experience (absorption/active), an esthetic experience (immersion/ passive) or an escapist experience (immersion/active).

11.2.2. *A typology of the value of the patient experience*

Based on the original work on the value of the consumption experience by Holbrook [HOL 94] and Pine and Gilmore [PIN 98], a typology of the value of the patient experience is proposed based on extrinsic/intrinsic and active/reactive dimensions. This is based on a theoretical reflection on the perceived value of the experience oriented toward the patient, and involves four components of the value of the patient experience (see Figure 11.1): the socio-educational value, the value of excellence, the value of communitas and the esthetic value. This typology thus highlights four ways of enhancing the experience lived by the patient.

The *socio-educational value* corresponds to the symbolic and social meaning that the experience has for the patient, through the status of patient (or sick person) that this experience confers on them, integrating the educational dimension of the experience which consists of learning to manage this patient (or sick person) status and any resulting care. For patients who value the socio-educational nature of the experience, through its extrinsic dimension (experience understood as a means and not an end in itself), the experience can be promoted by better support for the patient in the management of their patient (or sick) status and the active participation of the patient.

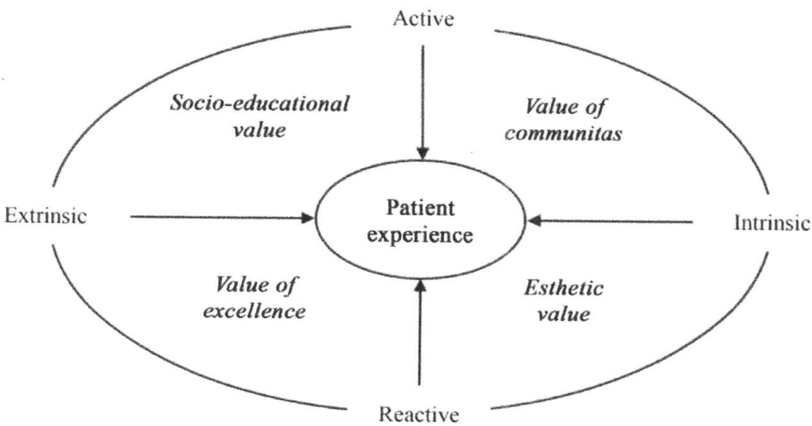

Figure 11.1. *Typology of the value of the patient experience*

The *value of excellence* reflects a reactive attitude in which the patient values the know-how and expertise of caregivers in caring for and supporting them and their family. Perceived excellence reinforces trust in caregivers and reassures the patient. The patient then values the experience from a utilitarian perspective. Patients who value the excellence of experience, through its extrinsic and reactive dimension, will be more receptive to the skills and reputation of the care team. Minvielle [MIN 18], in his study of the dynamics of collective work in the healthcare sector, identifies the need to develop organizational skills in addition to medical skills. Valuing experience here does not necessarily involve active patient participation. The patient responds passively to the experience.

In the *value of communitas*, the patient experience is valued for its own sake, for the experiential stimulation it provides, through the spirit of communitas, social links and sharing with other patients. The patient participates in a collective experience, notably through group sessions or activities that can reinforce their sense of belonging to a social group. For patients who value communitas, the intrinsic value of the patient experience (experience seen as an end in itself), the social dimension is a determining factor in the patient experience. The patient will particularly value interactions with people with whom they are in immediate contact (e.g. carers or other patients) who can play an important role in influencing the patient experience, for example by informing them about the service to come, serving as a staging post for the patient or acting as a distractor or disrupter. Valuing the patient experience through harmony also relies on the patient's active participation, and valuing the experience can be enhanced by a co-productive approach with patients.

The esthetic value of the experience refers to the patient's interpretation of the environment and to the sensory experience that arouses the patient's emotions (e.g. the appearance of the surroundings, smells, lighting, music, ergonomics of the premises, catering). For patients who value the esthetic value of the experience, through its intrinsic and reactive dimension, the appropriation of the experience can be facilitated by taking into account the patient's experiential environment. Aesthetic elements can be used to create a reassuring universe and a pleasant atmosphere for the patient by recreating familiar landmarks. In this case, the experience does not require the patient's active participation. Instead, the patient is more receptive to the experiential environment offered.

11.2.3. *Experience value as a lever for appropriation of the patient experience*

When entering a healthcare facility for the first time, the patient finds themselves in a vulnerable situation, in a new universe likely to be a source of stress and negative emotions. This immersion in an unusual experiential context, sometimes experienced by the patient, plunges them into a symbolic and emotional system that healthcare establishments need to better master in order to make the patient experience as pleasant as possible.

According to Carù and Cova [CAR 03], immersion is an important moment experienced by the consumer resulting from a process of the experience being appropriated. While the concept of immersion is understood in marketing as "a thematized, enclosed and secure situation" in hyperreal contexts [CAR 03], it is more, in the context of the patient experience, about supporting patient immersion and promoting access to an optimal and meaningful experience. As Pine and Gilmore [PIN 98] point out, the experience is subjective, experienced from the inside by the individual, but it is possible to act on the circumstances and environment of the experience. It therefore seems essential to take into consideration the levers for enhancing the patient experience in order to improve the appropriation of the experience by patients and thus promote their adherence and compliance [COU 16].

The patient experience should therefore be understood more in terms of how it is valued and experienced by the patient, through the components of patient experience, based on the extrinsic/intrinsic and active/reactive dimensions of value.

When extrinsic value is influential for the patient (socio-educational value; value of excellence), the experience is seen as a means to an end, not an end in itself. In this case, the patient will particularly value elements external to the experience itself, such as educational information or the skills of the caregivers. When the intrinsic value of the experience predominates (communitas value; esthetic value), the patient will be more sensitive to the social and aesthetic dimensions of the experience.

Enhancing the patient experience can be based on the patient's active participation (socio-educational value; communitas value). Recent research emphasizes the need to develop an organizational culture that supports and promotes active patient participation in the management and production of their healthcare journey [MIN 18]. Mifsud et al. [MIF 19] recommend encouraging the active participation of patients in healthcare programs, as this enables them to take psychological ownership of their program, thus promoting adherence. However, not all patients value this participation in the co-production of their experience in the same way. The appropriation of the experience does not necessarily involve active patient participation, when the patient values the experience in the reactive dimension, responding passively to the experience (value of excellence; esthetic value).

11.3. Conclusion

Understanding the patient experience is a major academic and managerial challenge. The service logic inherent in healthcare services can evolve toward a more experiential approach, and the theoretical framework of the experiential model – initially developed by Holbrook and Hirschman [HOL 82] – can be extended beyond the search for gratifying and hedonic experiences, to the patient experience. The typology of the value of patient experience highlights four ways in which patients value their experience: socio-educational value, excellence value, communitas value and esthetic value. This typology is based on the two extrinsic/intrinsic and active/reactive dimensions of value, which can be relevant levers for appropriating the patient experience.

This theoretical reflection on the value of the patient experience paves the way for strategic and operational managerial applications concerning the healthcare journey to promote compliance with therapeutic patient education programs and improve patient well-being and experience. An interesting managerial perspective concerns patient segmentation and the positioning of the healthcare offering.

Patients are traditionally differentiated by their clinical, genetic and biological characteristics to define therapeutic strategies, but the patient-centered care movement, which introduces the need to take into account patients' needs, demands and preferences, is increasingly complementing this clinical approach [MIN 18]. Patient classification based on value components of the patient experience would enable strategic thinking to take into account the way in which each patient values their experience. The patient experience value approach can also be used to identify areas for positioning the healthcare offering. A therapeutic program could thus position itself around one or more components of the value of the experience, optimizing the experience according to how the patient values it (spaces for meetings and exchanges between patients for the value of communitas or a more utilitarian approach emphasizing the quality of care for the value of excellence, for example).

However, a number of questions remain unanswered. We need to explore whether the different perceived values of the patient experience can be combined, and whether they take on fluctuating roles over the course of the same patient journey; in other words, whether one value is predominant at certain points in the pathway, or whether it is a more global valuation of each patient's experience. Practitioners can explore opportunities for improvement in the patient journey by drawing on patients' experience, based on real-life situations and the feelings reported by patients, beyond the pathology itself. We need to develop a culture of collaboration with patients within healthcare establishments in order to adapt practices to take better account of the patient experience, but also collaboration between healthcare establishments to develop exchanges on practices.

It is also important to remember that the experiential approach considers the consumer experience from a longitudinal perspective: anticipation, purchase, experience and memory [ARN 02]. The patient experience can similarly be understood from a longitudinal perspective. Can perceived value evolve over the course of the patient's experience? Spanjol et al. [SPA 15] have shown the importance of integrating the temporal element into prolonged service experiences in the context of patient medication compliance. The question of anticipating the future patient experience also arises. Could anticipating the patient experience, which is likely to be associated with negative emotions, leave traces in affective memory that would be reactivated and integrated into the actual experience, thus degrading the patient experience as it unfolds in real time? What is more, the patient experience is not limited to what happens at the point of consultation or hospitalization, but includes all interactions upstream (anticipation) and downstream (return home). Spanjol et al. [SPA 15] have shown that much of the extended co-production with patients takes place outside the organization of services. The patient experience must therefore be considered in a broader spectrum, which raises the question of the continuity of the patient experience outside healthcare structures. This includes the use of digital tools and hybrid physical/digital experiences.

Finally, the typology of patient experience is based on theoretical reflection on self-oriented perceived value. It would be interesting to complete this reflection on perceived value oriented toward others, particularly appropriate in the context of patient support, by studying the perceived value of the patient experience oriented toward the patient's family and caregivers.

11.4. References

[AND 18] ANDERSON S., NASR L., RAYBURN S.W., "Transformative service research and service design: Synergistic effects in healthcare", *The Service Industries Journal*, vol. 38, no. 1/2, pp. 99–113, 2018.

[ARN 02] ARNOULD E.J., PRICE L., ZINKHAN G.M., *Consumers*, McGraw Hill, Irwin, 2002.

[BEC 20] BECKER L., JAAKKOLA E., "Customer experience: Fundamental premises and implications for research", *Journal of the Academy of Marketing Science*, vol. 48, no. 4, pp. 630–648, 2020.

[BEN 17] BENOIT C., *L'expérience patient, La levée d'un tabou pour une meilleure prise en charge des patients*, Arnaud Franel Editions, Paris, 2017.

[CAR 03] CARÙ A., COVA B., "Approche empirique de l'immersion dans l'expérience de consommation : les opérations d'appropriation", *Recherche et Applications en Marketing*, vol. 18, no. 2, pp. 47–65, 2003.

[COU 16] COUTELLE-BRILLET P., DES GARETS V., MAUBISSON L. et al., "L'appropriation d'une innovation thérapeutique dans le cadre d'une maladie chronique : enjeux individuels et organisationnels", *Journal de Gestion et d'Economie Médicales*, vol. 34, no. 4, pp. 195–213, 2016.

[FIL 22] FILSER M., ROEDERER C., "L'expérience et après ?", in FILSER M., ROEDERER C. (eds), *L'expérience : objet académique et réalités managériales*, EMS, Caen, 2022.

[GAB 14] GABRIEL P., DIVARD R., LE GALL-ELY M. et al., *Marketing des services*, Dunod, Paris, 2014.

[HOL 82] HOLBROOK M.B., HIRSCHMAN E.C., "The experiential aspects of consumption: consumer fantasies, feelings, and fun", *Journal of Consumer Research*, vol. 9, no. 2, pp. 132–140, 1982.

[HOL 94] HOLBROOK M.B., "The nature of customer value: An axiology of services in the consumption experience", in RUST R.T., OLIVER R.L. (eds), *Service Quality: New Directions in Theory and Practice*, Sage, Thousand Oaks, 1994.

[LAB 21] LABBÉ-PINLON B., LOMBART C., BERGER V. et al., "Mesure de la valeur perçue de l'Éducation Thérapeutique en oncologie", *Journal de gestion et d'économie de la sante*, vol. 5, no. 5, pp. 229–254, 2021.

[LLO 97] LLOSA S., "L'analyse de la contribution des éléments du service à la satisfaction : un modèle tétraclasse", *Décisions Marketing*, vol. 10, pp. 81–88, 1997.

[MER 09] MERDINGER-RUMPLER C., "Contribution des éléments de service à la satisfaction du patient hospitalisé : une application du modèle tétraclasse", *Décisions Marketing*, vol. 53, pp. 43–52, 2009.

[MIF 19] MIFSUD M., MOLINES M., CASES A.S. et al., "It's MY health care program: enhancing patient adherence through psychological ownership", *Social Science & Medicine*, vol. 232, pp. 307–315, 2019.

[MIN 18] MINVIELLE E., *Le patient et le système : en quête d'une organisation sur mesure : approches innovantes du parcours de santé*, Seli Arslan, Paris, 2018.

[OLI 81] OLIVER R.L., "Measurement and evaluation of satisfaction processes in retail settings", *Journal of Retailing*, vol. 57, pp. 25–48, 1981.

[OLI 97] OLIVER R.L., *Satisfaction: A Behavioral Perspective on the Consumer*, McGraw Hill, New York, 1997.

[PIN 98] PINE J., GILMORE J.H., "Welcome to the experience economy", *Harvard Business Review*, vol. 76, no. 4, pp. 97–105, 1998.

[RIV 12] RIVIÈRE A., MENCARELLI R., "Vers une clarification théorique de la notion de valeur perçue en marketing", *Recherche et Applications en Marketing*, vol. 27, no. 3, pp. 97–123, 2012.

[SPA 15] SPANJOL J., CUI A.S., NAKATA C. et al., "Co-production of prolonged, complex, and negative services: An examination of medication adherence in chronically ill individuals", *Journal of Service Research*, vol. 18, no. 3, pp. 284–302, 2015.

[WHI 10] WHITE C.J., "The impact of emotions on service quality, satisfaction, and positive word-of-mouth intentions over time", *Journal of Marketing Management*, vol. 26, no. 5/6, pp. 381–394, 2010.

12

Adopting Ethical Sales Behavior

In buyer–seller B2B relationships, salespeople are often the interface of the relationship. This is why the question of ethics in sales behavior is so important. Ethics require an individual to behave in accordance with the rules of philosophical morality, in particular what is considered right or wrong. In sales, ethical behavior refers to a set of social standards such as fairness, honesty and transparency in dealings with customers. Roman and Munuera define ethical behavior as "fair and honest actions that enable the salesperson to foster long-term relationships with customers based on customer satisfaction and trust" [ROM 05]. These actions include selling products that are truly adapted to customers' needs, providing accurate product information and selling without pressure. However, salespeople are regularly confronted with situations that force them to arbitrate between multiple interests, linked to their organization's objectives, their own sales objectives and the customer's interests. This sometimes leads to unethical behavior.

The first part of this chapter focuses on how unethical behavior emerges, pointing out the dilemmas faced by salespeople and explaining how influence techniques can be misused to manipulate customers. The second part sheds light on ethical sales behavior and the conditions that foster its emergence, and shows that ethics enhance salespeople's well-being, customer satisfaction and sales performance.

12.1. Unethical temptation among salespeople

Unethical behavior is the result of dilemmas faced by salespeople. In order to win customer orders, they may have to turn certain principles of influence into manipulative techniques.

Chapter written by Eric JULIENNE.

12.1.1. *Salespeople's ethical dilemmas*

There are a variety of situations that expose salespeople to ethical dilemmas more than other professions. Lavorata and Nilles (2005) give an example of a scenario that exposes the salesperson to a dilemma [LAV 05]:

> You have sold a photocopier to one of your customers. You realize that you have given them inaccurate information about this machine, in particular about an option that was necessary for the customer, such as automatic sheet stapling, which is no longer available on this new machine. The contract has already been signed by the various parties involved, and has just been invoiced. How do you react?

The dilemma arises from the need for the salesperson to choose between the sometimes conflicting interests of the customer, the employer and themselves.

Several factors encourage unethical behavior [HAN 09]:

– Salespeople are the interface between the buying and selling organizations, so it is normal for ethical conflicts to arise when it comes to finding the right balance between the interests of the two organizations.

– Salespeople often work very independently; their distance from their hierarchy reduces ethical constraints and the sense of belonging to a group, with its expected normative influences in ethical matters.

– Salespeople are under intense pressure to achieve their sales targets, and ethical issues arise from this pressure.

– Sales managers have little regard for ethical transgressions when salespeople are meeting sales targets, especially when they themselves are under pressure from the bottom line.

– Salespeople are often involved in negotiations with their customers that lead them to exaggerate and dishonestly justify their positions.

Box 12.1 tells the real-life story of an ethical dilemma and illustrates the factors that encourage unethical behavior.

> My name is Elliot. I am a B2B salesman for a well-known computer manufacturer. I was consulted by the IT director of an SME about replacing a machine from a rival supplier. So I searched my range for the machine best suited to the customer's performance needs. I spotted a model that should theoretically be suitable in view of its technical specifications, but I had serious doubts as to whether the performance was really sufficient, as there is often a discrepancy between the advertised features and the actual performance. Ethically, it would have been better to advise the customer to choose a

higher performance machine. But this would have increased the price and seriously compromised the chances of making the sale in the face of numerous competitors who were very aggressive on price. I was behind on my sales targets, and a quick calculation made me half-think what I could earn in commissions if I made the sale. What is more, my manager used to say that the most important thing is to sell, and then deal with the problems – that is how business is done, otherwise it does not get done. All the salespeople in the team are steeped in this "chasing" culture, with little regard for customer satisfaction. It is about who can show the most value to management by demonstrating their ability to land new contracts, or "new business" as they call it...

Faced with the dilemma of whether to protect the customer's interests or make the sale, I decided in favor of the sale, and so produced a quotation with the undersized model. Unfortunately for me, I still missed the sale. Sometime later, on the occasion of another visit to this customer, the IT manager said to me: "You deliberately undersized the machine you proposed in your quotation, but I realized it and it didn't work". I have always felt ashamed of this conversation, coupled with an impression of commercial clumsiness, which probably contributed to the failure of this negotiation.

Box 12.1. *Real-life story of an ethical dilemma*

Among the unethical procedures used by salespeople, the literature includes the abusive use of the principles of influence developed by social psychologist Cialdini [CIA 21].

12.1.2. *The six principles of influence according to Cialdini*

Cialdini explains the six principles of influence that help salespeople to close a sale, to get the famous "yes" from a customer. Cialdini is not interested in the rational, objective arguments that appeal to the customer's conscious reason, but in the cognitive biases that influence the decision-making process. We are all – citizens, consumers or B2B customers – subjected to a deluge of information that is impossible to process and analyze, given the limits of our cognitive capacities. So how can we make a rational decision that takes all criteria into account? To compensate for the limits of our reasoning, the human brain borrows mental shortcuts, which can be summed up in six main principles:

– According to *the principle of reciprocity*, an individual who receives a gift or favor incurs a kind of psychological debt, and feels a moral obligation to repay that debt. A commercial gesture, for example, can encourage loyalty. A major effort in negotiating a contract may, in return, lead to a greater willingness to compromise on the part of the customer.

– *The principle of commitment and coherence* states that most individuals wish to be and appear to those around them to be coherent in their words, beliefs, attitudes and actions. This is why obtaining a first commitment from a customer (the acceptance of a first visit or order) leads to the hope of obtaining a second commitment, in the same direction and perhaps even of greater magnitude. For example, if the customer accepts the principle of a product trial, it would make sense for them to place an order if they are satisfied; otherwise, it would be difficult for them to justify their decision to try it out.

– According to *the principle of social proof*, individuals tend to refer to the behavior of others to know what they should think or do themselves. When you are unsure of what behavior to adopt or what decision to make, imitating others is reassuring, especially when they are numerous and similar to you. On the Internet, customer reviews are a good illustration of the principle of social proof. Similarly, in B2B, testimonials from former customers influence the decisions of prospective customers.

– *The principle of friendship* is based on the fact that people tend to accept requests from those they know and appreciate. It is hard to refuse a favor or service requested by a friend. So if the salesperson has succeeded in making a friend of their customer, it will be easier for them to obtain information about the customer's organization or competitors, and also easier to obtain orders from the customer. In B2C, sales meetings (Tupperware, Avon, Thermomix, etc.) are a perfect illustration of this principle: they are conducted by a brand ambassador "host" who invites their circle of friends or acquaintances to meetings at their home.

– *The principle of authority* stipulates that humans – who are by nature social animals – are naturally inclined to accept the requests of a person who, by virtue of their expertise, knowledge, wisdom or power, embodies authority. The car driver obeys the uniformed policeman. The student obeys the teacher's orders. The salesperson who embodies this authority – through their expertise, their product knowledge diplomas, their suit, or even their car – increases their ability to influence the customer.

– Finally, according to *the principle of scarcity*, individuals value more those opportunities which seem to be not very accessible or available. This principle derives directly from the psychological mechanism of reactance, which makes us desire things more when they are rare or unavailable, thus reducing our freedom of choice. In commercial terms, displaying a limited stock of products tends to speed up the customer's decision-making process ("hurry up before they run out!"), as does highlighting a promotional program ("a price reduction valid only this week").

The principles of influence can be used by salespeople as instruments of manipulation. This raises the question of the boundary between the two.

12.1.3. *Influence or manipulation: what are the differences?*

The principles of influence set out by Cialdini can be used by the salesperson in an entirely ethical way. For example, reciprocity and friendship are at the heart of any sincere relationship. It is normal for the salesperson to highlight the positive opinions of other customers in order to convince them, or to inform them of the current (and soon to end!) promotional program in order to encourage them to buy, and to show them how not to let a great opportunity pass them by. These behaviors are ethical whenever the seller's intention is benevolent, the technique used to influence helps the customer make the best decision and the resulting sharing of value is equitable [LAC 83].

On the other hand, unethical behavior occurs when the principle of influence is falsified, when it is fabricated by the seller in order to obtain the order. Setting an artificially high price and granting a large discount in the hope of obtaining an order (principle of reciprocity) is unethical, as is the fabrication of false customer reviews (the principle of social proof) or the display of a limited stock of products (the principle of scarcity) when in fact there is stock in reserve.

In this way, the principles of influence can be hijacked to become principles of manipulation. However, we propose to distinguish them using two criteria:

– Manipulation is based on lies, dissimulation and dishonesty, whereas ethical influence exploits a situation without distorting it (e.g. product stock is really limited).

– Manipulation involves the manipulator sacrificing the customer's interests for their own benefit, thus creating a blatant imbalance in the sharing of value. Ethical influence, on the other hand, is based on the intention to share value equitably.

Salespeople would be wrong to give up using the principles of influence when it is ethical to do so, because they are sales accelerators, helping them to achieve their objectives without sacrificing the customer's interests. Unfortunately, ethical thinking is too often sidelined when it comes to presenting the principles of influence. Numerous blogs and books teach salespeople how to influence their customers, without warning them that ethics should be at the heart of the method. Cialdini's original intention was, on the contrary, to give customers the weapons to better thwart attempts at manipulation by unscrupulous salespeople [CIA 21].

Unethical temptation stems from the attempt to generate short-term sales. But it would be inaccurate to think that dishonesty always benefits salespeople and the organizations that employ them, because it generates long-term costs. Victims of manipulation usually end up realizing that they have been cheated, and this has longer term repercussions on the supplier's reputation and sales. What is more, honest salespeople can experience psychological discomfort if they work in an organization that, in one way or another, encourages dishonesty. This can lead to hidden costs (job dissatisfaction, absenteeism, turnover, etc.). Conversely, while unscrupulous salespeople have no problem working in such an organization, their dishonesty is also likely to be directed at their employer, creating a general climate of mistrust that forces the latter to set up costly systems for over-monitoring, etc., which dishonest salespeople do their best to circumvent! There are so many hidden costs that argue in favor of ethics. Organizational efficiency reasons add up to moral reasons.

The first part of this chapter explains what unethical behavior is, the dilemmas that explain it and the differences between influence and manipulation. The second part focuses on ethical behavior.

12.2. Creating ethical behavior

First, we show that customer-oriented selling is at the heart of ethical behavior. Then, we look at the factors that encourage its adoption. Finally, we highlight the positive consequences of ethical selling for all stakeholders.

12.2.1. *Customer orientation at the heart of sales ethics*

The customer-oriented salesperson's main aim is to develop long-term customer satisfaction. They want to help customers make purchasing decisions that truly meet their needs. They prefer to establish a climate of trust and mutual engagement with their customers, rather than using sales tricks and gimmicks with the sole motivation of generating short-term sales.

Customer orientation is not simply a state of mind, it manifests itself through a set of the salesperson's behaviors [HOM 11]: listening to the customer attentively to clearly identify their needs, adapting the presentation and proposal to the needs expressed, influencing customers by providing objective and transparent information on the benefits of products and services, managing conflicts that arise cooperatively by finding a solution that is fair to both parties and genuinely taking the customer's interests into account. Far from Cialdini's principles, the influence of the customer-oriented salesperson stems from these behaviors, which help to establish a climate of trust. A study by Julienne and Llosa categorizes customer-oriented behaviors as the salesperson's basic relational skills, that is, those required by customers [JUL 21]. In other words, customer orientation is a prerequisite for any lasting business relationship.

Sales orientation is the opposite of customer orientation. It means focusing on the product rather than the customer, pushing the product by embellishing the reality, selling as much as possible without worrying whether it meets the customer's needs or will satisfy them in the long term.

Box 12.2 provides a scheme for measuring customer orientation and sales orientation. The wording of the items itself shows that customer orientation is ethical and sales orientation is not.

What the customer-oriented salesperson says:

– I try to figure out what customer needs are;

– A good employee has to have the customer's best interest in mind;

– I try to bring a customer with a problem together with a product/service that helps solve that problem;

– I offer the product/service that is best suited to the customer's problem;

– I try to find out what kind of products/services will be most helpful to a customer.

What the sales-oriented salesperson says:

– I try to sell as much as I can rather than to satisfy my customer;

– It is necessary to stretch the truth in describing a product to a customer;

– I try to sell a customer all I can convince them to buy, even if I think it is more than a wise customer would buy;

– I paint too rosy a picture of my products/services to make them sound as good as possible;

– I decide what product/service to offer on the basis of what I can convince customers to accept, not on the basis of what will satisfy them in the long run.

Box 12.2. *Sellers' orientation scheme [THO 01]*

Traditionally, one stage considered particularly difficult for sales-oriented salespeople is that of closing the sale (hence the profusion of Cialdini-inspired techniques for obtaining the final order). The customer-oriented salesperson reduces this difficulty, as they spend time understanding the customer's needs and propose an adapted solution. There is no need to force the sale, which is concluded more naturally. This way of selling requires more mutual investment and time on the part of both the seller and the customer, but it creates value for both parties. Customer-oriented selling is effective not only for generating short-term sales, but also for creating a climate of trust conducive to building a lasting relationship.

In reading these lines, the sales practitioner may wonder whether customer orientation is compatible with the principles of influence. In other words, can both be used in the same sales meeting? When influence principles are used without customer orientation, they arouse suspicion in the customer ("are they trying to manipulate me?"). However, when they are combined with customer orientation, the customer perceives the salesperson's ethical character, which triggers the act of buying without generating the feeling of being manipulated. The customer-oriented salesperson therefore achieves more sales in the short term when they use the principles of influence ethically, and does so without damaging the climate of trust essential to the long-term relationship [JUL 17].

12.2.2. *How can the ethical behavior of salespeople be developed?*

Several factors contribute to the development of ethical sales behavior. They are located either at the level of the organization or at the level of the individual [FER 07]:

– The ethical climate of the organization involves the salespeople's perceptions about their organization's practices, procedures, norms and values that concern ethics and give salespeople an indication of what behavior is considered acceptable [JAR 15]. More specifically, the ethical climate is manifested, for example, by the existence of a written code of ethics, by management's clearly stated willingness to enforce it and sanction any deviant behavior accordingly, or by the existence of ethics training programs. Lavorata proposes a four-dimensional scale for measuring the ethical climate [LAV 07]: corporate ethical procedures, peer behavior, sales practices and compensation plans;

– Managers also contribute to developing ethical sales behavior [JAR 15]. As salespeople refer to these ethical behaviors as a model to be followed, they contribute to the socialization of salespeople, showing them what the company's norms and values are, as well as which behaviors are acceptable and which are not.

– The sales force compensation system consists of a set of rules that encourage salespeople to achieve the organization's objectives through the attainment of their own targets. Fixed remuneration is recommended when organizations wish to encourage salespeople to adopt a long-term orientation and spend time serving customers to develop sales in the future. In this case, the organization alone assumes the risk of lost sales, giving the salesperson more freedom to act ethically toward the customer. Conversely, remuneration with a high variable component, in the form of commissions, encourages salespeople to make short-term sales without taking the customer's interest into consideration, thus increasing the risk of unethical behavior [ROM 05].

– The sales force control system enables managers to evaluate not only sales performance, but also the achievement of more qualitative objectives, such as customer satisfaction or customer follow-up. When the control system can evaluate not only the achievement of objectives, but also the behavior of salespeople, then it can take into account how salespeople achieve sales targets, and issue mandatory ethical rules.

– The seller's cognitive moral development (CMD) is an individual explanatory variable. According to CMD theory [KOH 69], the moral decision-making process becomes more complex and sophisticated as individuals develop. There are six stages of development. In stages one and two, individuals are primarily concerned with punishment and reward. In stages three and four, the individual conforms to the moral rules emanating from society or the group to which they belong. In stages five and six, individuals are guided by their own convictions, by values or principles considered universal. Confronted with an ethical dilemma, the salesperson makes a decision with reference to the stage of development they are at: the higher the stage, the more ethical the behavior [ING 07].

– Finally, age is the last factor to explain salespeople's ethical behavior. Older salespeople tend to have stricter ethics, a less permissive interpretation of ethical rules, more advanced moral reflection and more experience in resolving ethical dilemmas. This link between age and ethical behavior has been established by a number of studies, but it is weaker than the influence of other factors.

12.2.3. *Ethics and business performance: how compatible are they?*

A central question debated by practitioners and researchers alike is whether ethical sales behavior enhances or detracts from salespeople's performance.

For some, there is an incompatibility, a tendency to arbitrate in favor of sales at the expense of ethics when ethical dilemmas arise, an idea according to which being too ethical is detrimental to performance.

While unethical behavior may win orders in the short term, most studies show that, in the longer term, ethics contribute to better business performance [HAN 09, EVA 12, BAT 15].

Figure 12.1 illustrates this point. The existence of an ethical climate and the resulting ethical behaviors improve salespeople's satisfaction. This in turn reduces their intention to leave their employer, lowers their stress levels and boosts their performance.

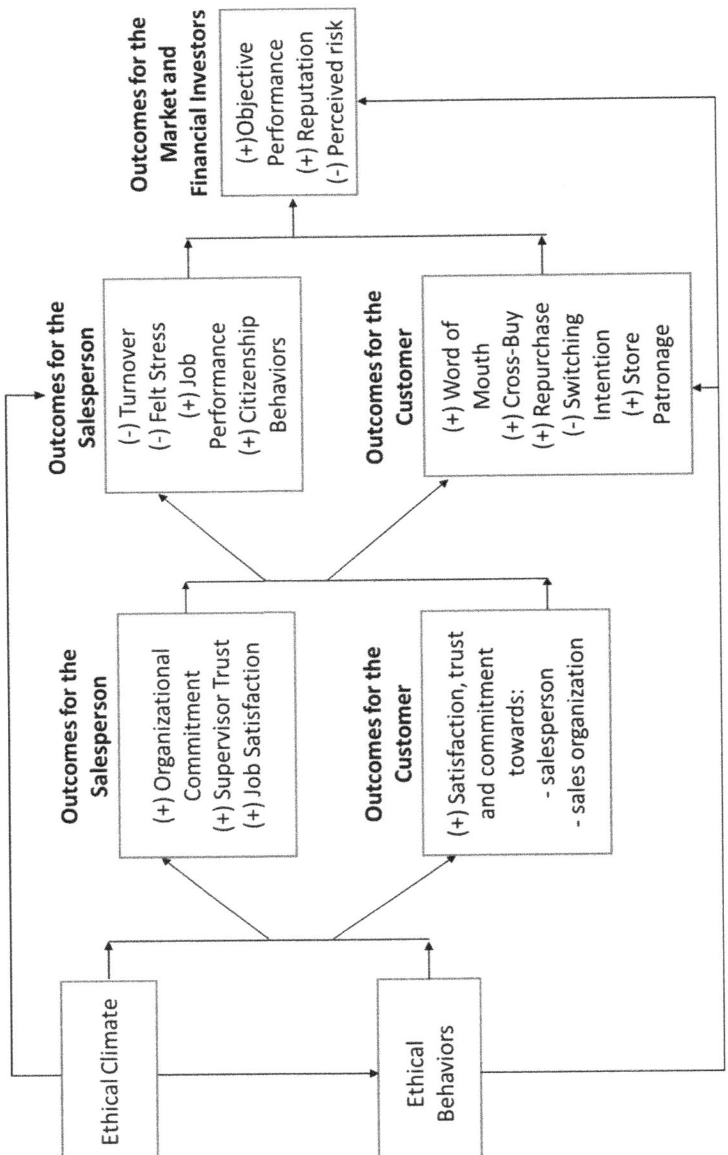

Figure 12.1. *Ethics improve performance [EVA 12]*

On the customer side, the perception of ethical behavior increases satisfaction, trust and commitment, and consequently promotes positive word-of-mouth, cross-selling, repurchase and loyalty, while decreasing the intention to leave the company for another supplier.

In the end, the company as a whole increases its performance, improves its reputation and reduces the perceived risk for both customers and financial investors.

12.3. Conclusion

To conclude this chapter on the ethical behavior of salespeople, it is appropriate to summarize and draw some lessons from the marketing literature about salespeople and sales organizations.

Three lessons concern salespeople:

– Salespeople's unethical tendencies come from the dilemmas they face. If they had no dilemmas, it would be easy for them to behave ethically.

– Salespeople often use techniques derived from Cialdini's principles of influence to close the sale, which in itself poses no problem. However, the ethical question arises when these techniques are based on lies and an unbalanced sharing of value. In this case, influence becomes manipulation.

– Customer orientation is ethical by nature, because it places customer satisfaction as an absolute priority and takes a long-term view of the relationship. It is this sales behavior that should be encouraged.

The adoption of ethical behavior is not the sole responsibility of salespeople. Sales organizations must transform themselves to embrace ethical salespeople and build sustainable growth through a shared interest with their customers. Here, we have three lessons for organizations:

– Management must play its full part in creating the right conditions, in particular an ethical climate (embodied, for example, in the code of ethics), the management style (which inspires salespeople and builds loyalty), a control system geared to behavior (and not just sales performance), a compensation system (which should not give excessive weight to variable pay, lest it reinforce ethical dilemmas) and the recruitment of salespeople (by including the level of moral development as a selection criterion).

– The ethical issue would be quickly settled if it were incompatible with commercial performance. Unethical behavior probably allows for some short-term commercial success, but in the longer term it ruins the quality of customer relations and the company's reputation.

– Finally, ethics is not just a question of corporate social responsibility; it is a key element of customer strategy and should be integrated into sales training programs as a performance factor, in the same way as prospecting, communication and adaptability.

The adoption of ethical behavior is vital for society as a whole, which overwhelmingly rejects deviant behavior. It is everyone's responsibility at both individual and organizational levels.

12.4. References

[BAT 15] BATEMAN C., VALENTINE S., "The impact of salesperson customer orientation on the evaluation of a salesperson's ethical treatment, trust in the salesperson, and intentions to purchase", *Journal of Personal Selling & Sales Management*, vol. 35, no. 2, pp. 125–142, 2015.

[CIA 21] CIALDINI R., *Influence New and Expanded: The Psychology of Persuasion*, Harper Business, New York, 2021.

[EVA 12] EVANS K.R., MCFARLAND R.G., DIETZ B. et al., "Advancing sales performance research: A focus on five underresearched topic areas", *Journal of Personal Selling & Sales Management*, vol. 32, no. 1, pp. 89–105, 2012.

[FER 07] FERRELL O.C., JOHNSTON M.W., FERRELL L., "A framework for personal selling and sales management ethical decision making", *Journal of Personal Selling & Sales Management*, vol. 27, no. 4, pp. 291–299, 2007.

[HAN 09] HANSEN J.D., RIGGLE R.J., "Ethical salesperson behavior in sales relationships", *Journal of Personal Selling & Sales Management*, vol. 29, no. 2, pp. 151–166, 2009.

[HOM 11] HOMBURG C., MÜLLER M., KLARMANN M., "When should the customer really be king? On the optimum level of salesperson customer orientation in sales encounters", *Journal of Marketing*, vol. 75, no. 2, pp. 55–74, 2011.

[ING 07] INGRAM T.N., LAFORGE R.W., SCHWEPKER C.H., "Salesperson ethical decision making: The impact of sales leadership and sales management control strategy", *Journal of Personal Selling & Sales Management*, vol. 27, no. 4, pp. 301–315, 2007.

[JAR 15] JARAMILLO F., BANDE B., VARELA J., "Servant leadership and ethics: A dyadic examination of supervisor behaviors and salesperson perceptions", *Journal of Personal Selling & Sales Management*, vol. 35, no. 2, pp. 108–124, 2015.

[JUL 21] JULIENNE E., LLOSA S., "How to build good relationship quality with artisan and shopkeeper customers: A tetraclass analysis", *Décisions Marketing*, vol. 101, no. 1, pp. 189–212, 2021.

[KOH 69] KOHLBERG L., "Stage and sequence: The cognitive developmental approach to socialization", in GOSLIN D. (ed.), *Handbook of Socialization Theory and Research*, Rand McNally, Chicago, 1969.

[LAC 83] LACZNIAK G.R., "Framework for analyzing marketing ethics", *Journal of Macromarketing*, vol. 3, no. 1, pp. 7–18, 1983.

[LAV 05] LAVORATA L., NILLÈS J.-J., PONTIER S., "La méthode des scénarios : une méthode qualitative innovante pour le marketing. Application au comportement éthique du vendeur en B to B", *Décisions marketing*, no. 37, pp. 67–75, 2005.

[LAV 07] LAVORATA L., "Proposal for a measurement scale of the ethical climate in business: A study in the area of B-to-B selling", *Recherche et Applications en Marketing (English Edition)*, vol. 22, no. 1, pp. 1–23, 2007.

[ROM 05] ROMÁN S., MUNUERA J.L., "Determinants and consequences of ethical behaviour: an empirical study of salespeople", *European Journal of Marketing*, vol. 39, no. 5/6, pp. 473-495, 2005.

[THO 01] THOMAS R.W., SOUTAR G.N., RYAN M.M., "The selling orientation-customer orientation (SOCO) scale: A proposed short form", *Journal of Personal Selling & Sales Management*, vol. 21, no. 1, pp. 63–69, 2001.

13

Customer Relationships as a Factor of Resistance: The Case of Smart Feedback Tools

The advent of the Internet of Things (IoT) has led to a proliferation of connected objects, enabling people and their behavior to be tracked. Brands have responded to this trend by offering their customers complementary services, generally free of charge, based on smart feedback tools. As connected objects, smart feedback tools enable a brand's customers to monitor their consumption in real time, and to set personal goals in relation to that consumption. By giving consumers more control over their consumption, these connected objects are undeniably a promise of empowerment. Empowerment here refers to the set of perceptions that individuals have regarding their ability to exercise control over their activities and the socio-technical environment associated with these activities [MEN 99]. In particular, smart feedback tools facilitate the transition to more sober consumption patterns by enabling consumers to track the volume of their consumption. However, these tools are also perceived by consumers as a threat and an infringement on their freedom, thus justifying forms of resistance ranging from avoidance to public protest.

To better understand the various facets of consumer acceptance of smart feedback tools, a detailed description of these tools and their dynamics for penetrating certain markets is first provided. This description makes it possible to grasp the wide variety of private consumer data that these tools aim to collect, and to understand the relevance of a classification of these tools based on the nature of the feedback they offer customers. Second, the smart feedback tool is presented from the angle of a brand relationship investment aimed at strengthening customer loyalty and engagement. Finally, an analysis of the forms of resistance to which smart

---

Chapter written by Françoise SIMON and Virginie SCHWEITZER.

feedback tools give rise is carried out. In particular, it shows how consumer distrust feeds on perceptions of individual vulnerability and loss of power generated by these tools.

13.1. The rise of smart feedback tools

13.1.1. *Definition of smart feedback tools*

A smart feedback tool can be defined as a connected device for tracking one's own consumption, enabling the consumer to monitor personal indicators in real time, put them into perspective by visualizing the level of attainment of targeted objectives, historical data or social benchmarks, and update their preferences [SCH 22].

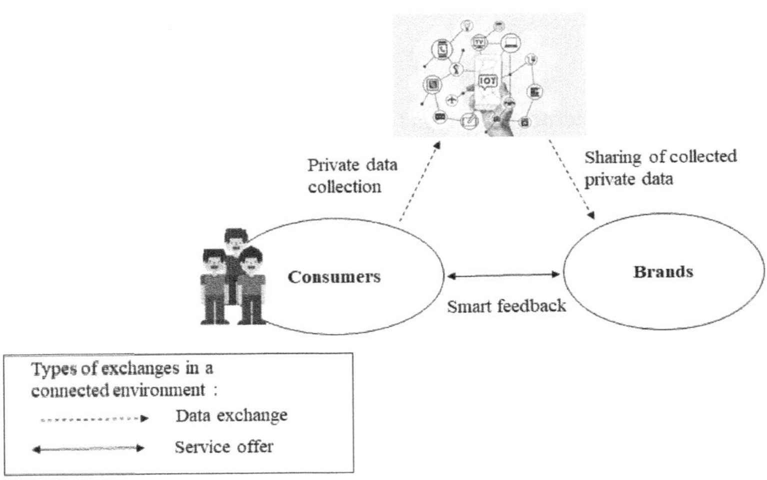

Figure 13.1. *Nature of interactions when using smart feedback tools*

The operation of smart feedback tools is based on the collection of private data that customers must first agree to share with brands. As connected devices, these tools then interact with other objects and/or actors to provide feedback (see Figure 13.1). Unlike self-contained connected devices, which are able to act on collected data without further human intervention (like smart autonomous fridges capable of ordering missing food products based on their real-time content analysis) [LAN 21], smart feedback tools involve the customer's participation in the realization of the service. This involves implementing targeted consumption behaviors that enable them to achieve their objectives in line with the feedback they receive.

A growing number of brands today offer smart feedback tools. In 2022, for example, the global market for smart fitness watches was expected to grow from USD 35.1 billion to 98.7 billion between 2020 and 2026, according to Expert Market Research.

Generally speaking, when they request feedback, individuals are looking for two types of information content: a diagnosis of the extent to which they have achieved their goals, and advice on how to implement the actions they need to progress [SCH 22]. Consequently, a smart feedback object must be able to provide the customer with both types of content: on the one hand, indicating whether the targeted behavioral objective has been achieved, and, on the other hand, specifying the nature of any discrepancies between actual and expected behavior in order to provide avenues for improvement. For example, smart sport watches indicate in real time the milestones that need to be reached to reach the targeted daily physical activity goals and also suggest activities that could help achieve them.

In addition, a smart feedback tool can enable you to compare your own performance with that of your peers. This feature, known as "normative feedback", enriches the feedback content [HAS 19]. In the case of smart sport watches, for example, customers can compare their level of physical activity and performance with other users, even in specific sporting disciplines.

13.1.2. *Deployment dynamics by sector*

The deployment of smart feedback tools reflects contrasting dynamics from one sector to another. While they are mainly present in the retail and healthcare sectors, three other sectors have also deployed smart feedback tools as complementary elements of brand offerings.

13.1.2.1. *Distribution*

In the retail sector, customers can use self-scanners allowing them to check their purchases in real time. By way of example, convenience chain 7-Eleven deployed a self-scanning and payment application in nearly 3,000 stores in the United States in 2021, enabling it to reach 50 million customers signed up to its loyalty program. Some *haptic mobile payment devices*, moreover, send individuals alerts in the form of a vibration when the amount of their purchases exceeds a certain set threshold.

In another example, customers can take advantage of *smart virtual closets* capable of identifying their mood and/or weather conditions in real time to advise them on how to choose and organize their outfits. The Vera app, created in France in 2019, invites customers to photograph the items in their closet, which the app categorizes and recognizes thanks to artificial intelligence, in order to suggest three outfits each day, taking into account the weather situation in particular.

Finally, retailer applications enriched with geolocation tools, also described as *geo-tracking apps* [RIE 21], enable customers to optimize their shopping journey in shopping centers with real-time recommendations linked to their purchasing preferences. In this context, Singapore's NomadX store has been offering facial recognition since 2018, so that when customers approach a digital screen installed at the point of sale, they can receive recommendations based on both their online and physical store purchase history.

13.1.2.2. *Health*

In the healthcare sector, feedback tools enable customers to track their physiological parameters or physical activities. Some *M-health apps* now offer real-time medical follow-ups for diabetes, obesity or asthma.

In 2022, pharmaceutical giant Roche launched the "Accuchek Sugar View" self-monitoring device for diabetic patients. This device enables patients to spot-test their blood sugar levels by photographing a strip analyzed by a dedicated mobile app.

Smart fitness watches, whose worldwide sales were expected to reach 48 million units by 2021, track the physical activities of their wearers.

Finally, *bio-feedback tools* inform individuals in real time of their emotional state, improving their ability to recognize stimuli transmitted by their own body, with a view to reducing anxiety-related symptoms.

13.1.2.3. *Housing, tourism and transport sectors*

In the housing sector, in 2022, 90% of households in France could access details of their energy consumption hour by hour, thanks to smart meters, and identify energy-intensive appliances in the home.

Just as in retail, *geo-tracking apps* based on geolocation and customer preferences offer the possibility of personalized tourist experiences thanks to targeted recommendations.

Lastly, in the transport sector, *smart cars* collect data on vehicle journeys and driving, providing feedback on traffic and vehicle conditions, as well as on the customer's control of the vehicle. As part of the "Scoop" project initiated by the French government and local authorities, the Renault and PSA groups equipped several thousand vehicles with such feedback tools in 2018 to test the performance of the communication system between vehicles and their environment on the roads of five French departments. Smart cars are also intended to ultimately enable the setting of personalized insurance rates based on individual driving.

13.1.3. *The collection of multiple types of private data*

The smart feedback tools on the market collect a wide variety of personal data, depending on the objectives they are designed to achieve. These may include details of a customer's shopping basket, their geolocation and movements, as well as their emotions and interests (see Table 13.1).

	Categories	**Type of personal data collected from the customer**
Distribution	Self-scanner	Shopping cart contents
	Haptic payment system	Shopping cart amount and amount available in bank accounts
	Geo-tracking app	Geolocation and preferences
	Smart virtual closet	Emotional state, weather and preferences
Health	M-health app	Physiological parameters
	Smart fitness watch	Physical activity
	Bio-feedback tool	Emotional state
Habitat	Smart meter	Detailed energy consumption
Tourism	Geo-tracking app	Geolocation and preferences
Transport	Smart car	Journeys and driving behavior

Table 13.1. *Data collected by smart feedback tools*

13.1.4. *Toward a classification based on the nature of feedback*

A classification of smart feedback tools can be proposed on the basis of two dimensions of feedback given to the customer. The first dimension describes the depth of the feedback, which can be basic, consisting of an assessment of whether the customer has achieved their objectives, or elaborated, when it is enriched with recommendations for achieving objectives. The second dimension reflects the presence or absence of comparison mechanisms: feedback limited to oneself or taking into account the performance of peers, thus contributing to "normative" feedback.

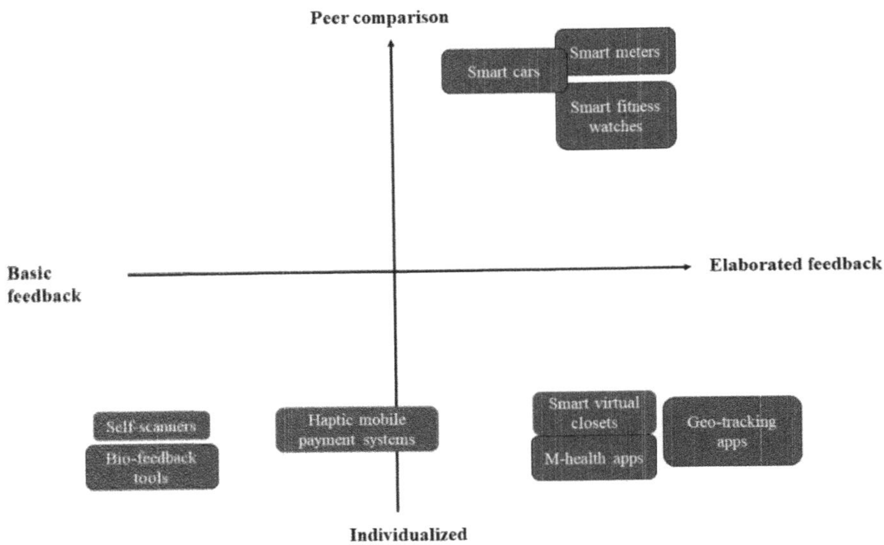

Figure 13.2. *Types of feedback associated with smart feedback tools (adapted from [SCH 22])*

An examination of the main smart feedback tools according to this classification (see Figure 13.2) shows that prescriptive feedback is still in the minority, as it is currently only offered in the context of smart fitness watches, smart meters and smart cars. However, with most smart feedback tools, brands are able to offer elaborated feedback with advice on how to achieve the goals set by the user, in addition to information on the deviation from the target. Brands can also limit themselves to providing basic feedback in the form of real-time behavioral information: this is the case with self-scanners, haptic payment systems and bio-feedback tools.

13.2. A brand relationship investment

13.2.1. *Relational investments supporting customer relationships*

Smart feedback tools are frequently offered free of charge by brands to their customers. For example, sports shoe manufacturer ASICS offers its customers the Runkeeper application. As a smart fitness watch, it provides access to basic performance data such as distance covered and calories burned, and enables progressive challenges to be formulated, the achievement of which is documented by the application. Moreover, energy suppliers use smart meters to provide their customers with applications that enable them to track their energy consumption in real time, by electrical appliance, and to benefit from personalized advice on how to reduce energy consumption.

Offered free of charge, a smart feedback tool is a brand relationship investment. This concept, defined by De Wulf and colleagues [DEW 01], corresponds to a customer's perception of the intensity of the resources, efforts and attention that the brand devotes to maintaining or improving their commercial relationship. These relational investments made by the brand cannot be recovered if the customer leaves the brand. Insofar as smart feedback tools are a complementary service offered to the customer, they constitute a relational brand investment to improve customer relationships.

Among the relational effects expected from a smart feedback tool, four benefits for the brand can be distinguished [SIM 15]. The first concerns the improvement of customer satisfaction in the use of the brand's products, as the smart feedback tool enables them to optimize their consumption in line with their personal objectives. The second aims to improve the brand's image in areas such as benevolence and social responsibility. This aspect is important because it enables the brand to show that it is helping its customers to control the volume of their consumption of resources or products, by providing them with real-time traceability of this consumption. In this way, the brand contributes to society's drive for sober consumption. The third is linked to the social benchmarks offered by the tool, including advice given to the customer. This feature tends to encourage customer commitment to the brand, especially if the brand knows how to link the social benchmarks to the brand communities it animates on its social pages. Finally, the availability of the smart feedback tool can provoke a feeling of gratitude in the customer, triggering reciprocal mechanisms in favor of the brand.

13.2.2. *Smart feedback tools as a promise of empowerment*

While the smart feedback tool is clearly a brand relationship investment, this relational investment is nonetheless associated here with a specific brand promise, namely that of customer empowerment of its customers.

In marketing research, the concept of "psychological empowerment" has been mobilized as a means of addressing the consumer's quest for power through the use of an artifact [SCH 21]. In this context, psychological empowerment describes the internal state of an individual who gives themself the means to act on their own in order to achieve the objectives they have set themself, by taking advantage of the resources offered by a tool [SPR 95, MEN 99]. The construct integrates a cognitive core that encompasses the beliefs that individuals hold concerning four facets of empowerment:

– the congruence of the activities undertaken with their personal goals and values;

– their skill in using the artifact;

– their autonomy in terms of the initiation, control and regulation of their actions;

– the impact their activities with the artifact can have on themselves and their community.

Conversely, consumers' beliefs about a loss of power in at least one facet of empowerment can be referred to as disempowerment.

Insofar as the smart feedback tool responds to an individual expectation of control over one's own consumption, it satisfies several facets of psychological empowerment. These include the congruence of the activities undertaken with the individual's values and meeting their needs for autonomy. As for impact and perceived competence, these are highly dependent on the performance of the tool and the acquired competence of the client. Aware of the empowerment potential of smart feedback tools, brands often often emphasize this benefit. Enedis, for example, promotes the Linky smart meter with this promise: "Control your energy with the Linky electric meter".

13.3. Consumer resistance to smart feedback tools

13.3.1. *Multiple sources of disempowerment*

While smart feedback tools can empower a brand's customers, they can also give rise to situations of disempowerment, whether occasional or permanent. Four main sources of disempowerment linked to smart feedback tools can be distinguished: tool imposition contexts, customer self-disclosure, normative pressures and perceived manipulation.

13.3.1.1. *Imposition contexts*

Imposition contexts refer to situations in which the customer is forced to use the smart feedback tool to access the brand's offering. In a number of cases, this imposition takes the form of forced substitution. For example, in some European countries, customers of electricity suppliers have not been able to keep their traditional electricity meters and have had to exchange them for smart meters. Similarly, in some retail outlets, self-checkout (for less than five items, for example) is no longer accessible, and has instead been replaced by a self-scanning device available at the store entrance. This type of imposition is perceived by customers as a loss of freedom and autonomy.

13.3.1.2. *The customer's personal disclosure*

A recurring concern for consumers is the potential for connected objects, including smart feedback tools, to compromise and invade their privacy. Here, consumers invoke the metaphorical term "Big Brother" to express the feeling of being watched by an invisible and intrusive presence, likely to give public or commercial entities significant access to their private data [SAV 13]. More generally, perceptions of personal exposure as a result of the private data collected by smart feedback tools induce a state of vulnerability and loss of power in many consumers.

13.3.1.3. *Normative pressures*

A growing number of smart feedback tools include forms of social benchmarking, enabling users to compare their performance in terms of goal attainment with that of other consumers whose consumption situation has been identified by the tool as being close to their own. The presentation of benchmark results is often associated with normative messages such as "Congratulations! You're one of the 10% of our community who have achieved this performance" or "Dear customer! This week, you scored 20 points less than last week. Let us help you get back on track". While information from social benchmarks is sought after by consumers, its repetition over time, combined with messages of a normative nature, can result in the perception of pressure to commit to behavior, giving players the feeling of a loss of control and personal freedom, and even a certain weariness [BRO 20].

13.3.1.4. *Perceived manipulation*

As this is a particular kind of relational investment involving the collection of detailed data on consumer behavior in their daily lives, the smart feedback tool may give rise to mistrust on the part of the customer. The very nature of the exchange with the brand may be questioned by the customer, based on the suspicion of a hidden interest on the part of the brand in the deployment of the tool [KIR 07]. In particular, the fear of less favorable pricing policies down the road, with the brand using its greater knowledge of customer expectations to charge higher prices on the most popular segments of the offer, may explain the customer's feeling of greater vulnerability in the face of the brand's reinforced power.

13.3.2. *Forms of resistance*

Consumer resistance can be seen as a manifestation of opposition in a situation perceived as oppressive, or as an individual's propensity to oppose [ROU 07]. It can take various forms: from apathy to avoidance of the solution proposed by the brand, possibly including brand denigration or collective actions directed against the brand.

In the case of smart feedback tools, consumer resistance is fueled by the situations of disempowerment they feel they are experiencing, and it is thus associated with manifestations of reactance. Psychological reactance is a motivational state oriented toward oppositional behavior in order to preserve a personal freedom that has been suppressed or is threatened with disappearance [BRE 89]. To restore their threatened freedom, individuals tend to harbor a stronger preference for the threatened choice, to denigrate the source of the threat and to implement oppositional actions in order to regain a sense of control.

Among resistance actions at a strictly individual level, we frequently find apathy toward the tool, where the customer voluntarily settles into a state of passivity, no longer paying much attention to the messages delivered by the app [BRO 20]. Avoidance is a more active form of resistance, in which the customer unsubscribes or uninstalls the smart feedback tool. In the case of smart electricity meters, some customers (of energy companies) have also physically opposed the installation of the new meter in their homes.

On a collective level, other forms of resistance may emerge. First, high levels of psychological reactance can lead to brand denigration through negative word-of-mouth in close circles and/or on social networks, particularly within brand communities associated with the smart feedback tool. More rarely, actions led by social actors are implemented, particularly in contexts where the tool is imposed on customers. For example, during the roll-out of the Linky smart meter in France, pressure groups and ad hoc associations highlighted the futility of replacing the traditional meter. Under pressure from their residents, municipalities have also fought against the tool by taking decisions concerning the deployment of the smart meter on their territory, ranging from allowing their constituents to decide for themselves whether or not to accept the installation of the new meter, to a total ban on the installation of the meter in the municipality [CHA 20].

13.4. Conclusion

Promoted by brands as individual empowerment devices, smart feedback tools are becoming increasingly popular with consumers, as demonstrated by the explosion of connected applications in the health, retail and home sectors. In particular, these tools are invaluable assets in the current context of transitioning consumption patterns toward greater sufficiency and sustainability.

At the same time, however, these tools are fueling mechanisms of individual and collective mistrust due to the volume and variety of private consumer data they are able to collect and analyze. More broadly, they lead consumers to question the nature of the exchange with brands. In particular, brands' intentions are challenged when they offer relationship investments, the granting of which is conditional on the customer's consent to provide ongoing information about the details of their daily life.

What is more, the increased knowledge of brands' business practices by customers makes them particularly lucid about tactics aimed at imposing this type of tool on customers under the guise of making available features that would be more attractive because they are "smart". More generally, it seems that the accusation of "kind washing" by brands is becoming increasingly widespread among consumers, especially insofar as the prerequisite for benefiting from the brand's supposed "benevolence" is to entrust it with the many details of one's private life. It therefore seems likely that the market will award a premium to virtuous companies capable of offering smart feedback solutions that are flexible, transparent and renegotiable at any time.

However, some private data are associated with increased risks of manipulation by brands. This is particularly true when consumers suspect that companies are using data collected by smart feedback tools to set personalized prices. The same is true of energy resources, which represent a large budget for households and fuel fears of personalized pricing to their detriment. In this case, smart feedback tools can lead to movements of collective resistance, as witnessed by public protests against smart meters for water and energy [CHA 20].

13.5. References

[BRE 89] BREHM J.W., "Psychological reactance: theory and applications", *ACR North American Advances*, vol. 16, pp. 72–75, 1989.

[BRO 20] BROHMAN K., ADDAS S., DIXON J. et al., "Cascading feedback: A longitudinal study of a feedback ecosystem for telemonitoring patients with chronic disease", *MIS Quarterly*, vol. 44, pp. 421–450, 2020.

[CHA 20] CHAMARET C., STEYER V., MAYER J.C. et al., "'Hands off my meter!' when municipalities resist smart meters: Linking arguments and degrees of resistance", *Energy Policy*, vol. 144, pp. 111–556, 2020.

[DEW 01] DE WULF K., ODEKERKEN-SCHRÖDER G., IACOBUCCI D. et al., "Investments in consumer relationships: A cross-country and cross-industry exploration", *Journal of Marketing*, vol. 65, no. 4, pp. 33–50, 2001.

[HAS 19] HASSAN L., DIAS A., HAMARI J., "How motivational feedback increases user's benefits and continued use: A study on gamification, quantified-self and social networking", *International Journal of Information Management*, vol. 46, pp. 151–162, 2019.

[KIR 07] KIRMANI A., ZHU R., "Vigilant against manipulation: the effect of regulatory focus on the use of persuasion knowledge", *Journal of Marketing Research*, vol. 44, no. 4, pp. 688–701, 2007.

[LAN 21] LANGLEY D., VAN DOORN J., NG I.C.L. et al., "The Internet of Everything: Smart things and their impact on business models", *Journal of Business Research*, vol. 122, pp. 853–863, 2021.

[MEN 99] MENON S.T., "Psychological empowerment: definition, measurement, and validation", *Canadian Journal of Behavioural Science*, vol. 31, no. 3, pp. 161–164, 1999.

[RIE 21] RIEGGER A.S., KLEIN J.F., MERFELD K. et al., "Technology-enabled personalization in retail stores: Understanding drivers and barriers", *Journal of Business Research*, vol. 123, pp. 140–155, 2021.

[ROU 07] ROUX D., "A résistance du consommateur : proposition d'un cadre d'analyse", *Recherche et applications en marketing (French Edition)*, vol. 22, no. 4, pp. 59–80, 2007.

[SAV 13] SAVIRIMUTHU J., "Smart meters and the information panopticon: Beyond the rhetoric of compliance", *International Review of Law, Computers & Technology*, vol. 27, no. 1/2, pp. 161–186, 2013.

[SCH 21] SCHWEITZER V., SIMON F., "Self-construals as the locus of consumer paradoxical empowerment in self-service retail technology environments", *Journal of Business Research*, vol. 126, pp. 291–306, 2021.

[SCH 22] SCHWEITZER V., "Characterizing smart tracking-based self-service technologies (STB SSTs) and their acceptance antecedents: A systematic literature review", *European Marketing Academy Annual Conference*, Budapest, Hungary, 2022.

[SIM 15] SIMON F., TOSSAN V., CONNAN-GUESQUIÈRE C., "The relative impact of gratitude and transactional satisfaction on post-complaint consumer response", *Marketing Letters*, vol. 26, no. 2, pp. 153–164, 2015.

[SPR 95] SPREITZER G., "Psychological empowerment in the workplace: Dimensions, measurement, and validation", *Academy of Management Journal*, vol. 38, no. 5, pp. 1442–1465, 1995.

14

Customer Relations in the Social and Solidarity Economy

14.1. Managing customer relations in social and solidarity economy organizations

In an open letter to the French Secretary of State for the Social and Solidarity Economy and Associative Life, the Social and Solidarity Economy (SSE) Lab proposed making this sector an economic standard[1], based on limited profitability and stakeholder participation in governance (such as customers and members). In this context, can customer relations be the same as in conventional commercial organizations?

The aim of this chapter is to provide some answers through the prism of:

– the concept of commitment: this is central to the customer relationship and can be defined as the willingness of those involved to pursue a long-term, valued relationship [MOR 09];

– the roles assumed by customers.

Section 14.1.1 of this chapter looks at the ways in which democratic governance is manifested in customer relationship management within SSE organizations, the particularities of which are highlighted. In the second part, we present the roles played by customers in two organizations: La Louve, a collaborative supermarket, and Enercoop Languedoc-Roussillon, a producer and supplier of green energy. What emerges is the central role played by affective engagement, which translates into shared objectives and values between customers and organizations.

Chapter written by Hajar EL KARMOUNI and Alix POELS.

1 See: https://www.carenews.com/le-labo-de-l-ess/news/l-ess-norme-de-l-economie.

14.1.1. *Democratic governance of SSE organizations and customer relations*

The law of July 31, 2014, defines the SSE as a mode of enterprise and economic development adapted to all areas of human activity. It is adhered to by legal entities under private law that meet the following cumulative conditions: a purpose other than profit-sharing; "democratic governance, defined and organized by the statutes, providing for information and participation, with this expression being not solely linked to the capital contribution of associates, employees, and stakeholders in the company's operations"; and, finally, limited profit-making.

SSEs include "legal entities under private law constituted as cooperatives, mutual societies, foundations or associations governed by the law of July 1 1901". By virtue of their statutes, SSE organizations must integrate a wide range of stakeholders, including customers. Qualified differently according to the organization (members, shareholders, cooperators, etc.), depending on the statutes, they can be given different roles. At the very least, they have a deliberative vote at general meetings. However, for conventional companies, the extension of marketing to other interlocutors is an initiative of the company that decides to enter into relations with other audiences (which is most often done within the framework of a CSR policy of stakeholder integration) [MAY 12]; in the SSE, it is necessary to statutorily integrate the customer. Consequently, SSE organizations adopt an "extensive marketing" approach [MAY 12], placing the customer as an internal stakeholder within the organization. In this context, how do customers become involved and participate in defining the relationship that concerns them?

The question of customer participation and roles within companies is not new [BON 12]. In marketing, it lies at the crossroads of three main streams: service marketing, innovation marketing and relationship marketing. These studies show that customer participation is often guided by the implementation of systems that invite individuals to participate in specific, predetermined aspects [DUB 09], from a relational perspective, with a view to capturing and retaining customers [HAR 17]. In service marketing, for example, the customer is seen as a contributor, and this participation is characterized by its intensity and content [LL0 11]. The customer can take on two types of role:

– an intra-role, that is, what the customer must do for the service to take place (check-in for a flight, for example);

– an extra-role, not necessary to the production of the service, but related to the customer's positive behavior, including actions such as promoting the brand (positive word-of-mouth) or helping to improve customer relations (by responding to a satisfaction questionnaire, for example).

The customer is then conceived as a "voluntary" collaborator whose motivations may be intrinsic (interest or pleasure in the activity performed for the company) or extrinsic (obtaining rewards beyond the activity performed) in order to co-create value [BON 12].

In the case of SSE organizations, the value created primarily concerns the members, who are themselves the beneficiaries of the service provided. For example, cooperatives pursue an economic and/or social goal for the benefit of their customers and members: "The cooperative is a company formed by several people who voluntarily join together to satisfy their economic or social needs through joint effort and the provision of the necessary means…"[2]. In these organizations, and more broadly, the roles taken on by customers include a transformative dimension affecting consumption and production processes, in a logic of consumer expression and decision-making. These roles can be likened to a form of political engagement [DUB 05], "and in this case, participation is a political process that has to do with the question of empowerment"[3] [BER 14, p. 93]. The consumers' voice is heard directly in decision-making forums linked to the cooperative's governance production system and consumption.

Access to membership, for example, opens up a realm of choice that not only concerns the properties of services or products, but also the organization's governance and strategic choices. In the next two sections, we look at how this relationship operates in two types of SSE organization: a consumer cooperative, using the example of the La Louve cooperative supermarket, and a collective interest cooperative company (SCIC for the French term *sociétés coopératives d'intérêt collectif*), using the example of Enercoop Languedoc-Roussillon.

14.2. CRM in consumer cooperatives: the case of La Louve

14.2.1. *The cooperative: definition and articles of association*

A cooperative is defined as "a company formed by several people who voluntarily join together to satisfy their economic or social needs through joint effort and the provision of the necessary means. It operates in all branches of human activity, and respects the following principles: voluntary membership open to all, democratic governance, economic participation of its members, training of said members and cooperation with other cooperatives" (law 47-1175, article 1). There are several types and statuses of cooperative in France, such as enterprise cooperatives (enterprises

2 Law no. 47-1775 of September 10, 1947.

3 Empowerment refers to a "Process that enables individuals to become aware of their ability to act and access more power"; see Zappi, L."“empowerment", nouvel horizon de la politique de la ville", *Le Monde*, February 7, 2013. Available at: http://www.lemonde.fr/société/article/2013/02/07/1827820_3224.html.

mutualize services essential to guaranteeing their independence and the stability of their business models, as in the case of agricultural, retail, craft, transport and maritime cooperatives), user cooperatives (members are the individual beneficiaries of the goods and services produced by the cooperative), consumer cooperatives (cooperative banks, housing projects and residents' banks, cooperative supermarkets), production cooperatives (cooperative production businesses (SCOPs), business and employment cooperatives (CAE)), and multi-society cooperatives (collective interest cooperative companies (SCICs)). They generate sales of EUR 329 billion and employ 1.3 million people. One French person in three is a member of at least one cooperative[4].

Consumer cooperatives appeared in France at the beginning of the 19th century, after similar experiments had been successful in other European countries, notably Great Britain with the pioneering Rochdale Equitable Pioneers Society in 1844 [GID 04]. This cooperative pursued two main objectives [DUB 04, pp. 21–22]:

– providing poor households with access to quality products, while allowing them to benefit from the profits generated by sales. Thus, "with a small capital base fed by small but regular member contributions, the cooperative buys wholesale groceries that are resold at cost" [TOU 05, p. 26];

– involving cooperators in the management of business activities by granting them voting rights.

The first consumer cooperatives had to provide their members with everything they could possibly need, so that they did not have to spend outside the cooperative. The needs of the working-class family were restricted, and the time available for shopping was too limited to allow them to visit several stores [GID 04].

The movement grew considerably until the 1960s. At that time, cooperatives constituted the most powerful food distribution network in France. Essentially grouping together local stores, they sold at the same price as traditional chain stores, but then redistributed most of their profits to their cooperative members in the form of rebates.

After almost disappearing from the retail landscape, consumer cooperatives have reappeared over the last 10 years, mainly in the form of cooperative supermarkets.

By 2021, some 100 projects could be identified in France and several other European countries, in both urban and rural areas. Their mission: to offer quality products at a lower cost by involving members. Members are the store's owners, volunteers and exclusive customers. Decision-maker, customer, citizen and worker, the customer simultaneously represents several of the organization's stakeholders all at the same time.

Box 14.1. *Focus on the consumer cooperative*

4 Panorama des coopératives, 2022. Available at: https://www.entreprises.coop/system/files/inline-files/CoopFR-Panorama_2022_0.pdf.

14.2.2. *La Louve cooperative supermarket*

In France, La Louve is the pioneering model emblematic of this consumer cooperative revival. The supermarket, which opened its doors in 2016, has imported to the European continent the participatory model born in the United States in the 1970s with the Park Slope Food Coop.

> We weren't satisfied with the food on offer, so we decided to set up our own supermarket.[5]

This translated quote comes from the homepage of La Louve's website. From the outset, the supermarket has positioned itself as an alternative to the "food offer" proposed by other distribution channels. The difference between the project and the criticized model is then explained:

> La Louve offers quality food at reduced prices, mostly organic, local and artisanal. Anyone can shop there, all they have to do is become a cooperator and participate in the running of the store.[6]

To take advantage of this "quality, low-cost, mostly organic, local and artisanal" food[7], the consumer needs to participate in the organization's operations for 3 h a month. The organization thus claims to be a cooperative and participative supermarket.

The cooperative approach is expressed first and foremost through the purchase of shares, with a minimum investment of EUR 100 (i.e. 10 cooperative shares) to become a member, and a reduced entry fee for those on minimum social benefits, who can buy just one share – an investment of EUR 10. Participation involves devoting three consecutive hours of work every 4 weeks to the cooperative. There are numerous tasks to be carried out, and they aim to ensure self-management of all the activities required to run the cooperative: using the till, stocking, cleaning, administration; the operational tasks required to run a supermarket. This self-management model also makes it possible to limit the payroll (there were only 10 employees at La Louve in 2019, mainly in charge of administration and purchasing) and, thanks to the absence of marketing costs and shareholders to remunerate, to charge reasonable prices, 15%–40% lower than in other distribution channels for similar products.

---

5 La Louve supermarket website, available at: https://cooplalouve.fr.

6 *Ibid.*

7 *Ibid.*

14.2.3. *Taking on the intra-role: from consumer to cooperator through work*

The founders of La Louve want to anchor the cooperative spirit in their members. In doing so, they encourage cooperators to take on an intra-role. The cooperator has to be a worker in order to have customer status. This enables them to voice their needs and take action to satisfy them.

The terms "consumer" or "customer" are decried. They are the antithesis of the concept of cooperator: a consumer is "passive", whereas a La Louve cooperator is expected to be "active". Commitment (giving one's time, taking physical action) is a *sine qua non* of cooperation.

> When we opened La Louve we wanted "zero customers". We didn't want customers, we wanted cooperators, and that's a different thing. A cooperator is a person with the real sense that the supermarket is theirs, and that changes things. For example, if there's a problem, it's up to the customer to complain and say: "Ah, it's not working" and give the power to solve the problem to someone else, whereas it's us, it's you yourself who can go down and see if the product is there, and it's a totally different spirit… We don't really like the word consumer. It's a very passive concept. In a way, you have certain privileges: you can say that you don't have the work to do, you can say: "I don't like it, so I'll spend my money elsewhere", but in reality, you also lose the whole decision-making aspect, if you don't give your classic supermarket any possibility of saying: "Ah, I don't like this kind of product" or "Why don't we offer this kind of product in our supermarket" or, with the profits from our supermarket, do we want to do something good for the neighborhood? That's not something you can do with a capitalist supermarket, whereas at La Louve that's exactly what we can do. (Co-founder of La Louve)

According to the concept of its founders, it is by providing work that the member acquires the status of cooperator. Work is central to the cooperative's existence, with a statutory injunction to provide 3 hours of work every 4 weeks. If a cooperator fails to take up their intra-role, for example, if they fail to fill their slot for 2 months in a row, their supermarket access card is automatically blocked, preventing them from shopping.

14.2.4. *Between customers and cooperative status*

This 1,450 m² supermarket offers a range of 5,000 product references. The architecture and interior layout meet the standards expected of a supermarket: raw concrete with a smooth cement floor on three levels. The customer flow is well thought-out. The first floor is devoted to reception, checkouts, fruit and vegetables and cold storage (dairy, meat, frozen foods, delicatessen), as well as part of the grocery store. It also includes the members' office. The rest of the grocery store is located in the basement, alongside the cleaning, hygiene, stationery and baby products departments. A wing is dedicated to bulk products.

However, unlike a supermarket, the cooperative's members are involved in the choice of products. Some of them are members of the "shopping" working group, filling in a suggestion booklet, but they also make their own purchases:

> In fact, votes on products are purchases; if you like the products, you buy them; otherwise, you don't, and you remove them from the supermarket. It's very democratic, in fact. (Co-founder of La Louve)

The product offering is not built up by suppliers, sales representatives or range agreements, but by the choices of cooperative members, with no superiority between product categories (organic, non-organic, from multinationals or local producers, from short or conventional distribution channels, etc.).

While this model is spreading to a number of French and European cities, certain limitations have been highlighted. At La Louve and other cooperative supermarkets, long-term commitment is not guaranteed. While some volunteers are highly committed, this investment does not compensate for the disinvestment of others, and the salaried team is gradually finding its tasks grow heavier and its prerogatives widen, leaving less room for cooperators.

At the same time, the over-investment of cooperators tends to be rewarded by participation in decision-making by joining the various working groups (those relating to operation, such as that of member management, or those managing the governance of the supermarket, such as the "agenda" committee whose mission is to set the agendas for general assemblies), or by taking part in the cooperative's governing bodies as a reward for their commitment. An informal hierarchy is thus established between the various members.

14.3. Organizing customer relations in a collective interest cooperative company: the case of Enercoop Languedoc-Roussillon

14.3.1. *The collective interest cooperative company: definition and articles of association*

Created following the publication of law no. 2001-624 of July 17, 2001, and numbering 1,060 by 2021, collective interest cooperative companies (SCICs) are part of the social and solidarity-based economy, based on a democratic ("one person = one vote") and non-profit approach (collective ownership of production tools, limited sharing of dividends and obligation to deposit part of surpluses in non-transferable reserves) [DEM 03, p. 69]. Two major features differentiate these enterprises from other cooperative statutes:

– multi-partnership, which must be organized around a minimum of three categories, two of which are mandatory: employees and users (often consumers);

– cooperative activities must respond to collective needs within a territory or economic sector. One of the main challenges to the governance of SCICs is to bring together the varied interests of players with multiple logics (individuals, institutions, organizations) – who play different roles and maintain different relationships with regard to cooperative activities [MAR 05] – in order to bring to life a collective project that reconciles economic and social performance.

14.3.2. *The SCIC Enercoop Languedoc-Roussillon*

Enercoop Languedoc-Roussillon (Enercoop LR) is part of a network of regional SCICs. This network is coordinated by a central entity based in Île-de-France, which is responsible for the collective project at a national level. "National" Enercoop was founded in 2005, with the main aim of reclaiming the energy sector for citizens. In addition to offering "green, local and socially responsible" electricity to individuals, professionals and local authorities, Enercoop aims to develop new means of producing energy from renewable sources and to control energy consumption from a territorial base. Enercoop Languedoc-Roussillon has been leading this collective project in the Occitanie region since 2011. The supply activity is managed by the national cooperative; the Occitan cooperative is therefore considered as a provider of business to the network for each new electricity meter subscription. Enercoop Languedoc-Roussillon's activities also include a design office dedicated to engineering services (especially around the implementation of photovoltaic power stations), support for citizens' renewable energy production projects and training in public and private higher education establishments.

Enercoop LR presents itself as an alternative citizen organization in the energy sector, contributing to and exploring the principles of cooperation and social utility in various ways:

– by designing a new model of energy production, decentralized and shared via the inclusion of local authorities and citizens in decision-making and investment (Enercoop LR activity report, 2014);

– by instilling a civic character in energy transition practices (Enercoop LR activity report, 2015);

– in internal and external collaboration with energy players in the Occitanie region and nationally:

> Collaboration, that's the key word of our work and our hopes: collaboration between each Enercoop LR player – producers, consumers, employees, partners, communities – to invent an energy transition where every citizen, every entity that has the desire to get involved, to try an action, to understand what it means, can act in a concrete and immediate way. (Chairman of the Board of Directors, Management Report, 2013)

Enercoop LR has 2,155 members, organized into six colleges: holders, producers, local authorities, partners, employees and consumers (the latter representing 98% of the membership). These member–consumers participate in the life of Enercoop LR in a variety of ways: they can get involved in governance (voting at the Annual General Meeting, participation in the Board of Directors and/or other decision-making bodies), or in transition actions at the crossroads between the organization and other local players. Participation can be financial (the acquisition of shares being the gateway to membership), but can also be linked to communication or commercial support.

14.3.3. *A commitment that translates into extra-roles conditioned by the organization's economic times*

The extra-roles assumed by Enercoop LR's customers have evolved in line with the SCIC's economic development phases, and have been central to ensuring the organization's sustainability. Thus, during its launch phase between 2012 and 2015, Enercoop LR was strongly supported by Enercoop National, which remunerated the organization on the number of incoming contracts. This model drives them to rapidly develop the number of customers and sales leads intensively. However, employees in charge of customer relations reject the name "salespeople" and instead use the term "facilitators" of the energy transition. They see becoming an Enercoop customer as a concrete way of helping to transform consumption patterns, and as a first level of commitment.

> I don't like this job, I couldn't be a salesperson in another structure [...]. Facilitator at the limit... I help people make the transition [...] we try to understand the person's needs and above all to give them um... as much information as possible, in the most sincere way possible [...] to be as transparent as possible, as sincere as possible and um... to speak from the heart. (Individual business development manager)

Increasing the number of members is also a major challenge for the SCIC during this period, as it builds up its initial capital. Customers and cooperative members are therefore first and foremost financiers.

Between 2016 and 2018, the SCIC went through a "growth crisis" (Enercoop LR activity report, 2017) characterized by a rapid increase in the number of customers and members but with a deficit on its balance sheet. This phase saw a multiplication of the roles devolved to customers and members. In addition to their financial commitment and participation in annual general meetings, they can take part in trade fairs and festivals, or even organize screenings and debates on the subject of transition. In concrete terms, they can canvass and recruit new customers and members. However, the SCIC's strategy for animating cooperative life and for the ways in which customers and members can participate remains embryonic.

> Without a clear strategy for the short, medium and long term, we don't know what we're building and what we're building for. And we've never built a real strategy. [...] And what about cooperative life? What do we want to do with it? Do we want to have a great network of ambassadors? Do we want to have x number of local groups? Is our aim to train all our members so that they're all up to speed and understand all the issues involved in the energy transition? Clearly, we've never made that clear to ourselves. So... we made progress [...]. Today, cooperative life in Languedoc-Roussillon is supported neither by the employees nor by the Board of Directors! So, at a certain point, it's impossible. (Cooperative life manager)

Consultation and deliberation mechanisms such as cooperative meetings have been set up, as well as a network of ambassadors[8] working with Enercoop LR on a voluntary basis. However, these events were poorly attended. Enercoop LR then

8 This network, set up by the SCIC, is made up of members who are very involved in supporting the salaried team in its communication and prospecting missions.

began to reflect on its capacity to mobilize by aligning itself with the concerns of its customers and members, so as to think of member participation not on a regional scale (Occitanie) but on a very local scale, that is, as close as possible geographically to its customers and members, with the aim of increasing the skills of the territories (citizens, collectives, local authorities).

From 2019 onwards, the SCIC has become economically consolidated, and this phase is marked by its ability to spread its model across the Occitan territory. A raison d'être is redefined for the cooperative:

> Enercoop LR implements a sustainable energy model for, by and with all the citizens and players in our territories, in a logic of Enercoop cooperation: we are a human tool enabling everyone to understand, decide and act in this direction, to access local energy of renewable origin, and to produce it collectively. (Enercoop LR Activity Report, 2020)

The organization is renewing its commitment to empowering customers and members by reflecting on their roles and democratic participation. The range of activities on offer is diversified (webinars on the workings of the energy market, visits to production sites, training days for members wishing to become "ambassadors", themed walks), and customers and members are invited to imagine and build participation mechanisms. What emerges is a strategy for animating cooperative life in which member-policyholders and customers are invited to participate in an inclusive way, notably through working groups. Gradually, the organization has moved from imposing roles on customers to orchestrating participation.

14.4. Conclusion

In the two organizations studied, intra-roles [LLO 19] are more or less predominant. Thus, within the La Louve cooperative, access to customer status (cooperator in the organization's own language) is conditional on voluntary work time. It is this role that determines access to the cooperative's offer, and is thought to ensure members' commitment over time. Extra-roles [LLO 19], for their part, are necessary for the long-term survival of both cooperatives: participation in working groups at La Louve, for example, or volunteer time at fairs and exhibitions for Enercoop LR. The challenge remains for SSE organizations to ensure the endorsement of these two roles over time.

These extra-roles give greater latitude to customers and greater freedom of action in SSE organizations than in the context of conventional companies. While extra-roles are classically linked to the positive behavior of the customer toward the chain or the brand, via positive word-of-mouth for example, the extra-roles within La Louve as within Enercoop LR allow customers to take back power by integrating a transformative dimension of their consumption and production processes, in a logic of expression and decision. Finally, customer commitment, far from being limited to an instrumental commitment (that is to say a balance between costs and benefits allowing one to decide whether or not to continue the relationship) is more oriented toward alignment between the shared values of the organization and customers, which constitutes a significant challenge for these organizations.

14.5. References

[BER 14] BERNARD F., "Imaginaire, participation, engagement et empowerment. Des notions pour penser la relation entre risques et changements", *Communication et organisation. Revue scientifique francophone en Communication organisationnelle*, vol. 45, pp. 87–98, 2014.

[BON 12] BONNEMAIZON A., CADENAT S., BENOIT-MOREAU F. et al., "“Client exécutant", "assistant marketing opérationnel", "relais" ou "apporteur de solutions" : dis-moi ce que tu fais, je te dirai qui tu es !", *Management Avenir*, vol. 2, no. 52, pp. 175–193, 2012.

[DEM 03] DEMOUSTIER D., *L'économie sociale et solidaire : s'associer pour entreprendre autrement*, Syros, Paris, 2003.

[DUB 04] DUBUISSON-QUELLIER S., LAMINE C., "Faire le marché autrement. L'abonnement à un panier de fruits et de légumes comme forme d'engagement politique des consommateurs", *Sciences de la Société*, vol. 62, pp. 145–167, 2004.

[DUB 09] DUBUISSON-QUELLIER S., *La consommation engagée*, Presses de la Fondation Nationale des Sciences Politiques, Paris, 2009.

[GID 04] GIDE C., *Les sociétés coopératives de consommation*, Librairie de la société du Recueil Sirey, Paris, 1904.

[HAR 17] HARMELING C.M., MOFFETT J.W., ARNOLD M.J. et al., "Toward a theory of customer engagement marketing", *Journal of the Academy of Marketing Science*, vol. 45, pp. 312–335, 2017.

[LLO 19] LLOSA S., NICOD L., "The augmented customer relationship: The increasing importance of the customer's role", in N'GOALA G., PEZ-PÉRARD V., PRIM-ALLAZ I. (eds), *Augmented Customer Strategy: CRM in the Digital Age*, ISTE Ltd, London and John Wiley & Sons, New York, 2019.

[MAR 05] MARGADO A., "La SCIC, une coopérative encore en devenir", *Revue internationale de l'économie sociale (RECMA)*, no. 295, pp. 38–49, 2005.

[MAY 12] MAYAUX F., "Le marketing au service des organisations de l'économie sociale et solidaire", in BAYLE E. (ed.), *Management des entreprises de l'économie sociale et solidaire. Identités plurielles et spécificités*, De Boeck Supérieur, Louvain-la-Neuve, pp. 157–179, 2012.

[MOR 94] MORGAN R.M., HUNT D.S., "The commitment-trust theory of relationship marketing", *Journal of Marketing*, vol. 3, no. 58, pp. 20–38, 1994.

[TOU 05] TOUCAS P., DREYFUS M., *Les coopérateurs : deux siècles de pratiques coopératives,* Editions de l'Atelier, Paris, 2005.

15

Purpose Corporations and Customer Strategy: Toward a Strategy of Customer Education and Empowerment?

15.1. Purpose corporations: a response to customers' expectations of "responsible" capitalism

15.1.1. *Customer demand for "enhanced" corporate social responsibility*

Numerous studies have recently shown that customers expect companies to assume, within the framework of a social and environmental responsibility that we could describe as "enhanced", not only the negative impact that their activities may have on the environment but also a genuine political role in the city. As early as 2018, in a study carried out by Havas Paris[1], 60% of French people considered that "companies today have a more important role than governments in creating a better future", and 73% of them considered that they have "more power than ever to transform society". Large corporations, whose economic weight sometimes equals a country's GDP, could take over from the state in embracing major societal challenges. According to the barometer of the Observatoire des sociétés à mission[2], in 2022, "67% of French people expect business leaders to take over from the government when the latter is struggling to solve societal problems". At a time when societal needs are colossal (health, improved housing, better nutrition, help for the

Chapter written by Isabelle PRIM-ALLAZ and Martine SÉVILLE.

1 See: https://www.lesechos.fr/idees-debats/cercle/changer-la-vie-de-la-politique-aux-marques-130307.

2 See: https://www.observatoiredessocietesamission.com/.

elderly, greater financial security, less damage to the environment, etc.), it is clear that these are, in fact, not completely fulfilled by the conventional economy [POR 11]. Companies, true "agents of civilization", as Hatchuel describes them, noting that it "is not the State which invented the railway or the smartphone", are now often recognized as major sources of profound transformation of society by their stakeholders, notably their shareholders and their customers.

All in all, companies have been given and are taking on a genuine "collective creative mission" in the face of major societal challenges, which some of them have decided to embody by setting up new systems (e.g. societal dividends[3]) and adopting a new form of company, the purpose corporation.

15.1.2. *Companies with a mission to meet customer expectations?*

15.1.2.1. *A developing phenomenon, but not so new worldwide*

Until 2019, the date of the PACTE Act[4] (see below), French law was limited to distinguishing private companies in the commercial sector from those in the social and solidarity economy (presented in the previous chapter). Private companies all had the same legal status, that of "joint-stock" companies, whose main objective, as set out in their articles of association, was above all to serve the interests of their shareholders. The assessment of these companies was essentially based on the measurement of their economic and financial performance (sales growth rates, economic and financial profitability rates, etc.).

However, as early as the 1980s, new thinking began to emerge in the United States about the very purpose of corporate activity – their "raison d'être". In the United States, new statutes such as purpose or benefit corporations have emerged[5] [AUT 20]. These companies explicitly state their intention to pursue a dual purpose, the pursuit of profit AND the pursuit of a positive impact on society, by enshrining this mission in their articles of association. A manifesto published in 2019 by a group of American executives, for example, reiterates the primary interest of companies in investing in their employees, offering value to customers, treating suppliers fairly and supporting the frontiers in which they operate[6].

---

3 See: https://www.francetransactions.com/actus/news-banques/dividende-societal-credit-mutuel.html.

4 PACTE – *plan d'action pour la croissance et la transformation des entreprises*. A French plan of action for the growth and transformation of businesses.

5 These are known as B-Corp companies.

6 See: https://fr.businessam.be/business-roundtable-responsabilisation-entreprises/.

15.1.2.2. *The PACTE Act law in France and the emergence of privately owned "purpose" corporations*

With the introduction of the concept of the "purpose corporation", France's PACTE law[7], passed in May 2019, changes the definition of a company in the Civil Code by breaking with the sole interest of the partners and specifying that the company, which remains a company financed by private capital, "must be managed in its social interest, taking into consideration the social and environmental issues of its activity" (Article 1833 of the Civil Code)[8].

As a result, companies have an autonomous interest that goes beyond that of the individuals who make them up. The PACTE law thus calls on managers to consider the social and environmental issues at stake in their activity, and to include them in their management decisions in the interests of civil society[9].

The purpose corporation implies a commitment on the part of stakeholders and, in particular, shareholders, to place social and environmental objectives at the heart of the corporate project, at least at the same level as economic objectives [AUT 20, COR 20]. The PACTE law added a paragraph to article 1835 of the French Civil Code, allowing companies to define a raison d'être and incorporate it into their articles of association.

Inclusion in the statutes:

1) a raison d'être;

2) one or more social and environmental objectives that the company is committed to pursuing in the course of its business;

3) procedures for monitoring the execution of the assignment, including the creation of an assignment committee (or an assignment coordinator for companies with fewer than 50 employees), separate from the corporate bodies and comprising at least one employee.

Verification by an independent third-party organization every two years (three years for companies with fewer than 50 employees) that targets are being met.

Box 15.1. *Conditions for obtaining the purpose corporation status*[10]

7 See: https://www.legifrance.gouv.fr/jorf/id/JORFTEXT000038496102/.

8 See: https://www.entreprisesamission.org/la-loi-pacte/.

9 *Ibid.*

10 See: https://www.observatoiredessocietesamission.com/wp-content/uploads/2022/03/barometre-societes-a-mission-1.pdf.

15.1.2.3. *Raison d'être and objectives of purpose corporations*

The definition of a raison d'être remains flexible and specific to each company. This raison d'être must reflect a real project for the company over the long term. It is a real opportunity to involve a wide range of stakeholders in the process[11]. By defining a precise raison d'être and clear underlying objectives, the company with a mission defines a kind of code of conduct known to all, and which presupposes a collective commitment (see Figure 15.1).

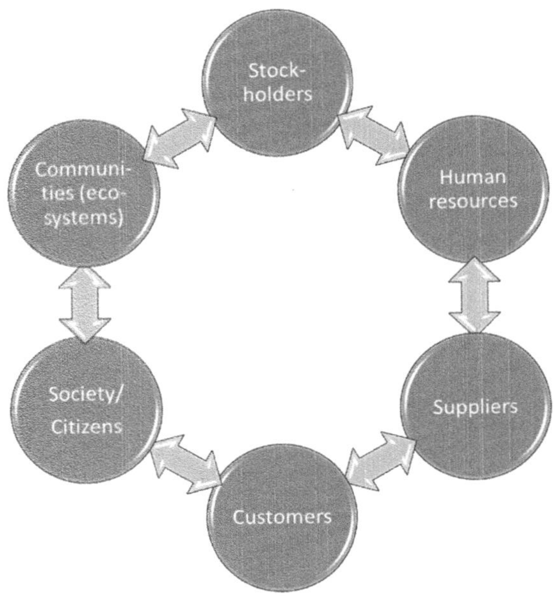

Figure 15.1. *Potential stakeholders in the mission*

The mission is made up of "a raison d'être (defining the company's identity, its usefulness to society and the future it wishes to help build), associated social and environmental objectives, and a governance structure that protects the given purpose"[12]. These objectives constitute an operational guide to conduct, as shown in Box 15.2.

11 See: https://www.entreprisesamission.org/la-loi-pacte/.

12 See: https://www.observatoiredessocietesamission.com/wp-content/uploads/2022/03/barometre-societes-a-mission-5.pdf.

Raison d'être

The company's raison d'être is to enable everyone to experience life to the full, leaving no footprints other than their own.

Objectives

The social and environmental objectives that the company is committed to pursuing in the course of its business, within the meaning of the 2nd article L.210*10 of the French Commercial Code, are as follows:

– designing sustainable products using recycled or certified raw materials;

– using suppliers who guarantee their compliance with the United Nations Global Compact principles;

– encouraging and promoting environmentally friendly behavior among employees by adapting workplaces and organizing internal environmental awareness campaigns;

– implementing actions to raise awareness of the circular economy and environmental protection among customers, and give them the opportunity to take action at their own level;

– participating in and supporting environmental protection initiatives, notably aimed at preserving forests, biodiversity and eagles.

Box 15.2. *Example of a raison d'être and related objectives – the case of Aigle (retail, outdoor wear)*

More specifically, in the course of writing this chapter, we studied 270 purpose corporations[13]. The main missions they pursue are the following (a raison d'être can be coded in several dimensions): social benefit (67% of companies studied), environmental protection (64%), financial performance (14%), reasons internal to the organization, particularly in the HR dimension (10%) or even ethics (6%).

These raisons d'être touch on a variety of major societal challenges, while taking into account the need for economic sustainability.

By making this raison d'être explicit, purpose corporations thus seem to provide an initial response to customer demand for "enhanced" social and environmental

13 To complete this chapter, we carried out an analysis of the raisons d'être (and related objectives) of the purpose corporations listed at https://www.observatoiredessocietesamission.com/societes-a-mission-referencees/, at the end of June 2022. Of the 660 companies listed, 270 were available and then analyzed.

responsibility. However, what role can/should they play in the definition and realization of this mission?

The role of shareholders in purpose corporations has, in fact, been widely debated while the role of customers in this transition to the purpose corporation has much less discussed. Is it conceivable that customers are content to express a demand for "enhanced" corporate social and environmental responsibility, without being more involved in defining the company's mission, or even in carrying it out?

In this chapter, we begin by showing that assuming a societal mission means managing the "customer loyalty paradox" – a real challenge for the long-term survival of these companies, which are in fact undergoing a profound transformation of their business model; we then go on to analyze the extent to which consumers are themselves associated with the achievement of their mission in the discourse of these companies; finally, we propose a genuine strategy for empowering customers within these companies with a mission.

15.2. The "customer loyalty paradox" in purpose corporations

Purpose corporations are hybrid organizations that have to reconcile two logics: an economic logic to meet the profitability objectives necessary for their survival, and a societal, social and environmental logic. This balancing act is a difficult one, as the company is constantly at risk of "schizophrenia" as it is torn between different, sometimes even contradictory, objectives (see Table 15.1).

When transforming a company into a purpose corporation, the search for this difficult balance complicates the relationship with the customer (see section 15.2.1), even if this transformation meets some of the company's CSR requirements and is itself a tool for winning new customers and building loyalty (see section 15.2.2).

Business and marketing objectives	Purpose corporation objectives
Short-term: financial profitability and customer satisfaction	In the long term: implement a set of means in a sustainable and proactive manner to best embrace one or more societal causes – environmental or social – even if it means reducing or reorienting customer choices and increasing prices Establish performance indicators linked to the mission, which may conflict with economic performance indicators

Business and marketing objectives	Corporate mission objectives
Strive for differentiation to achieve the most profitable competitive positioning possible and be perceived as different by the customer	No competitive positioning, no differentiation, no open competition on societal objectives. On the contrary, it is about looking for a community of practices and interests that makes it possible to embrace the societal mission "together". This implies forging special partnerships with companies or organizations that themselves have a mission (financial institutions with a mission, suppliers of companies with a mission). The risk, however, is of building an ecosystem between these different companies that is so intertwined that it no longer leaves much room for freedom to customers, who become extremely captive
Risk of losing financial partners and loyal customers if the company is too mission-focused; possible need to find new customers more in tune with the social mission	Risk of losing legitimacy if no coherent, credible mission strategy

Table 15.1. *The difficult balance of the purpose corporation between different objectives and associated risks*

15.2.1. *The transition to a purpose corporation: a challenge for customer relations*

For companies that are not "born" as purpose corporations, but that become them, the transition to this status goes hand in hand with an adaptation of their business model. In particular, the value proposition made to customers must integrate this societal mission. Carrefour's "Act for Food" initiative is in line with the mission that the company has given itself by becoming a purpose corporation:

> To offer our customers quality services, products and food accessible to all through all distribution channels. Thanks to the skills of our employees, our responsible and multicultural approach, our local roots and our ability to adapt to production and consumption patterns, we aim to be a leader in the food transition for all.

However, while the company is implementing numerous internal actions to fulfill this mission, it is doing little to communicate its new status to its customers.

As part of this transformation, purpose corporations have to deal with a paradox, which we call the "customer loyalty paradox": by becoming a purpose corporation, it responds in some way to increasingly stringent customer demands in terms of corporate social responsibility (CSR), but many of its existing customers are in danger of drifting away as a result of the transformation of its value proposition. Customers who were previously loyal may find themselves destabilized in several ways:

– they may not adhere to the mission put forward by the company and/or may lose interest in it;

– they may consider the transition to this new status as opportunistic and insincere and interpret it as missionwashing[14];

– they may no longer fit into offers that have evolved as a result of the new mission: withdrawal of certain products or services that are incompatible with the mission, such as, for example, products deemed too polluting (choice editing), or price changes (e.g. relocation of production resulting in higher labor costs).

Thus, when Camif, a house furniture reseller, which had become a purpose corporation, refused to implement the Black Friday operation by closing its online sales site on that day, considering that it went against its mission entitled "Offering Products and Services for the Home, for the Benefit of People and the Planet", the company risked seeing some of its loyal customers criticize it for not offering them advantageous prices, like competitors. Camif, by adopting this action in 2017[15], closing its online sales site on this day of mass promotion – an action now followed by 1,200 brands[16] – showed that it trusts its customers by making them aware of their responsibilities with regard to over-consumption (see Box 15.3).

No Black Friday, just disconnect!

On Black Friday [since 2017], we close our website and Camif goes offline for the planet! Why? Simply because there is no plan B for the planet. It is our first home, so let us protect it! This is the strongest gesture an e-commerce site can make. Zero sales. An absolute refusal to over-consume on this long-awaited day. Yes, it is a powerful act, because we want to raise awareness of responsible, reasoned consumption. More local, more sustainable, more civic-minded. But what about you? What will you be doing on Black Friday? Join us in #JeMeDeconnectePourLaPlanete (I'm Disconnecting for the Planet).

Box 15.3. *Camif and the refusal to participate in Black Friday*[17]

14 In reference to the term "greenwashing", which refers to companies that try to give themselves an eco-responsible image, far removed from the reality of their business.

15 See: https://camif.fr/lesbelleshistoires/pas-de-black-friday-deconnecte.html.

16 Initiated by another purpose corporation, Faguo. See: https://www.makefridaygreenagain.com/.

17 See: https://camif.fr/lesbelleshistoires/pas-de-black-friday-deconnecte.html.

CEO Emery Jacquillat puts it this way: “We’ve decided not to do it, and not to be part of this over-consumption that runs counter to our values. It’s not good for our wallet, nor that of our customers”, and nor for the planet!

15.2.2. *The transition to a purpose corporation: a tool for winning and building loyalty*

The definition and implementation of a mission can now be seen as an argument for building loyalty for a clientele gradually attached to the issue of CSR and for attracting a new clientele sensitive to these arguments, and the efforts of the company to assume its political role in the community. This clientele can be considered as buycott-oriented[18] [PRI 12].

According to some authors who have worked on the implementation of business models in hybrid organizations such as B-corp companies [DAV 18, DAV 19], their target audience corresponds to “more conscious customers, with the aim of educating, raising awareness and reinforcing their role as consumers while improving their well-being. Prices are higher than average, which their customers can afford. Relationships with customers are morally driven and built on emotional bonds, highlighting what customers choose as correct” [TAB 21, p. 4]. Transforming the company into a purpose corporation may thus, if it fails to convince its loyal customers, require a new customer segmentation and targeting strategy, geared more toward niches of consumers sensitive to “sustainable” dimensions [DAV 18].

In this respect, studies carried out on B-corp companies provide some interesting insights. The first is that, while the transition to B-corp status increases overall sales for these companies in the short term [PAE 21], the real leverage effect of this transformation on sales occurs in the medium term. Although the reasons for the time interval required for the effects on sales to stabilize are not specified in this work, we can put forward the hypothesis that a balance needs to be struck between the departure of certain customers unconvinced by this new status and the arrival of new customers attracted by this strategy.

This can be seen, for example, at Elizia Conseil, whose mission is to “defend our commitments to society by offering the best consulting services to players with a strong social impact”, and where “over 50% of our clients are non-profit organizations, resolutely committed to a more inclusive society” (source: Elizia Conseil).

---

18 The term “buycott” refers to the idea of choosing a product or service for its responsible characteristics, as opposed to boycott, which is the rejection of an offer because it is not responsible.

In France, no study, to our knowledge, has analyzed the risk of losing previously loyal customers, nor the importance of the arrival of new customers associated with the company's transformation into a purpose corporation. It is clear, however, that the transition to a purpose corporation requires the company to make its customers aware of, or convince them of, the importance of its social mission, in particular of the fact that there are other beneficiaries of the company's activity (those of the societal mission) besides itself – and to make them potentially accept a higher price, necessary for the company to be able to assume its mission [DAV 18], a new offer or even partnerships with other purpose corporations. This new ecosystem may seem to impose itself on customers, so it is essential to involve them in the mission in one way or another. Some companies use their most committed customers as ambassadors.

As a result, there is a real need for communication, conviction, education and empowerment of customers to build loyalty and attract new customers. This work can forge a new relationship marketing strategy more centered on morality and affective ties [DAV 18, TAB 21], in which the end customer is both a beneficiary of the company's activity, in that they consume its products and services, and an actor/contributor to the company's social mission.

15.3. Toward a new relationship marketing strategy

In order to overcome the "customer loyalty paradox", the company needs to rethink its relational marketing approach, raising customer awareness and educating them to ensure that they not only adhere to the company's mission, but are also involved in defining and carrying it out. The aim is to develop a strategy of customer empowerment (in the sense of Spreitzer [SPR 95]) based on information, communication regarding the objectives and results of these actions and empowerment in the face of major societal challenges. The Aigle company, for example, has set itself the objective of "implementing awareness-raising actions for customers in relation to the circular economy and environmental protection, and giving them the opportunity to take action at their own level".

15.3.1. *Purpose corporations: (re)thinking customer relations*

A purpose corporation, by committing itself to fulfilling a societal objective while remaining sustainable and profitable, will no longer seek to maintain a captive customer base by encouraging the growth and renewal of their consumption through a classic strategy of persuasion. On the contrary, it will seek to act, through the role it is trying to play in the face of contemporary challenges, in their long-term interests, and to reciprocally encourage their responsible behavior by activating their "moral" motivations to a greater extent. It must therefore create a relationship of trust with its customers, who must be convinced of the value of such an approach, and make them true partners in the accomplishment of its mission, which is far from the traditional techniques of persuasion [COU 16]. The relationship is therefore part of a long-term vision, a mutual commitment and a relationship of trust, all of which form the basis of relationship marketing. While relationship marketing is generally defined as the establishment, development and maintenance of a mutually successful exchange relationship [MOR 94], the notion of "success" takes on a different meaning in the context of enhanced CSR and purpose corporations. The promotion of "sustainable" consumption cannot, in fact, go hand in hand with ever-increasing consumption; it also presupposes acceptance on the part of customers of a sharing of value extended to new stakeholders such as the beneficiaries of the mission.

Crédit Mutuel Arkéa, a French bank, highlights this notion of extended value sharing in its mission statement: "To this end, we have chosen to be a cooperative and collaborative bank that promotes a balanced sharing of value with its members, customers, employees, partners and communities. We are a socially responsible, ethical and inclusive company, and we take great care to respect our environment".

All in all, while relationship marketing and purpose corporations share the same fundamentals, the way in which they reach out to customers and convince them seems to differ from what conventional companies can do, particularly in terms of the place that relationship marketing should give to the customer in this relationship of mutual commitment to a mission. The customer's role may be simply to accept the new mission by accepting the new marketing conditions: modification of the offer, price increase, appearance of new partners who are themselves purpose corporations. It is a form of minimum participation which presupposes on the part of the purpose corporation a promotion and justification strategy around the mission and its interest (see section 15.3.2). The customer can also be supported by the purpose corporation, which educates, informs and helps them to transform (see section 15.3.3). In this way, customers gain skills and autonomy of action; they become empowered. Finally, customers can be invited to become more involved in the realization of the company's mission, either as co-creators of a new offering or as ambassadors of the mission and related offering (see section 15.3.4). As an example, Camif launched a Camifathon around circular economy experts, French manufacturers, designers and customers to brainstorm new collections [CHR 17].

15.3.2. *A renewed promotion and justification strategy around the raisons d'être of purpose corporations*

Companies with a mission need to build their promotion strategy around their raison d'être, with customers taken as witnesses, or even enlisted, for the company's major challenges.

Some purpose corporations emphasize this "collective", "doing things together" dimension in their raison d'être; for example, Crédit Mutuel Alliance Nationale: "*Together, Listen, Act*", or Botanic: "*Together, let's find the path back to nature.* [...] We unite a community of enthusiasts (experts and customers) who share their know-how. We act at the heart of a network of partners, creating, producing, selecting, distributing and advising on more natural products and solutions".

Of the 270 raisons d'être analyzed for this research, 35% cite the customer or the offer made to the customer as the reason for their mission. Some B2B companies define their raison d'être as helping their own customers to achieve their mission, as shown in Box 15.4.

> We are convinced that sustainable economic performance can only exist in a sustainable world: a world that prioritizes the fulfilment and dignity of human beings, as well as the restoration and preservation of the environment. We need to move society towards more society-based, socially and environmentally sustainable models, and finance is one of the most powerful levers for addressing this challenge. We support our customers in the challenge of bringing together financial, social and environmental objectives, so that through their capital and their commitment, they can contribute to building a better world. Our aim is to create a humane and responsible family office that makes a positive impact on its customers, employees and partners, and whose ethical values create economic value. So, together with all our stakeholders, we want to be leaders in setting the highest economic, social and environmental standards. We want to lead the way in integrating a global, social, societal and sustainable approach throughout the value chain.

Box 15.4. *Example of customer-related mission: Jahier Pneumatics*

An analysis of the objectives associated with these raisons d'être, according to the elements of customer strategy they reflect, reveals 10 dimensions: helping the customer to transform toward something more sustainable (18% of companies); educating the customer (14%); developing the customer's degree of empowerment (10%); improving the quality of the offer (9%); creating and developing trust (7%); generating or increasing customer satisfaction (5%); developing a long-term relationship (4%); integrating the customer into the organization (3%); choosing customers in line with the mission (2%); improving customer relations (1%).

The first four dimensions correspond well to the objectives of raising customer awareness, educating them about the mission and involving them in defining and carrying it out.

15.3.3. *Customer awareness and education: a renewed corporate branding strategy*

The purpose corporation, through its raison d'être, takes on a strong, unique organizational identity. This means promoting this identity on the basis of a renewed corporate branding strategy, potentially embodied by the leader thus invested with a new role. It must make its customers aware of the causes it supports and encourage them to take responsibility for their behavior. It must also highlight the alignment of the company's business model with the mission it has set itself, and make the public aware of the efforts it is making, and that its customers agree to make with it, to fulfill this mission. As Jessica Kruger, founder of LUXTRA, a B-corp for sustainable clothing, has stated: "Our B-corp status has become a big part of our identity, so rather than our communication simply being 'buy this new pink bag', we engage with customers by talking about bigger issues and add value to their lives through education. It leaves an impression".[19] Patagonia's "Don't buy this jacket" campaign[20] is part of the same approach. Poponi et al. [POP 19] speak of the need to adopt an "awareness-raising perspective". Camif has set itself the goal of "informing, raising awareness and empowering [customers] to consume more responsibly". Poponi et al. [POP 19] and Tabares [TAB 21] suggest that B-corp-type companies should develop global communications centered on stories of success and failure to create emotional and affective bonds with customers and a shared experience of moral commitment to the mission. Camif is doing just that, talking about the "great stories"[21] surrounding the closure of its site on Black Friday.

The work of persuasion or communication may involve a rethink of the classic mass communication strategy in favor of more targeted communication, or communication that is more focused on the players or those responsible for the mission, such as the managers who embody the mission, or the customers themselves as ambassadors.

15.3.4. *A customer education strategy for mutual learning and commitment to the mission*

There are a number of rationales and related objectives that demonstrate how purpose corporations seek to reinforce the education of their customers toward more

19 See: https://www.transitionearth.co/2021/02/24/what-is-a-b-corp-and-will-it-ever-matter-to-consumers/.

20 See: https://eu.patagonia.com/fr/fr/stories/dont-buy-this-jacket-black-friday-and-the-new-york-times/story-18615.html.

21 See: https://camif.fr/lesbelleshistoires/pas-de-black-friday-deconnecte.html.

responsible behavior, in line with the mission the company has endorsed. To name but three:

– "Inform, raise awareness and provide the means for more responsible consumption" (Camif's objective).

– "Its mission is to provide its customers and stakeholders with concrete, pragmatic solutions to help them better manage the production and recovery of waste from construction activities. This mission takes the form of waste prevention consulting, waste sorting education, the design of sorting and promotion tools, collection services tailored to the constraints of the construction industry and adapted to site constraints, and the selection of ecologically efficient recycling channels in terms of distance and industrial processes" (Tri'n'collect's mission).

– "Make second-hand a reflex" (Il Etait Plusieurs Fois's mission).

Together, these activities aim to raise awareness and, through new behaviors, improve the social footprint of both the company with a mission and its customers: improvements at the heart of today's social and environmental challenges.

15.3.5. *Helping customers transform*

Many purpose corporations, especially consulting firms, are asserting their commitment to helping customers transform toward more sustainable models. For example:

– "Promote environmentally friendly solutions for our customers' projects" (Elcimal's objective).

– "Our raison d'être is to undertake transformations for a desirable economy. As entrepreneurs in the field of management consulting, and as players in the unique development of their companies, we are committed to the strategic, cultural and technological transformation of our customers. As the bearers of a responsible vision of business and industry, we work alongside them to build sustainable success, combining performance and contribution to the community" (Kea & Partners's mission statement).

In addition to raising awareness, the purpose corporation has an interest, as with stockholders, in involving customers more closely in the very definition of the mission and its realization.

15.3.6. *Encouraging customer involvement in defining and carrying out the company's mission*

Involvement in the very definition of the mission and the means to achieve it for customers is undoubtedly one way of overcoming the paradox of customer loyalty mentioned earlier. This commitment presupposes a rethinking of the customer's role in relation to the four pillars of the purpose corporation and, more generally, in the governance of these companies.

15.3.6.1. *Rethinking the customer's role in relation to the four pillars of the purpose corporation*

Customers must be able to intervene in the four pillars of a purpose corporation[22]. These include the definition of the mission, objectives, commitments and responsibilities through a customer-education strategy; corporate governance of these companies through the participation of customers in strategic decisions; and, finally, the evaluation of these companies through the opinion they can give on their ability to carry out the societal objective of the raison d'être, the marketing objective of differentiated positioning and the more general objective of profitability. The role of the customer must reflect an alignment between the strategy defined in the context of adopting the status of a purpose corporation, the resulting objectives, the organizational resources mobilized and the customer strategy adopted [PRI 19].

This alignment takes the form of organizational or management choices, such as Camif's decision to re-internalize its call center to ensure that the processing of requests is consistent with the company's mission[23], or MAIF's (an insurance company) decision not to commit its employees to sales, so as not to create a misalignment between the interests of the employee and those of the customer. Consistency must be recognized by all stakeholders. These new resources are sometimes important sources of managerial innovation. At Camif, for example, a service for locating repairers, recyclers and resource centers was set up after employees pointed out, during the creation of a collaborative budget, that Camif's mission to advocate a responsible consumption model favoring the circular economy was incomplete, as it focused only on "consuming better" and not on "consuming less" [AUT 20].

---

22 See: https://www2.deloitte.com/content/dam/Deloitte/fr/Documents/sustainability-services/deloitte_companies-a-mission-2019.pdf.

23 CAMIF's mission: "To offer products and services for the home that benefit people and the planet. Mobilize our ecosystem (consumers, employees, suppliers, partners, local players), collaborate and act to invent new models of consumption, production and organization".

15.3.6.2. *A new role for customers in the governance of purpose corporations to promote transparency and evaluation*

Many of today's customers demand proof of a company's commitment to its stated mission.

The success of platforms such as YUCA and SCanUp, as well as those arriving in other sectors (such as Clear Fashion in apparel), is forcing companies to transform themselves and their products. Global Report Initiative (GRI) indicators, as well as reports from organizations that assess purpose corporations (B-Lab for B-Corp companies, independent third-party reports for purpose corporations) on various dimensions, provide customers with a set of proof elements that the company has no control over. The company is thus urged to be perfectly transparent about its actions and their impact, in line with the mission it has set itself. Purpose corporations are helped in this by their legal framework, which requires the creation of a mission committee. The U.S. B-Corp Act requires the creation of a committee of independent experts whose purpose is to verify that the objectives corresponding to the mission have indeed been pursued. In this way, an obligation of means is imposed, which means that the results do not necessarily achieve the objectives initially set.

By 2022, 79% of purpose corporations had integrated at least one external stakeholder into their governance process. These included experts and researchers, as well as customers and shareholders. There is no single model for the composition of a mission committee, which reflects the identity and ambition of each company[24]. However, Vileva et al. [VIL 21] have shown that even when the raisons d'être were consumer-focused, B-corp companies did not transform their governance in depth; this remained made up of founders and shareholders without involving or incorporating customers. This is a point that needs to be rethought by companies contemplating their transition to a purpose-based status.

More generally, customers need to be convinced that the company is doing everything in its power to achieve its dual goals of social responsibility and economic performance. This proof that a purpose corporation is doing everything in its power to embrace its mission to the full must be given to customers on a regular basis and is a prerequisite for establishing a relationship of mutual trust between the company and its customers. Otherwise, the purpose corporation runs the risk of missionwashing, just like greenwashing. A high level of transparency is therefore essential: transparency regarding the commitments and promises made by products, and transparency regarding the actions taken to fulfill its mission. Acionnys formation, for example, has set itself the objective of "guaranteeing the

24 See: https://www.entreprisesamission.org/la-loi-pacte/.

independence of its capital, for the benefit of its staff and in the interests of its customers; never compromising on honesty and transparency with respect to its customers and the market; working to maximize the usefulness and impact of the assignments carried out; being ethically irreproachable in the exercise of its profession". The presence of client representatives on engagement committees would reinforce this transparency, as it would enable closer links to be forged between the company's decision-makers and its clients.

In conclusion, in a purpose corporation, the customer-buyer would become an active customer, taking on a role in the company's mission. This presupposes a genuine commitment on the part of the customer of a purpose corporation, as well as the acquisition of new skills. Does this mean that the customers of purpose corporations have a special profile? Would they themselves have new expectations of marketing? Research into the behavior of customers of purpose corporations and their commitment, as well as these companies' approach to marketing, must now be undertaken in order to get to know these customers better and measure their degree of loyalty to these companies and their willingness to be empowered in the company's mission.

15.4. References

[AUT 20] AUTISSIER D., *Entreprises à mission et raison d'être : changer l'entreprise pour un monde plus durable*, Dunod, Paris, 2020.

[CHR 21] CHRISTIAN D., TOUVARD F., *L'entreprise à mission : concept novateur ou effet de mode ?*, Mardaga, Brussels, 2021.

[COR 20] CORIAT B., TORO M., "Nutri'zaza, la malnutrition et le service du bien commun : histoire d'une entreprise sociale hybride à "Objet Social Exclusif"", *Entreprise & Société*, vol. 6, pp. 85–103, 2020.

[COU 16] COUPET A., DORMAGEN E., "Au-delà de la RSE, l'entreprise progressiste", *Gestion HEC Montréal*, vol. 41, no. 3, pp. 25–29, 2016.

[DAV 18] DAVIES I.A., CHAMBERS L., "Integrating hybridity and business model theory in sustainable entrepreneurship", *Journal of Cleaner Production*, vol. 177, pp. 378–386, 2018.

[DAV 19] DAVIES I.A., DOHERTY B., "Balancing a hybrid business model: the search for equilibrium at Cafédirect", *Journal of Business Ethics*, vol. 157, no. 4, pp. 1043–1066, 2019.

[MOR 94] MORGAN R.M., HUNT S.D., "The commitment-trust theory of relationship marketing", *Journal of Marketing*, vol. 58, no. 3, pp. 20–38, 1994.

[PAE 21] PAELMAN V., VAN CAUWENBERGE P., VANDER BAUWHEDE H., "The impact of B corp certification on growth", *Sustainability*, vol. 13, no. 13, p. 7191, doi: 10.3390/su13137191, 2021.

[POP 19] POPONI S., COLANTONI A., CIVIDINO S.R. et al., "The stakeholders' perspective within the B Corp certification for a circular approach", *Sustainability*, vol. 11, no. 6, pp. 1584, 2019.

[POR 11] PORTER M.E., KRAMER M.R., "Creating shared value: Redefining capitalism and the role of the corporation in society", *Harvard Business Review*, vol. 89, no. 1/2, pp. 62–77, 2011.

[PRI 12] PRIM-ALLAZ I., "La résistance des consommateurs et le marketing", in MARTINET A.-C. (ed.), *Le management au cœur de la société : mutations et ruptures,* Vuibert, Paris, 2012.

[PRI 19] PRIM-ALLAZ I., VOLLE P., "Organizing the augmented customer relationship", in N'GOALA G., PEZ V., PRIM-ALLAZ I. (eds), *Augmented Customer Strategy: CRM in the Digital Age*, ISTE Ltd, London and John Wiley & Sons, New York, 2019.

[SPR 95] SPREITZER G.M., "Psychological empowerment in the workplace: Dimensions, measurement, and validation", *Academy of Management Journal*, vol. 38, no. 5, pp. 1442–1465, 1995.

[TAB 21] TABARES S., "Certified B corporations: An approach to tensions of sustainable-driven hybrid business models in an emerging economy", *Journal of Cleaner Production*, vol. 317, pp. 128380, 2021.

[VIL 21] VILLELA M., BULGACOV S., MORGAN G., "B Corp certification and its impact on organizations over time", *Journal of Business Ethics*, vol. 170, no. 2, pp. 343–357, 2021.

16

Complex Customer Experience Management with Multi-stakeholders

The advent of new information and communication technologies at the turn of the 1990s had a lasting impact on the customer's relationship with the company. It gave rise to a multiplication of communication and marketing channels (such as the Web, cellphones, etc.), as well as complexity in customer journeys, which have become cross-channel or omni-channel and no longer linear. In addition, the 2000s witnessed large-scale intermediation phenomena linked to the arrival of platforms on extremely varied markets: the take-away food market and the vacation rental market, for example. All these developments generate growing interrelationships between stakeholders within experiential ecosystems (Box 16.1).

Companies have a pressing need to manage the complexity generated by these fundamental changes. Customer experience management as a theoretical field has evolved considerably in recent years to take account of these changes. It is no longer a question of analyzing the behavior of actors, customers, partners, companies, etc., in isolation from one another, but rather of adopting a networked perspective to grasp these interrelationships.

This chapter outlines the marketing literature on customer experience and its management. It reviews the origins of the customer experience concept, before proposing a shift from a customer-centric perspective to a multi-stakeholder perspective. Finally, it discusses the crucial role of value propositions as both a descriptor and driver of stakeholder alignment in experiential contexts. Throughout the chapter, we use the case of FranceGaz, a supplier of bottled and natural gas, to illustrate each of the concepts in practice.

Chapter written by Amélie MARTIN.

The following case study highlights the complexity and number of actors involved in customer experience management. To this end, we can define the experiential ecosystem as the network of stakeholders with a direct or indirect influence on the design, management and/or delivery of customer journeys. This experiential ecosystem is represented here as the focal company, in whose name the experience is delivered to the end customer. The following case study is that of a tank and cylinder gas supplier we call FranceGaz*. We have reconstructed its experiential ecosystem on the basis of an interview with the organization's head of customer journey management and secondary data collection (annual reports, internal documents, websites, general and specialized press articles).

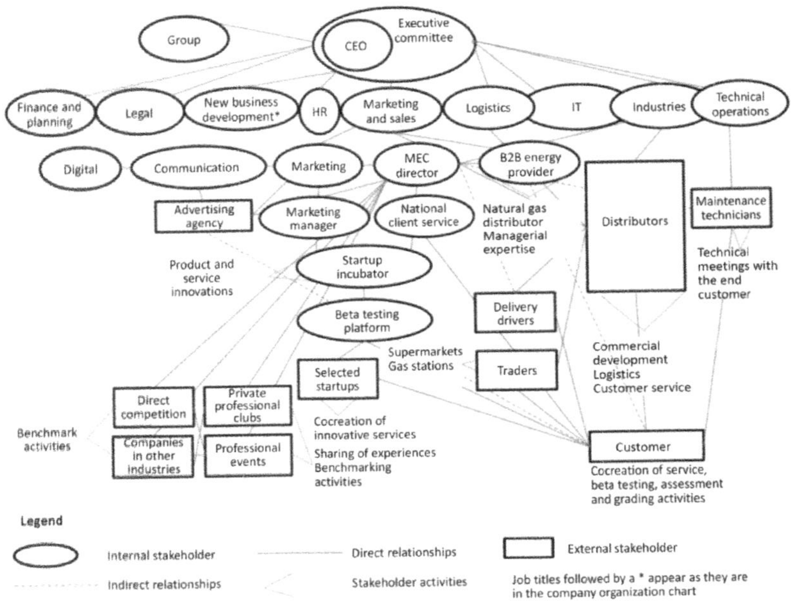

Figure 16.1. *A supplier's experiential ecosystem of bottled and tanked gas*

Box 16.1. *Customer experience management and experiential ecosystem. *Names have been changed*

16.1. From customer experience to its management

Hungry at lunchtime, you go out into the street and choose a restaurant in which to eat. You enjoy your meal, exchange a few words with the waiter or waitress, settle the bill and get back to work. Planning your next vacation, you carefully choose a hotel to stay in. You read online customer reviews, compare rates across booking platforms and so on. You finally settle on a hotel and take the opportunity to sign up for a boat trip offered by the hotel. You will not be staying there for several months, but making this reservation already projects you into the experience. What do these two stories have in common? In both cases, you are living a consumption experience, otherwise known as a customer experience.

16.1.1. *The origins of the customer experience*

The customer experience takes place in all our acts of consumption, from the everyday (shopping, for example) to the more exceptional (buying a car, going on a trip). It occurs when a set of interactions occurs between a customer and all or part of a company, product or service, provoking one or more reactions.

The customer experience is strictly personal: the consumption experience you have in a restaurant will undoubtedly differ at least in part from that of the colleague with whom you shared your meal. This difference is explained in particular by your socio-demographic (based on social or demographic particularities) and psychographic (based on lifestyle, beliefs, values or personality) characteristics, which may differ significantly from those of your colleague.

Customer experience also involves the consumer at different levels: rational, emotional, sensory, physical and spiritual [GEN 07].

16.1.2. *A first approach to customer experience management*

Customer experience management is the strategy designed to manage this experience. The focus here is on the organizational aspects of the customer experience. The traditional top-down marketing perspective, in which the organization is conceptualized as mastering all aspects of the customer experience, is overtaken by another approach. The experience arises from factors controlled by the organization (e.g. elements of the marketing mix and point-of-sale atmosphere), but also from factors outside its direct control (e.g. consumer-related factors, situational moderators and the social environment) [JON 99, BAC 06, VER 09]. Box 16.2 presents the context of the FranceGaz company and its internal stakeholders.

The case of bottled and tanked gas supplier FranceGaz* allows us to highlight the main stakeholder groups involved in the customer experience. This box deals with internal stakeholders at the group and company level. Box 16.3 deals with external stakeholders at the level of the network of stakeholders that make up the experiential ecosystem.

FranceGaz* company background

Founded in 1931 by two French engineers, FranceGaz has been an Alpha* subsidiary since 2015. The second-largest distributor of liquefied petroleum gas in France, FranceGaz holds a 25% market share in a market of 2 million tons. The company operates from 46 depots, distributing its products to 250,000 B2C customers, 16,000 points of sale (gas cylinder resellers) and 10,000 B2B customers in the cylinder segment. Every year, an average of 4 million customers use FranceGaz cylinders. FranceGaz sources its liquefied petroleum gas from several suppliers in France, Belgium, Spain and Germany: exploration-production and refining companies and import and supply terminals. Internally, FranceGaz relies on an experienced management team and a high-quality sales, marketing and operating infrastructure. FranceGaz is a well-known brand among French gas consumers.

Group level

Alpha, the group that has owned FranceGaz since 2015, defines the overall strategic direction and uses portfolio synergies to develop new offerings. For example, Alpha acquired EuroGaz* (a French company specializing in natural gas distribution) in 2017. Leveraging EuroGaz's brand, experienced management teams and industry expertise, FranceGaz has launched a new natural gas and electricity offering for its B2C customers.

Company level

The management team decided to give the company a strong customer experience focus in 2014. To this end, it created the position of Director of Customer Experience Management. The Director of Customer Experience draws on internal infrastructure and management teams. She works closely with the marketing division and assumes direct responsibility for national customer service.

Box 16.2. *Internal stakeholders. *Names have been changed*

16.1.3. *The customer journey approach and value co-creation*

Mobilizing customer journeys allows us to conceptualize the customer experience with the organization over time. The customer journey schematically divides the customer experience into three main phases: the pre-purchase phase, the purchase phase and the post-purchase phase. During each phase, consumers encounter a number of touch points. These are individual contacts of a verbal (contact personnel, advertising) or non-verbal (product use) nature that take place between the organization and the consumer during the experience. There are four types of touch point: brand-owned (created, controlled and managed by the organization), partner-owned (created jointly with the brand), consumer-owned and social/external (outside the organization's control) [LEM 16].

The customer experience is necessarily multi-stakeholder in that it arises from factors and takes place in places both inside and outside organizational control. Stakeholders in this context are subjects, entities, organizations, etc., who have a stake in and/or engage in activities that have an influence on the customer experience (Box 16.1). In the academic and professional worlds, attention remains focused mainly on the consumer and the organization, leaving the other stakeholders involved in the shadows. We can explain this underlying trend by the fact that the majority of researchers and practitioners rely on a traditional view of the market, which de facto circumscribes the customer experience to the consumer–company dyad [AKA 15]. Considering the experiential ecosystem in its entirety in order to manage potential positive or negative externalities requires a different approach.

16.2. Integrating stakeholders in customer experience management

16.2.1. *Moving beyond customer-centric experience management*

The business network approach goes beyond this traditional perspective. It considers the organization as embedded in a network of market and non-market relationships which both constrain and authorize its performance [GRA 85]. In marketing, business networks are frequently mobilized by two currents of research: service-dominant logic and industrial marketing and purchasing groups. Researchers working in the field of service-dominant logic have established the axiom that service forms the basis of exchange, and that value is co-created by multiple players, including the end consumer [VAR 04, VAR 16]. Thus, all the actors involved are integrators of resources and providers of mutual services. Institutions and institutional arrangements play a coordinating role in value co-creation. Business networks are customer-oriented, relational and market-driven. Their boundaries are porous, and traditional market roles are often transcended: for example, consumers are also co-producers. Organizations create value through cooperation and coordination, underpinned by institutions such as rules, beliefs and norms.

16.2.2. *Toward customer experience management focused on stakeholders*

The work on industrial marketing and purchasing groups, on the other hand, emphasizes the coopetition and co-creation of value taking place in business relationships [FOR 12]. Organizations integrate the resources they lack through interactions with a variety of business network actors, with the aim of co-creating value [RIT 04]. Business networks are conceptualized as being of infinite size and complexity and focused on relationships between actors. Organizations define their own network boundaries, intentionally or not, depending on the scope of their influence. They strive to manage their position and control the network to achieve their own objectives. Here, the main obstacle to value co-creation lies in the risk of falling into hierarchical network governance [FOR 12]. In this perspective, all organizations are intermediaries, occupying a unique position between their suppliers and their customers. Conversely, all network players can be both supplementors and competitors [RIT 04]. Box 16.3 shows FranceGaz's external stakeholders.

The case of FranceGaz*, a supplier of bottled and tanked gas, enables us to highlight external stakeholders at the level of the stakeholder network that constitutes the experiential eco-system.

FranceGaz has forged partnerships with players in the housing construction and renovation sector, as well as with equipment manufacturers: Gazinox (gas connection equipment), Camping Gaz (outdoor cooking specialist), Inotech (professional cooking appliances) and Boos-tHEAT (thermal compressors).

The company has also developed a start-up incubator linked to a beta-test platform. The latter is an interface between FranceGaz, selected start-ups and customers, enabling the co-creation of innovative services (e.g. a wood pellet delivery service co-created with start-up TankYou).

The Customer Experience Director relies on the company's five historical distributors: RiGaz* and FilGaz* (both subsidiaries) and PoGaz*, PruGaz* and Avgaz* (appointed by FranceGaz). Mandated distributors take charge of key strategic activities: logistics, business development and customer services. They provide FranceGaz services to end-users through salaried delivery drivers and contracts with resellers (e.g. supermarkets, service stations). The Customer Experience Department uses communication tools to clearly communicate the value proposition to these stakeholders (e.g. workshops, a commitment charter and customer service training sessions).

The customer experience is created by a key player: the maintenance technician. Reporting to the Technical Operations department, maintenance technicians are external service providers who must carry out annual checks on customers' tank gas installations. Although the Customer Experience Department has no direct control over these customer touch points operated by partners, it tries to convey both FranceGaz's value proposition and its singular customer culture through various communication tools (workshops and newsletters in particular).

Customers are, of course, key players in this network, as they engage in value co-creation activities through consumption experiences, service co-creation, beta-testing and feedback activities.

Finally, the Customer Experience Director participates in professional clubs and events, sharing experience and keeping an eye on the market. Direct competitors and companies in other sectors are also taken into account in both benchmarking and competitive intelligence activities. The knowledge acquired through these activities contributes to the development of new service offerings and practices.

Box 16.3. *External stakeholders. *Names have been changed*

16.3. Using value propositions to align stakeholders

16.3.1. *The need to align stakeholders*

The concept of organizational alignment emerged in the 1960s and established a link with corporate performance. Thus, increased performance results from an alignment between internal variables (e.g. organizational structure, governance) and external variables (e.g. environment, business context, market, etc.). Alignment is a term used to define the relationship between an organization and its environment. Organizational alignment implies that actors share a common set of representations and beliefs, as well as common – and some divergent – objectives.

Stakeholder alignment in an experiential ecosystem can be defined as the extent to which interdependent stakeholders, sharing certain common representations of the business network in which they operate, interact with each other to achieve distinct and common goals, the main objective being, in this perspective, the alignment of the customer journey's touch points.

16.3.2. *Value propositions as a tool for stakeholder alignment*

The concept of value proposition was first defined in the work of Lanning and Michaels [LAN 88]. In this customer-centric perspective, three steps must be followed by companies to create a value proposition. First, they must carry out an analysis of target customer groups according to the attributes they consider valuable. Second, companies must assess the opportunities associated with each identified customer segment, with the aim of delivering superior value to customers. Third, companies must define a value proposition that optimizes the opportunities identified in the second step. In this way, companies are able to deliver value to end-customers. In this perspective, the roles assumed by the stakeholders in the creation and delivery of value propositions are not taken into account. Focal companies, those in whose name customer experiences are delivered, predetermine value. They must strive to develop value propositions that will be delivered top-down to end-customers. The role of partners or alliances is not taken into account.

In the marketing literature, service-dominant logic extends this concept by adopting a stakeholder-centered vision of value propositions. In doing so, it highlights the role of value propositions and their importance in value co-creation processes [VAR 04, VAR 16]. From this perspective, value is always co-created by multiple stakeholders, including customers. The company cannot deliver value per se, but only offer customers value propositions. Thus, the concept of value proposition is defined as "an invitation from one actor to another to engage in service, or to align their connections and dispositions with one another" [CHA 15, p. 12]. In this line of research, value is not pre-determined by focal firms, but built on reciprocal promises of value including external stakeholders. In this way, value propositions are mutually determined [PAY 17]. The stakeholder-centric view of value propositions has shown that:

– knowledge sharing and dialogue between stakeholders shape value propositions;

– value propositions are reciprocal and play a role in balancing relationships with stakeholders;

– value propositions help co-create value within the business ecosystem.

According to Payne and Grow, we can distinguish four distinct dimensions of a value proposition: its perspective, its explicitness, its granularity and its focus in terms of value dimensions, [PAY 17].

Perspective analysis allows us to understand the level of involvement by external stakeholders in defining the value proposition. This can in fact be determined by the focal firm or it can be transitional: in this case, it will be determined largely by the focal company, but certain external stakeholders (partners, for example) may be consulted during this formulation phase. Finally, it can be mutually determined: in the latter case, the focal company fully mobilizes the external stakeholders making up its business network to define its value proposition.

The second dimension is the explicitness of the value proposition. It can be completely explicit: in this case, it will be written down in black and white and made public – via the focal company's website, for example. At the other extreme, it can be completely implicit. In this case, no internal or external document specifically mentions it.

The third dimension corresponds to the level of granularity at which the value proposition is developed. It can be developed at company or market level. The focal company may also choose to develop it at the customer segment level, or at the individual customer level in the case of ultra-customized offers. In the latter case, a specific value proposition will be developed for each identified marketing target.

Finally, the fourth dimension is the specific focus placed on certain value dimensions. Here, the emphasis may be on a single attribute of the product or on a broader benefit linked to environmental, economic and/or social concerns of interest to stakeholders in the ecosystem.

These four dimensions encapsulate the need for stakeholder alignment around the same conception of the target customer experience. Indeed, a value proposition determined by the focal, implicit company, developed for each consumer segment, emphasizing a specific attribute of the product on offer, requires the development of a customer journey where touch points are primarily operated by the focal company in order to deliver a fully consistent customer experience. In contrast, a mutually determined, explicit value proposition, developed at market level and emphasizing values that are meaningful to the players in its extended ecosystem, requires an effort to align stakeholders across the entire customer journey. Box 16.4 presents an analysis of FranceGaz's value proposition.

This box analyzes FranceGaz's value proposition and its dimensions.

The value proposition of FranceGaz

The company's core business is the supply, sale, marketing and distribution of liquefied petroleum gas. Since 2018, FranceGaz has launched a natural gas and electricity offer. FranceGaz's corporate mission is formulated as follows: "Our raison d'être: your everyday comfort".

Value proposition perspective

The perspective of FranceGaz's value proposition used to be supplier-driven – the company formulated its offer to customers in a top-down manner. In 2012, FranceGaz embarked on a major overhaul of its brand platform and moved to a transitional value proposition perspective. Through Voice of the Customer programs, customer surveys and, in a second phase, a participatory innovation platform involving start-ups and customers, the company focused on the customer experience. It has worked to gather information and feedback from customers, and to develop new service offerings: for example, a click and collect bottle service co-created with customers and start-up partners.

Explicit nature of the value proposition

FranceGaz uses a variety of tools and channels to communicate its value proposition to its stakeholders in a very explicit way. To internal stakeholders and partners, the value proposition is communicated through regular workshops and meetings, and an annual event called Green Day. This customer-focused event aims to reflect on the role played by everyone, employees and partners alike, in the customer experience. The value proposition is also communicated through internal communication tools (leaflets, charters, guides, weekly newsletters, etc.) aimed at both in-house staff and employees of partner distributors.

Granularity level

FranceGaz's value proposition is at the corporate level. The company has not developed specific value propositions aimed at different customer segments or market levels. Consequently, each stakeholder is provided with an identical value proposition.

Importance of value dimensions

FranceGaz focuses on three core values that shape its value proposition: proximity, quality and innovation. Thus, the company chooses to focus on the values that make the difference in the customer experience, rather than on product benefits alone.

Box 16.4. *Value propositions*

Value propositions thus play the role of strategic organizing principles. They are mobilized by focal companies to align stakeholders at all touch points structuring the customer journey. In themselves, the dimensions of value propositions can play the role of stakeholder alignment mechanisms.

The scope of value propositions also plays this key role. This scope can be defined along a *continuum* ranging from narrow to broad. There may be several ways of characterizing this scope: the number of stakeholders involved in the customer experience, the length of the customer journey, the number of touch points involved. One premise is that the broader the scope of the value proposition is, the more touch points escape the control of the focal company and/or are influenced by various stakeholders. Thus, the scope of the value proposition determines the need for alignment of the stakeholders making up the experiential ecosystem. Box 16.5 shows the scope of FranceGaz's value proposition.

The scope of FranceGaz's value proposition is broad: the company aims to do more than simply supply its customers with gas cylinders or fill up their tanks. It seeks to provide customers with day-to-day comfort. To deliver its value proposition, FranceGaz works closely with a variety of stakeholders and external stakeholders – including suppliers, partners and customers, as some parts of the customer journey beyond its direct control. Take the case of delivery: delivery drivers are subcontractors under the supervision of FranceGaz distributors, themselves partners mandated by the company. There is no direct link or formal agreement between FranceGaz and the delivery drivers. Nevertheless, drivers have direct contact with end customers and play a crucial role in the customer experience.

FranceGaz recognizes the role of different stakeholders in the customer journey. The company does not just work in dyads, for example, by working solely with distributors or with start-ups, but takes into account the interrelation of stakeholders. Indeed, FranceGaz recognizes both the influence of multiple stakeholders on customer experiences and their interdependence. For example, the company is aware of the crucial role played by the distributors it commissions in the customer experience. However, it is also aware of the key role played by delivery drivers, themselves sub-contractors to distributors, and develops communication tools and training programs specifically for distributors and delivery drivers alike. FranceGaz leverages its global value proposition to build a shared understanding of the customer experience across the network of stakeholders in which it operates. In doing so, the company strives to align the touch points of the customer journey by aligning the stakeholders who operate or influence them.

Box 16.5. *The scope of the value proposition*

16.4. Conclusion

This chapter introduces a multi-stakeholder perspective on customer experience which has several direct implications for managers. This experiential ecosystem approach enables us to redefine the scope of customer experience management.

Marketing managers are often focused on the customer journey segments under their direct control. This approach enables them to become aware of the experiential eco-system in which they operate. This mapping-based awareness gives managers the opportunity to delineate the experiential ecosystem by identifying all the stakeholders that make it up. It also enables them to analyze the relationships of each stakeholder with each other and with the end customer.

So, by thinking in these terms about customer experience management, marketing managers can identify opportunities for co-creation and coopetition, or threats of competition. They can also pinpoint sensitive or frictional points to which particular attention should be paid: in this respect, let us mention direct customer touch points that are not operated by the focal company but by an external stakeholder, such as suppliers, partners or franchisees, for example.

Finally, they can analyze the phenomena of intermediation and disintermediation taking place in their experiential ecosystem. This analysis makes it possible to identify the threat of a stakeholder inserting itself between the focal company and its customer in an intermediation process or the opportunity for disintermediation: the focal company recovers its sovereignty over a touch point previously controlled by an external stakeholder.

This chapter also explains the role of the value proposition as a descriptor and driver of stakeholder alignment. Indeed, the scope of the value proposition is a key characteristic that reflects the need for alignment and which managers must grasp. Since the value proposition is a strategic organizing principle, a major managerial responsibility lies in defining it. It goes without saying that this is accompanied by the development and maintenance of exchange relationships with the stakeholders in the experiential ecosystem.

16.5. References

[AKA 15] AKAKA M.A., VARGO S.L., SCHAU H.J., "The context of experience", *Journal of Service Management*, vol. 26/2, pp. 206–223, 2015.

[BAC 06] BÄCKSTRÖM K., JOHANSSON U., "Creating and consuming experiences in retail store environments: Comparing retailer and consumer perspectives", *Journal of Retailing and Consumer Services*, vol. 13/6, pp. 417–430, 2006.

[CHA 15] CHANDLER J.D., LUSCH R.F., "Service systems: A broadened framework and research agenda on value propositions, engagement, and service experience", *Journal of Service Research*, vol. 18/1, pp. 6–22, 2015.

[FOR 12] FORD D., GADDE L.-E., HAKANSSON H. et al., *Managing Business Relationships*, Wiley, Chichester, 2012.

[GEN 07] GENTILE C., SPILLER N., NOCI G., "How to sustain the customer experience: An overview of experience components that co-create value with the customer", *European Management Journal*, no. 25/5, pp. 395–410, 2007.

[GRA 85] GRANOVETTER M., "Economic action and the problem of embeddedness", *American Journal of Sociology*, vol. 91, pp. 481–510, 1985.

[JON 99] JONES M., "Entertaining shopping experiences: An exploratory investigation", *Journal of Retailing and Consumer Services*, no. 6/3, pp. 129–139, 1999.

[LAN 88] LANNING M.J., MICHAELS E.G., "A business is a value delivery system", *McKinsey Staff Paper*, vol. 41, pp. 1–16, 1988.

[LEM 16] LEMON K.N., VERHOEF P.C., "Understanding customer experience throughout the customer journey", *Journal of Marketing*, vol. 80, pp. 69–96, 2016.

[PAY 17] PAYNE A., FROW P., "The customer value proposition: Evolution, development, and application in marketing", *Journal of the Academy of Marketing Science*, vol. 45, pp. 467–489, doi: 10.1007/s11747-017-0523-z, 2017.

[RIT 04] RITTER T., WILKINSON I.F., JOHNSTON W.J., "Managing in complex business networks", *Industrial Marketing Management*, vol. 33, no. 3, pp. 175–183, doi: 10.1016/j.indmarman.2003.10.016, 2004.

[VAR 04] VARGO S.L., LUSCH R.F., "Evolving to a new dominant logic for marketing", *Journal of Marketing*, vol. 68, no. 1, pp. 1–17, doi: 10.1509/jmkg.68.1.1.24036, 2004.

[VAR 16] VARGO S.L., LUSCH R.F., "Institutions and axioms: An extension and update of service-dominant logic", *Journal of the Academy of Marketing Science*, vol. 44, pp. 5–23, doi: 10.1007/s11747-015-0456-3, 2016.

[VER 09] VERHOEF P.C. et al., "Customer experience creation: Determinants, dynamics and management strategies", *Journal of Retailing*, vol. 85, no. 1, pp. 31–41, doi: 10.1016/j.jretai.2008.11.001, 2009.

List of Authors

Loubaba BELAOUD
ThEMA
CY Cergy Paris University
France

Grégoire BOTHOREL
Numberly
1000Mercis Group
Paris
France

Léa CAUCHARD
MRM
University of Montpellier
France

Isabelle DABADIE
LARGEPA
Panthéon-Assas University Paris II
France

Thierry DELÉCOLLE
De Vinci Higher Education
Pôle Léonard de Vinci
Courbevoie
France

Jeoffrey DROUARD
GREDEG
Côte d'Azur University
France

Hajar EL KARMOUNI
IRG
UPEC
Créteil
France

Séverine ERHEL
LP3C
Rennes 2 University
France

Nathalie FLECK
DRM, CNRS
Paris Dauphine University
France

Valérie GUILLARD
DRM, CNRS
Paris Dauphine University
France

Florence JACOB
LEMNA
Nantes University
France

Eric JULIENNE
LITEM
University of Évry
Paris-Saclay University
France

Sarah LASRI
DRM, CNRS
Paris Dauphine University
France

Catherine LEJEALLE
ISC Paris
France

Sylvie LLOSA
CERGAM
IAE Aix-Marseille University
France

Cindy LOMBART
In Situ Lab
Audencia Business School
Nantes
France

Didier LOUIS
LEMNA
IUT Saint-Nazaire
Nantes University
France

Marianne LUMEAU
CREM
University of Rennes
France

Amélie MARTIN
Paris School of Business
France

Aïda MIMOUNI-CHAABANE
ThEMA
CY Cergy Paris University
France

Lionel NICOD
CERGAM
IUT Aix-Marseille University
France

Béatrice PARGUEL
DRM, CNRS
Paris Dauphine University
France

Virginie PEZ
LED
Paris 8 University Vincennes-Saint-Denis
France

Alix POELS
IRG
UPEC
Créteil
France

Isabelle PRIM-ALLAZ
Coactis
Lumière University Lyon 2
France

Valérie RENAUDIN
DRM, CNRS
Paris Dauphine University
France

Virginie SCHWEITZER
CREGO
University of Upper Alsace
France

Martine SÉVILLE
Coactis
Lumière University Lyon 2
France

Françoise SIMON
CREGO
University of Upper Alsace
France

Raphaël SUIRE
LEMNA
Nantes University
France

Stéphanie VERFAY
Coactis
Lumière University Lyon 2
France

Tom VILLENET
Magellan
IAE Lyon School of Management
Jean Moulin University Lyon 3
France

Pierre VOLLE
DRM, CNRS
Paris Dauphine University
France

Jean-Baptiste WELTÉ
Grego
IAE Dijon
University of Burgundy
France

Index

A, B

accessibility, 121, 123–125
  effective, 131, 132, 134, 136, 137, 139
appropriation, 152, 153
assortment/range, 17, 18
autonomy, 119, 121, 124, 125, 134, 178, 179
avatar, 71, 72, 74
behavior
  ethical, 157, 162, 164, 165, 167, 168
  responsible, 52
big data, 102
Black Friday, 15, 204, 209
blockchain, 72, 75, 77, 78
brands, 171–173, 176, 178, 180, 181
bulk, 33, 34, 37

C, D

capacity, 132, 137, 141
cause-related marketing, 35–37
cognitive moral development, 165
commercial performance, 167
communication, 206, 207, 209, 210
consent, 85, 86, 88, 93–96
cooperative, 185–187, 192, 193
corporate social responsibility (CSR), 27–31, 33, 35–37, 41, 42, 44–46, 48, 49, 51, 54, 202, 204, 207
customer, 15–18, 20–24
  data, 83
  experience management, 215–218, 225
  intimacy, 83
  journey, 109, 138, 139, 189, 216, 218, 223–225
  loyalty, 202, 206, 211
  orientation, 162–164, 167
  relations, 2, 3, 6, 8, 10, 11, 183, 184
dark patterns, 99–102, 104, 106–111
data
  first-party, 82
  second-party, 86
  third-party, 86
  vulnerability, 84
deconsumer practices, 4
design, 100–102, 104, 106, 108, 109, 111
digital literacy, 119–121
Digital Service Act, 110
direct marketing, 59
disability, 132, 134, 136

E, F

eco-friendliness, 64
ecological, 25
ecosystem, 216, 217, 219, 221–226
emailing, 59
employees, 16, 20, 23–25
empowerment, 171, 177, 178, 180, 202, 206, 213
engagement/commitment, 63, 64, 66
environment, 32–34, 36
equity, 123–125
ethical
  climate, 164, 165, 167
  dilemma, 158, 159, 165
experience
  customer, 72, 78, 137, 145, 215–221, 223–225
  patient, 145–154
  user, 115, 118
extra-role, 184, 191, 193
feedback, 171–179, 181

G, H, I

gift, 45, 47, 51, 53, 54
governance, 183–185, 190, 191, 200, 211, 212
  democratic, 183–185
health/healthcare, 145–149, 151–154
illectronism, 135
immersive universe, 73
inclusion, 132
  digital, 116, 118, 119, 121, 122, 124–127
inequalities, 119, 127
influence, 157, 159–162, 164, 167
intra-role, 184, 188, 193

L, M, N

loyalty, 27–37, 41–51, 54, 57, 59, 65, 66
manipulation, 100, 109, 157, 160, 161, 167
metaverse, 71–79
non-fungible token (NFT), 72, 73, 75, 76, 78
nudge, 102

O, P

organizational alignment, 221
over-consumption, 9, 59
PACTE, 198, 199
paradox, 16, 21, 24, 88
participation, 115, 117, 119, 124–126
patient, 145–149, 151–154
perception, 125
personalization, 83, 84, 89, 96
planetary limits, 57
positioning, 153, 154
prices, 17–19
privacy, 81, 84, 85, 88–90, 93–96, 179, 181
  paradox, 88
program
  loyalty, 41–54, 65
  prosocial, 53
promotion, 57
prosocial, 41, 52–54
proximity, 34–37
purpose corporation, 199, 200, 202, 203, 205, 206, 209–213

R, S

raison d’être, 198–201, 207–212
recognition, 124, 125
relationship investment, 171, 176, 177, 179
resistance, 178, 180, 181
retail, 15–17, 20, 21, 25
retailers, 15–21, 23–25
reward, 42–45, 47, 49, 51–54
satisfaction, 146, 147
second-hand goods, 1, 3–8, 10–12

self-scanning, 173, 179
sellers, 157–165, 167
service, 145, 146, 148, 153
  -dominant logic, 219, 222
skills, 4, 8, 10, 11
smart feedback, 171–173, 175–181
social, 25
  and solidarity economy (SSE), 183–185
sponsorship, 35–37
stakeholders, 199, 200, 207, 208, 210, 215–226
status, 64
structure, 42, 43, 46, 47, 53
sufficiency, 1, 4, 11, 12, 57, 63–68

T, U, V, W

trust, 87–90, 92, 93, 95, 96
typology, 150, 151, 153, 154
user, 146
value, 148–154
  co-creation, 218, 219, 221, 222
  creation, 11
  proposition, 221–226
vulnerability, 134–137, 139, 141
wastage, 19
Web 3.0, 76, 79
well-being, 42

Other titles from

iSTE

in

Innovation, Entrepreneurship and Management

2024

BRASSEUR Martine, BARTOLI Annie, CHABAUD Didier, GROUIEZ Pascal, ROUET Gilles
Inclusive Territories 2: Role of Institutions and Local Actors
(Territorial Entrepreneurship and Innovation Set – Volume 2)

COURIE-LEMEUR Aline
Innovation, Collective Intelligence and Resiliency in Healthcare Organizations
(Health and Innovation Set – Volume 4)

DIMOTIKALIS Yannis, SKIADIS Christos H.
Data Analysis and Related Applications 3: Theory and Practice – New Approaches
(Big Data, Artificial Intelligence and Data Analysis Set – Volume 11)

PARMENTIER Guy
Organizational Creative Capabilities: Management Factors, Processes and Devices
(Organizational Creativity Set – Volume 1)

RUIZ Émilie
The Creative Capabilities of Open Organizations
(Organizational Creativity Set – Volume 2)

VERNIER Marie-France
Eco-Design and Ecological Transition: Questioning the Economic Model
(Smart Innovation Set – Volume 42)

2023

BOLLINGER Sophie
Management Control and Creativity: Challenges of Managing Innovation Processes
(Smart Innovation Set – Volume 41)

BOUVIER-PATRON Paul
Frugal Innovation and Innovative Creation
(Smart Innovation Set – Volume 40)

BRASSEUR Martine, BARTOLI Annie, CHABAUD Didier, GROUIEZ Pascal, ROUET Gilles
Inclusive Territories 1: Role of Enterprises and Organizations
(Territorial Entrepreneurship and Innovation Set – Volume 1)

CASADELLA Vanessa, UZUNIDIS Dimitri
Agri-Innovations and Development Challenges: Engineering, Value Chains and Socio-economic Models
(Innovation in Engineering and Technology Set – Volume 8)

DARTIGUEPEYROU Carine, SALOFF-COSTE Michel
Futures: The Great Turn
(Innovation and Technology Set – Volume 18)

PEYROUX Élisabeth, RAIMOND Christine, VIEL Vincent, LAVIE Émilie
Development and Territorial Restructuring in an Era of Global Change: Theories, Approaches and Future Research Perspectives

SAULAIS Pierre
Knowledge and Ideation: Inventive Knowledge Analysis for Ideation Stimulation
(Innovation and Technology Set – Volume 17)

2022

AOUINAÏT Camille
Open Innovation Strategies
(Smart Innovation Set – Volume 39)

BOUCHÉ Geneviève
Productive Economy, Contributory Economy: Governance Tools for the Third Millennium
(Innovation and Technology Set – Volume 15)

BRUYÈRE Christelle
Caring Management in Health Organizations: A Lever for Crisis Management
(Health and Innovation Set – Volume 3)

ENJOLRAS Manon
Innovation and Export: The Joint Challenge of the Small Company
(Smart Innovation Set – Volume 37)

FLEURY Sylvain, RICHIR Simon
Immersive Technologies to Accelerate Innovation: How Virtual and Augmented Reality Enables the Co-Creation of Concepts
(Smart Innovation Set – Volume 38)

HELLER David
Valuation of the Liability Structure by Real Options
(Modern Finance, Management Innovation and Economic Growth Set – Volume 5)

MATHIEU Valérie
A Customer-oriented Manager for B2B Services: Principles and Implementation

MORALES Lucía, DZEVER Sam, TAYLOR Robert
Asia-Europe Industrial Connectivity in Times of Crisis
(Innovation and Technology Set – Volume 16)

NOËL Florent, SCHMIDT Géraldine
Employability and Industrial Mutations: Between Individual Trajectories and Organizational Strategic Planning
(Technological Changes and Human Resources Set – Volume 4)

DE SAINT JULIEN Odile
The Innovation Ecosystem as a Source of Value Creation: A Value Creation Lever for Open Innovation
(Diverse and Global Perspectives on Value Creation Set – Volume 4)

SALOFF-COSTE Michel
Innovation Ecosystems: The Future of Civilizations and the Civilization of the Future
(Innovation and Technology Set – Volume 14)

SOULÉ Bastien, HALLÉ Julie, VIGNAL Bénédicte, BOUTROY Éric, NIER Olivier
Innovation in Sport: Innovation Trajectories and Process Optimization
(Smart Innovation Set – Volume 35)

VALLIER Estelle
Innovation in Clusters: Science–Industry Relationships in the Face of Forced Advancement
(Smart Innovation Set – Volume 36)

VAYRE Emilie
Digitalization of Work: New Spaces and New Working Times
(Technological Changes and Human Resources Set – Volume 5)

ZAFEIRIS Konstantinos N, SKIADIS Christos H, DIMOTIKALIS Yannis, KARAGRIGORIOU Alex, KARAGRIGORIOU-VONTA Christina
Data Analysis and Related Applications 1: Computational, Algorithmic and Applied Economic Data Analysis
(Big Data, Artificial Intelligence and Data Analysis Set – Volume 9)
Data Analysis and Related Applications 2: Multivariate, Health and Demographic Data Analysis
(Big Data, Artificial Intelligence and Data Analysis Set – Volume 10)

2021

ACH Yves-Alain, RMADI-SAÏD Sandra
Financial Information and Brand Value: Reflections, Challenges and Limitations

ARCADE Jacques
Strategic Engineering
(Innovation and Technology Set – Volume 11)

BÉRANGER Jérôme, RIZOULIÈRES Roland
The Digital Revolution in Health
(Health and Innovation Set – Volume 2)

BOBILLIER CHAUMON Marc-Eric
Digital Transformations in the Challenge of Activity and Work: Understanding and Supporting Technological Changes
(Technological Changes and Human Resources Set – Volume 3)

BUCLET Nicolas
Territorial Ecology and Socio-ecological Transition
(Smart Innovation Set – Volume 34)

DIMOTIKALIS Yannis, KARAGRIGORIOU Alex, PARPOULA Christina, SKIADIS Christos H
Applied Modeling Techniques and Data Analysis 1: Computational Data Analysis Methods and Tools
(Big Data, Artificial Intelligence and Data Analysis Set - Volume 7)
Applied Modeling Techniques and Data Analysis 2: Financial, Demographic, Stochastic and Statistical Models and Methods
(Big Data, Artificial Intelligence and Data Analysis Set – Volume 8)

DISPAS Christophe, KAYANAKIS Georges, SERVEL Nicolas, STRIUKOVA Ludmila
Innovation and Financial Markets
(Innovation between Risk and Reward Set – Volume 7)

GAUDIN Thierry, MAUREL Marie-Christine, POMEROL Jean-Charles
Chance, Calculation and Life

GASMI Nacer
Corporate Innovation Strategies: Corporate Social Responsibility and Shared Value Creation
(Smart Innovation Set – Volume 33)

GIORGINI Pierre
The Contributory Revolution
(Innovation and Technology Set – Volume 13)

GOGLIN Christian
Emotions and Values in Equity Crowdfunding Investment Choices 1: Transdisciplinary Theoretical Approach
Emotions and Values in Equity Crowdfunding Investment Choices 2: Modeling and Empirical Study

GRENIER Corinne, OIRY Ewan
Altering Frontiers: Organizational Innovations in Healthcare
(Health and Innovation Set – Volume 1)

GUERRIER Claudine
Security and Its Challenges in the 21st Century
(Innovation and Technology Set – Volume 12)

HELLER David
Performance of Valuation Methods in Financial Transactions
(Modern Finance, Management Innovation and Economic Growth Set – Volume 4)

LEHMANN Paul-Jacques
Liberalism and Capitalism Today

LIMA Marcos
Entrepreneurship and Innovation Education: Frameworks and Tools
(Smart Innovation Set – Volume 32)

MACHADO Carolina, DAVIM J. Paulo
Sustainable Management for Managers and Engineers

MEUNIER François-Xavier
Dual Innovation Systems: Concepts, Tools and Methods
(Smart Innovation Set – Volume 31)

UZUNIDIS Dimitri, KASMI Fedoua, ADATTO Laurent
Innovation Economics, Engineering and Management Handbook 1: Main Themes
Innovation Economics, Engineering and Management Handbook 2: Special Themes

2020

ANDREOSSO-O'CALLAGHAN Bernadette, DZEVER Sam, JAUSSAUD Jacques, TAYLOR Robert
Sustainable Development and Energy Transition in Europe and Asia
(Innovation and Technology Set – Volume 9)

BEN SLIMANE Sonia, M'HENNI Hatem
Entrepreneurship and Development: Realities and Future Prospects
(Smart Innovation Set – Volume 30)

CHOUTEAU Marianne, FOREST Joëlle, NGUYEN Céline
Innovation for Society: The P.S.I. Approach
(Smart Innovation Set – Volume 28)

CORON Clotilde
Quantifying Human Resources: Uses and Analysis
(Technological Changes and Human Resources Set – Volume 2)

CORON Clotilde, GILBERT Patrick
Technological Change
(Technological Changes and Human Resources Set – Volume 1)

CERDIN Jean-Luc, PERETTI Jean-Marie
The Success of Apprenticeships: Views of Stakeholders on Training and Learning (Human Resources Management Set – Volume 3)

DELCHET-COCHET Karen
Circular Economy: From Waste Reduction to Value Creation
(Economic Growth Set – Volume 2)

DIDAY Edwin, GUAN Rong, SAPORTA Gilbert, WANG Huiwen
Advances in Data Science
(Big Data, Artificial Intelligence and Data Analysis Set – Volume 4)

DOS SANTOS PAULINO Victor
Innovation Trends in the Space Industry
(Smart Innovation Set – Volume 25)

GUILHON Bernard
Venture Capital and the Financing of Innovation
(Innovation Between Risk and Reward Set – Volume 6)

JURCZENKO Emmanuel
Machine Learning for Asset Management: New Developments and Financial Applications

LATOUCHE Pascal
Open Innovation: Human Set-up
(Innovation and Technology Set – Volume 10)

MAKRIDES Andreas, KARAGRIGORIOU Alex, SKIADAS Christos H.
Data Analysis and Applications 3: Computational, Classification, Financial, Statistical and Stochastic Methods
(Big Data, Artificial Intelligence and Data Analysis Set – Volume 5)
Data Analysis and Applications 4: Financial Data Analysis and Methods
(Big Data, Artificial Intelligence and Data Analysis Set – Volume 6)

MASSOTTE Pierre, CORSI Patrick
Complex Decision-Making in Economy and Finance

MICHAUD Thomas
Science Fiction and Innovation Design
(Innovation in Engineering and Technology Set – Volume 6)

MONINO Jean-Louis
Data Control: Major Challenge for the Digital Society
(Smart Innovation Set – Volume 29)

MORLAT Clément
Sustainable Productive System: Eco-development versus Sustainable Development (Smart Innovation Set – Volume 26)

SAULAIS Pierre, ERMINE Jean-Louis
Knowledge Management in Innovative Companies 2: Understanding and Deploying a KM Plan within a Learning Organization
(Smart Innovation Set – Volume 27)

UZUNIDIS Dimitri
Systemic Innovation: Entrepreneurial Strategies and Market Dynamics

2019

AMENDOLA Mario, GAFFARD Jean-Luc
Disorder and Public Concern Around Globalization

BARBAROUX Pierre
Disruptive Technology and Defence Innovation Ecosystems
(Innovation in Engineering and Technology Set – Volume 5)

DOU Henri, JUILLET Alain, CLERC Philippe
Strategic Intelligence for the Future 1: A New Strategic and Operational Approach
Strategic Intelligence for the Future 2: A New Information Function Approach

FRIKHA Azza
Measurement in Marketing: Operationalization of Latent Constructs

FRIMOUSSE Soufyane
Innovation and Agility in the Digital Age
(Human Resources Management Set – Volume 2)

GAY Claudine, SZOSTAK Bérangère L.
Innovation and Creativity in SMEs: Challenges, Evolutions and Prospects
(Smart Innovation Set – Volume 21)

GORIA Stéphane, HUMBERT Pierre, ROUSSEL Benoît
Information, Knowledge and Agile Creativity
(Smart Innovation Set – Volume 22)

HELLER David
Investment Decision-making Using Optional Models
(Economic Growth Set – Volume 2)

HELLER David, DE CHADIRAC Sylvain, HALAOUI Lana, JOUVET Camille
The Emergence of Start-ups
(Economic Growth Set – Volume 1)

HÉRAUD Jean-Alain, KERR Fiona, BURGER-HELMCHEN Thierry
Creative Management of Complex Systems
(Smart Innovation Set – Volume 19)

LATOUCHE Pascal
Open Innovation: Corporate Incubator
(Innovation and Technology Set – Volume 7)

LEHMANN Paul-Jacques
The Future of the Euro Currency

LEIGNEL Jean-Louis, MÉNAGER Emmanuel, YABLONSKY Serge
Sustainable Enterprise Performance: A Comprehensive Evaluation Method

LIÈVRE Pascal, AUBRY Monique, GAREL Gilles
Management of Extreme Situations: From Polar Expeditions to Exploration-Oriented Organizations

MILLOT Michel
Embarrassment of Product Choices 2: Towards a Society of Well-being

N'GOALA Gilles, PEZ-PÉRARD Virginie, PRIM-ALLAZ Isabelle
Augmented Customer Strategy: CRM in the Digital Age

NIKOLOVA Blagovesta
The RRI Challenge: Responsibilization in a State of Tension with Market Regulation
(Innovation and Responsibility Set – Volume 3)

PELLEGRIN-BOUCHER Estelle, ROY Pierre
Innovation in the Cultural and Creative Industries
(Innovation and Technology Set – Volume 8)

PRIOLON Joël
Financial Markets for Commodities

QUINIOU Matthieu
Blockchain: The Advent of Disintermediation

RAVIX Joël-Thomas, DESCHAMPS Marc
Innovation and Industrial Policies
(Innovation between Risk and Reward Set – Volume 5)

ROGER Alain, VINOT Didier
Skills Management: New Applications, New Questions
(Human Resources Management Set – Volume 1)

SAULAIS Pierre, ERMINE Jean-Louis
Knowledge Management in Innovative Companies 1: Understanding and Deploying a KM Plan within a Learning Organization
(Smart Innovation Set – Volume 23)

SERVAJEAN-HILST Romaric
Co-innovation Dynamics: The Management of Client-Supplier Interactions for Open Innovation
(Smart Innovation Set – Volume 20)

SKIADAS Christos H., BOZEMAN James R.
Data Analysis and Applications 1: Clustering and Regression, Modeling-estimating, Forecasting and Data Mining
(Big Data, Artificial Intelligence and Data Analysis Set – Volume 2)
Data Analysis and Applications 2: Utilization of Results in Europe and Other Topics
(Big Data, Artificial Intelligence and Data Analysis Set – Volume 3)

VIGEZZI Michel
World Industrialization: Shared Inventions, Competitive Innovations and Social Dynamics
(Smart Innovation Set – Volume 24)

2018

BURKHARDT Kirsten
Private Equity Firms: Their Role in the Formation of Strategic Alliances

CALLENS Stéphane
Creative Globalization
(Smart Innovation Set – Volume 16)

CASADELLA Vanessa
Innovation Systems in Emerging Economies: MINT – Mexico, Indonesia, Nigeria, Turkey
(Smart Innovation Set – Volume 18)

CHOUTEAU Marianne, FOREST Joëlle, NGUYEN Céline
Science, Technology and Innovation Culture
(Innovation in Engineering and Technology Set – Volume 3)

CORLOSQUET-HABART Marine, JANSSEN Jacques
Big Data for Insurance Companies
(Big Data, Artificial Intelligence and Data Analysis Set – Volume 1)

CROS Françoise
Innovation and Society
(Smart Innovation Set – Volume 15)

DEBREF Romain
Environmental Innovation and Ecodesign: Certainties and Controversies
(Smart Innovation Set – Volume 17)

DOMINGUEZ Noémie
SME Internationalization Strategies: Innovation to Conquer New Markets

ERMINE Jean-Louis
Knowledge Management: The Creative Loop
(Innovation and Technology Set – Volume 5)

GAUDIN Thierry, LACROIX Dominique, MAUREL Marie-Christine, POMEROL, Jean-Charles
Life Sciences, Information Sciences

GILBERT Patrick, BOBADILLA Natalia, GASTALDI Lise, LE BOULAIRE Martine, LELEBINA Olga
Innovation, Research and Development Management

VAN HOOREBEKE Delphine
The Management of Living Beings or Emo-management

IBRAHIMI Mohammed
Mergers & Acquisitions: Theory, Strategy, Finance

LEMAÎTRE Denis
Training Engineers for Innovation

LÉVY Aldo, BEN BOUHENI Faten, AMMI Chantal
Financial Management: USGAAP and IFRS Standards
(Innovation and Technology Set – Volume 6)

LOISY Catherine, COULET Jean-Claude
Competence and Program-based Approach in Training: Tools for Developing Responsible Activities
Innovation and Responsibility Set – Volume 1)

MILLOT Michel
Embarrassment of Product Choices 1: How to Consume Differently

PANSERA Mario, OWEN Richard
Innovation and Development: The Politics at the Bottom of the Pyramid
(Innovation and Responsibility Set – Volume 2)

RICHEZ Yves
Corporate Talent Detection and Development

SACHETTI Philippe, ZUPPINGER Thibaud
New Technologies and Branding
(Innovation and Technology Set – Volume 4)

SAMIER Henri
Intuition, Creativity, Innovation

TEMPLE Ludovic, COMPAORÉ SAWADOGO Eveline M.F.W.
Innovation Processes in Agro-Ecological Transitions in Developing Countries
(Innovation in Engineering and Technology Set – Volume 2)

UZUNIDIS Dimitri
Collective Innovation Processes: Principles and Practices
(Innovation in Engineering and Technology Set – Volume 4)

2017

AÏT-EL-HADJ Smaïl
The Ongoing Technological System
(Smart Innovation Set – Volume 11)

D'ANDRIA Aude, GABARRET Inés
Building 21st Century Entrepreneurship
(Innovation and Technology Set – Volume 2)

BAUDRY Marc, DUMONT Béatrice
Patents: Prompting or Restricting Innovation?
(Smart Innovation Set – Volume 12)

BÉRARD Céline, TEYSSIER Christine
Risk Management: Lever for SME Development and Stakeholder Value Creation

CHALENÇON Ludivine
Location Strategies and Value Creation of International Mergers and Acquisitions

CHAUVEL Danièle, BORZILLO Stefano
The Innovative Company: An Ill-defined Object
(Innovation between Risk and Reward Set – Volume 1)

CORSI Patrick
Going Past Limits To Growth

DAIDJ Nabyla
Cooperation, Coopetition and Innovation
(Innovation and Technology Set – Volume 3)

FERNEZ-WALCH Sandrine
The Multiple Facets of Innovation Project Management
(Innovation between Risk and Reward Set – Volume 4)

FOREST Joëlle
Creative Rationality and Innovation
(Smart Innovation Set – Volume 14)

GUILHON Bernard
Innovation and Production Ecosystems
(Innovation between Risk and Reward Set – Volume 2)

HAMMOUDI Abdelhakim, DAIDJ Nabyla
Game Theory Approach to Managerial Strategies and Value Creation
(Diverse and Global Perspectives on Value Creation Set – Volume 3)

LALLEMENT Rémi
Intellectual Property and Innovation Protection: New Practices and New Policy Issues
(Innovation between Risk and Reward Set – Volume 3)

LAPERCHE Blandine
Enterprise Knowledge Capital
(Smart Innovation Set – Volume 13)

LEBERT Didier, EL YOUNSI Hafida
International Specialization Dynamics
(Smart Innovation Set – Volume 9)

MAESSCHALCK Marc
Reflexive Governance for Research and Innovative Knowledge
(Responsible Research and Innovation Set – Volume 6)

MASSOTTE Pierre
Ethics in Social Networking and Business 1: Theory, Practice and Current Recommendations
Ethics in Social Networking and Business 2: The Future and Changing Paradigms

MASSOTTE Pierre, CORSI Patrick
Smart Decisions in Complex Systems

MEDINA Mercedes, HERRERO Mónica, URGELLÉS Alicia
Current and Emerging Issues in the Audiovisual Industry
(Diverse and Global Perspectives on Value Creation Set – Volume 1)

MICHAUD Thomas
Innovation, Between Science and Science Fiction
(Smart Innovation Set – Volume 10)

PELLÉ Sophie
Business, Innovation and Responsibility
(Responsible Research and Innovation Set – Volume 7)

SAVIGNAC Emmanuelle
The Gamification of Work: The Use of Games in the Workplace

SUGAHARA Satoshi, DAIDJ Nabyla, USHIO Sumitaka
Value Creation in Management Accounting and Strategic Management: An Integrated Approach
(Diverse and Global Perspectives on Value Creation Set –Volume 2)

UZUNIDIS Dimitri, SAULAIS Pierre
Innovation Engines: Entrepreneurs and Enterprises in a Turbulent World
(Innovation in Engineering and Technology Set – Volume 1)

2016

BARBAROUX Pierre, ATTOUR Amel, SCHENK Eric
Knowledge Management and Innovation
(Smart Innovation Set – Volume 6)

BEN BOUHENI Faten, AMMI Chantal, LEVY Aldo
Banking Governance, Performance And Risk-Taking: Conventional Banks Vs Islamic Banks

BOUTILLIER Sophie, CARRÉ Denis, LEVRATTO Nadine
Entrepreneurial Ecosystems
(Smart Innovation Set – Volume 2)

BOUTILLIER Sophie, UZUNIDIS Dimitri
The Entrepreneur
(Smart Innovation Set – Volume 8)

BOUVARD Patricia, SUZANNE Hervé
Collective Intelligence Development in Business

GALLAUD Delphine, LAPERCHE Blandine
Circular Economy, Industrial Ecology and Short Supply Chains
(Smart Innovation Set – Volume 4)

GUERRIER Claudine
Security and Privacy in the Digital Era
(Innovation and Technology Set – Volume 1)

MEGHOUAR Hicham
Corporate Takeover Targets

MONINO Jean-Louis, SEDKAOUI Soraya
Big Data, Open Data and Data Development
(Smart Innovation Set – Volume 3)

MOREL Laure, LE ROUX Serge
Fab Labs: Innovative User
(Smart Innovation Set – Volume 5)

PICARD Fabienne, TANGUY Corinne
Innovations and Techno-ecological Transition
(Smart Innovation Set – Volume 7)

2015

CASADELLA Vanessa, LIU Zeting, DIMITRI Uzunidis
Innovation Capabilities and Economic Development in Open Economies
(Smart Innovation Set – Volume 1)

CORLOSQUET-HABART Marine, GEHIN William, JANSSEN Jaques, MANCA Raimondo
Asset and Liabilities Management for Banks and Insurance Companies

CORSI Patrick, MORIN Dominique
Sequencing Apple's DNA

CORSI Patrick, NEAU Erwan
Innovation Capability Maturity Model

FAIVRE-TAVIGNOT Bénédicte
Social Business and Base of the Pyramid

GODÉ Cécile
Team Coordination in Extreme Environments

MAILLARD Pierre
Competitive Quality and Innovation

MASSOTTE Pierre, CORSI Patrick
Operationalizing Sustainability

MASSOTTE Pierre, CORSI Patrick
Sustainability Calling

2014

DUBÉ Jean, LEGROS Diègo
Spatial Econometrics Using Microdata

LESCA Humbert, LESCA Nicolas
Strategic Decisions and Weak Signals

2013

HABART-CORLOSQUET Marine, JANSSEN Jacques, MANCA Raimondo
VaR Methodology for Non-Gaussian Finance

2012

POMEROL Jean-Charles
Decision-Making and Action

SZYLAR Christian
UCITS Handbook

2011

LESCA Nicolas
Environmental Scanning and Sustainable Development

LESCA Nicolas, LESCA Humbert
Weak Signals for Strategic Intelligence: Anticipation Tool for Managers

MERCIER-LAURENT Eunika
Innovation Ecosystems

2010

SZYLAR Christian
Risk Management under UCITS III/IV

2009

COHEN Corine
Business Intelligence

ZANINETTI Jean-Marc
Sustainable Development in the USA

2008

CORSI Patrick, DULIEU Mike
The Marketing of Technology Intensive Products and Services

DZEVER Sam, JAUSSAUD Jacques, ANDREOSSO Bernadette
Evolving Corporate Structures and Cultures in Asia: Impact of Globalization

2007

AMMI Chantal
Global Consumer Behavior

2006

BOUGHZALA Imed, ERMINE Jean-Louis
Trends in Enterprise Knowledge Management

CORSI Patrick, CHRISTOFOL Hervé, RICHIR Simon, SAMIER Henri
Innovation Engineering: the power of intangible networks

Printed and bound by CPI Group (UK) Ltd, Croydon, CR0 4YY
13/09/2026
14961042-0005